GLOBALIZATION AND SURVEILLANCE

TIMOTHY ERIK STRÖM

ROWMAN & LITTLEFIELD
Lanham • Boulder • New York • London

Executive Editor: Susan McEachern
Assistant Editor: Katelyn Turner
Higher Education Channel Manager: Jonathan Raeder

Published by Rowman & Littlefield
An imprint of The Rowman & Littlefield Publishing Group, Inc.
4501 Forbes Boulevard, Suite 200, Lanham, Maryland 20706
www.rowman.com

6 Tinworth Street, London SE11 5AL, United Kingdom

British Library Cataloguing in Publication Information Available

Library of Congress Cataloging-in-Publication Data

Names: Ström, Timothy Erik, 1985- author.
Title: Globalization and surveillance / Timothy Erik Ström.
Description: Lanham : Rowman & Littlefield, [2020] | Includes bibliographical
  references and index.
Identifiers: LCCN 2019050119 (print) | LCCN 2019050120 (ebook) |
  ISBN 9781538123577 (cloth) | ISBN 9781538123584 (paperback) | ISBN
  9781538123591 (epub)
Subjects: LCSH: Electronic surveillance. | Globalization. | Privacy, Right of. | Personal
  information management.
Classification: LCC HV7936.T4 S77 2020 (print) | LCC HV7936.T4 (ebook) | DDC
  303.3—dc23
LC record available at https://lccn.loc.gov/2019050119
LC ebook record available at https://lccn.loc.gov/2019050120

For loving UB, and
—I am pleased to add—
dearest Mirolima.

CONTENTS

ACKNOWLEDGMENTS

Firstly, I must extend many thanks to my editors, Terrell Carver and Manfred Steger. The opportunity that they put forward, followed by their encouragement, support, and editorial guidance have been most helpful and warmly appreciated (likewise their tolerance of my inability to spell "phenomenon," or inability to distinguish between its plural or singular forms, among other common gaffes). Susan McEachern and Katelyn Turner from Rowman & Littlefield were fantastic to work with, and the five reviewers also gave good advice and much encouragement.

So many delightful people who I am honored to call friends have helped me to produce this book. In a multitude of ways—through enriching conversations, engaging encounters, and sharing meaningful moments—their love and support has been essential. As the task of listing them all is difficult, here follows a focused collection of people who helped in more direct ways with this project. At the University of Melbourne, I'd like to thank my research team there: Justin Clemens, Robert Hassan, Nicolas Hausdorf, Janice Richardson (of Monash), Ingrid Volkmer, and Karin Zhu. Likewise, thanks also to the students who took my subjects, Digital Politics and Global Media Policy and Governance at the University of Melbourne, and Global Political Economy at RMIT. I would like to extend thanks to the Arena collective, especially Alison Caddick and Paul James for their ongoing assistance and mentoring. I must also extend thanks to Jan Ström for proofreading a draft of the manuscript, in addition to being a fantastic mother—as well as to my father, Peter, and brother, Chris. A truly massive thanks must be extended to my loving partner, UB and our darling daughter, Mirolima. As the bulk of this book was written over the course of the first year of Miro's life, plainly none of this would have been possible without UB's unwavering care, warmth, support, advice, and love—this has been paramount. Furthermore, in addition to teaching me much about the human condition, Mirolima is also a source of much inspiration, and a very un-abstract argument for re-doubling efforts in the endless struggle for justice.

In addition to the fantastic people listed above—and many, many more unlisted—I would also like to thank the following artists for their various and brilliant albums, all of which have been among those in high rotation while working on this book: Alice Coltrane's *Ptah, the El Daoud*; ANOHNI's *Hopelessness*; Bill Laswell's *Panthalassa: The Music of Miles Davis 1969–1974*; Dirty Three, *Ocean Songs*; DJ Spooky's *Rebirth of a Nation*; Geoffrey Gurrumul Yunupingu, *Djarimirri (Child of the Rainbow)*; Grails' *Chalice Hymnal*; Kate Tempest's *Let Them Eat Chaos*; Lubomyr Melnyk's *Fallen Trees*; Mono's *Hymn to the Immortal Wind*; Nine Horses' *Snow Borne Sorrow*; Opeth's *Sorceress*; Russian Circles' *Guidance*; and Wolves in the Throne Room's *Thrice Woven*.

PRELUDE

"YOU'RE IN CONTROL"

This narrative begins with a commodity: a package arrives in the mail, a cardboard box with Amazon's smiling arrow logo emblazoned on it. Within this box lies another box, the inner one with a sleek design and stylistic photographs. Out from this second box wafts a strong smell of plastic, artificial cleanliness, a strange perfume that consumers associate with the "newness" of an electronic gadget. Lying there snugly in nonbiodegradable Styrofoam lies the commodity. It is a starkly designed silver cylinder with a ring emerging from its top, a ring embedded with light-emitting diodes (LEDs). It's a lamp, but not only a lamp; rather it is a networked computing-machine with lamp-like qualities, a condition referred to by marketers through attaching the prefix "smart." It goes by the strangely minimalistic name: "C by GE Sol."

This smart-lamp can be seen as an embodiment of early twenty-first-century globalization. It was designed by General Electric (GE), an American conglomerate founded by Thomas Edison—the famed "inventor" of the lightbulb in 1889. GE has consistently been one of the world's most powerful corporations, with its operations spreading from electrical devices to oil to weapons to finance. GE collaborated with other companies on the lamp, with the physical stuff of the device being assembled in a series of factories neatly obscured behind the three little, ubiquitous words: "Made in China." As China is currently by far the world's largest exporter, many goods bear this stamp, yet it often conceals more than it reveals. The factories of China's export zones are rife with dubious and degrading labor practices, including exceedingly long hours, forced overtime, unpaid work, grueling productivity quotas, child labor, dangerous working conditions, and authoritarian management. None of this makes it to the foreground in the construction of these devices that consumers "just can't live without." Likewise, it conceals the processes whereby minerals are mined around the world, plastics synthesized from oil, and brought together via polluting logistical chains, processes with immense and thoughtless ecological implications. Likewise, it also conceals complex long-term stories of world-historic transformations, great power struggles, and contested legacies of empire. All of this lurks behind the commodity and its apparent arrival from nowhere.[1]

Of the various companies that contribute to C by GE Sol, the one that makes it "smart"—and hence the one that forces its relevance to a book about surveillance—is the tech-giant Amazon. The lamp connects to Alexa, a piece of software, so-called artificial intelligence, developed by the firm in 2014 and currently the most popular "virtual assistant" on the market. The owner of a C by GE Sol can speak to Amazon's software via their lamp's microphone, issuing verbal communications and commands to the world-spanning computing-machine. One could say, "Alexa, lights on," and the machine should automatically comply by illuminating the LEDs. Playing into illusions of godlike power, the biblical phrase "let there be light" echoes across the commodity's advertisements and reviews. Alexa's abilities extend far beyond the adjustment of lighting levels; one can ask the lamp for recipes, the news, and the weather; it can order more commodities, play music, and tell a joke, in addition to many other features. It is a part of the broader phenomena often grouped under the much-hyped heading "Internet of Things."[2] To function, the lamp records every sound within range of its microphone, streaming it to Amazon's cloud computers for processing. There, voice recognition algorithms go through the audio files, extracting data and recording it in a searchable archive and, when relevant, actioning the request: placing an order, activating the light, and so on.

This is to say that the very function of a virtual assistant is constituted by surveillance.[3]

The surveillance recordings of voices are held digitized in Amazon's cloud storage facilities, the locations of which the firm sought to protect via layers of subsidiaries, pseudonyms, and outsourcing. Nevertheless, a leaked list revealed the exact locations of the data centers as of

2015, showing them to be spread in fifteen cities across nine countries in a global geography of power and tax evasion: Australia (Sydney), Brazil (Rio de Janeiro, São Paulo), China (Beijing, Nigxia), Germany (Frankfurt), Ireland (Dublin), Japan (Osaka, Tokyo), Luxembourg, Singapore, and the United States (Virginia, California, Oregon, Seattle).[4] Amazon's Alexa goes well beyond the smart-lamp market. It has been integrated into TVs built by Sony, refrigerators built by LG, speakers built by Marshall, and all 2018 cars produced by Ford, Toyota, and Volkswagen, among others. Furthermore, Amazon is not alone, it is joined by Apple's "Siri," Microsoft's "Cortana," and Alphabet's "Google Assistant," which populate an increasing range of smart-devices. They are united by the fact that all speak with female voices. Speaking only when spoken to, these feminized machines are programmed to be at their "little master's" beck and call, engaging with a pleasing subservience, adopting a tone that is polite, no matter the tone or topic leveled at it. These pseudo-female machines employ emotional and sentiment analysis software that attempts to automatically detect irritation in a little master's voice, hence prompting the cybernetic maidservant to offer an apology.

While a little master can, for a price, alter the lighting in their room, the "big masters" are busy reorganizing the universe. Take Amazon's CEO Jeff Bezos as a shining example. As the richest person in human history, he earns—as of October 2018—$8,961,187 per hour. It would take an Amazon worker, being paid Washington State's minimum wage of $11.50 per hour, ninety-one years of 24/7 work to make as much as their boss does in one hour.[5] The wealth gap between Bezos and his workers is greater than between a Pharaoh and his slaves: he is well beyond the 1% popularized by Occupy, rather he is the 0.00000001%. Considering how readily money translates into power under conditions of capitalism, facts like this serve to illustrate the staggering inequality of the early twenty-first century.[6]

The smart-lamp records everything within range of its speakers. If it sits on a bedside table, the lamp is privy to every conversation that unfolds around it; all the pillow talk and other bedroom soundscapes. This unprecedented window into people's private lives provides an extremely valuable resource, one facilitated in part by the flimsy and almost-never-read "privacy" policies. Corporations construct software to pore over this surveillance data, seeking to extract information that can be used to alter people's practices. Through targeted advertising and default suggestions, these assistants work to encourage people to engage in more and more consumerism, promoting commercial solutions to everything, and seeking to add in as many opportunities to extract profit as possible. Virtual assistants exert a pressure toward consumerism that is pervasive and structural, which stems from the very foundations of corporations' need to maximize profits for external shareholders. This will be discussed in greater depth in chapter 3, which looks at how surveillance and commodification are the secret to much of the power of the tech-titans.

In addition to the corporations, government spy agencies have backdoor access to this information, allowing the state to pry deep into people's private lives. As Edward Snowden's leaks revealed back in 2013, the tech-titans all actively collaborated with the shadowy National Security Agency (NSA) in allowing them access to their surveillance data.[7] This is unsurprising when one considers the long militaristic history of computing technology (chapter 2), and the fact that these firms remain major players in the increasingly lucrative business of military contracting. So much data is produced by these surveillance operations, that storing it has become a lucrative subsector of military contracting. The *Washington Post*—which is incidentally entirely owned by Bezos—reported that Amazon had opened a vast cloud-computing platform for the Pentagon, specifically designed to hold classified information obtained by the Central Intelligence Agency (CIA). For its work, Amazon is paid a tidy US$600 million of U.S. taxpayer dollars.[8]

The depth and breadth of the state's ability to pry into people's private spheres is unprecedented, with even the most malicious examples from history paling in comparison. For example, one of the most invasive, repressive, and effective surveillance states was East Germany (1949–1990). The formidable reach of its powerful secret police agency, known as the Stasi, paled in comparison to the potential for snooping.[9] Technology like C by GE Sol makes the Stasi's cigarette-box cameras and hidden tape recorders look like quaint relics. Indeed, the most ambitious Stasi agent likely could not imagine a world where people paid money to have their every private conversation recorded by powerful and distant forces.

Despite all of this, the marketing rhetoric of C by GE Sol seeks to shore up the little masters' positions by reminding them: "You're in control." This conclusion only holds if one prioritizes "convenience" above and beyond any other consideration; pondering the matter in deeper and more critical ways shows this to be dubious in the extreme. Rather than flipping a mechanical switch with one's finger to turn a light on or off, the new smart-lamps use automated, real-time surveillance that runs through an extremely energy-intensive and wasteful global system of privatized, networked computing-machines, processing layers and layers of algorithms and programs, serving the profit-maximizing interests of one of history's most powerful corporations, with backdoors built in for potentially/actually repressive state agencies to hack their way in. In this world of vast inequalities and massively uneven distributions of power, the concept of control is central, but its locus is not the little masters.

Questions of control are riddled with contradictions—one can both gain and lose it at the same time, with it being simultaneously concentrated and undermined. To analyze these contradictions, this book examines some of the practices, subjectivities, structures, and historical dynamics that have led us to this strange moment. As the next chapter explores, these developments have long historic roots. Curiously, the word "control" came into English at the beginning of capitalist modernity half a millennium ago, with it first referring to a bureaucratic mechanism for overseeing and verifying accounts—a "counter-roll"— which was used in the exercise of power and governance. Emerging at this pivotal moment in world history, and spreading intensively and extensively around the globe, control has long been intimately involved as a technique and technology of power. The smart-lamp serves as an entry point into these discussions on globalization and surveillance, for commodities such as the C by GE Sol are both increasingly common everyday objects and deeply complex and problematic apparatuses: how did we get to this point?

Chapter 1

Surveying Surveillance

Overseers, Enclosures, and Colonization

Globalization is plainly an enormously complex and contested term, one that has spawned an entire transdisciplinary field of inquiry known as global studies, dedicated academic journals such as *Globalizations*, and a rapidly expanding literature.[1] Likewise, surveillance is also an enormously complex and contested term, having also spawned the field of surveillance studies, dedicated journals such as *Surveillance & Society*, and a rapidly expanding literature.[2] The slender book you hold in your hands draws on these approaches as it weaves a narrative and addresses the critical intersection of these two complex concepts.

How has the intensification of globalization changed the nature and meaning of surveillance? And conversely, how has surveillance shaped the nature and meaning of globalization? Beginning with these broad questions, I understand "globalization" as a multi-dimensional phenomenon, a set of dynamic social processes, and relations that transform the organization of the world in ways that are simultaneously subjective and material. It is an often contradictory and always uneven process of reorganization, with the expansion and intensification of social relations across space and time. Often as these relations are extended, they are remade on more abstract levels, which has consequences for both social organization and subjectivity, and the organization of matter. These shifting forms of human practice produce various forms of homogenization, heterogenization, and hybridization. Globalization is a multi-dimensional social phenomenon, unfolding in economic, political, and cultural domains within nature.[3]

At is broadest, the word "surveillance" means to "watch over" something in order to project control down upon it. The word comes to English from Latin via French, with the Latin prefix *sur* meaning "over" or "above," hence it is significant for it implies a power relation in a hierarchical and centralized society: an overseer, a supervisor, a superintendent. The latter part of the word came from *vigil*, meaning to watch, to be alert, to be a watchman, to be vigilant. Back in Ancient Rome, this concept was bound up with paramilitary units of city watch called the *vigiles urbani*. Stationed in Rome, and other important trade cities, they were tasked with literally watching over the city, both from watchtowers and on armed patrols through the streets in order to uphold the status quo. The *vigiles* functioned as a form of police; their job was to maintain order in the streets, crack down on petty crime, fight fires, defend property, and hunt down runaway slaves. This force was put in place by Augustus (63 BCE–19 CE) the first emperor of the Roman Empire, and they were funded by a 4 percent tax on the sale of slaves.

Tracing the etymological roots of the word surveillance shows that it is fundamentally about social power. Two millennia ago it was used by a centralized power to defend and extend itself, upholding a status quo of domination and exploitation. As such, surveillance must be understood as being intimately bound up with the dynamics of social struggles. The powerful have long looked down on what they claimed as their territories and subjects, attempting to organize the world according to their own visions. These impositions of order have often been resisted by slaves, colonial subjects, workers, and dissidents, for ordinary people are active agents, not simply subjected to power; they can both embrace and oppose, conform and confront. This is significant, for I understand surveillance as the social process of "watching over" something for the purpose of projecting control over it. This interpretation is explicitly critical in the sense that it focuses on social power, with a focus on the role that surveillance has in enabling the concentration of power in social contexts of inequality.

The ancient *vigiles* embodied an aspect of the ambiguity that runs through the entire history of surveillance. They watched over the city for nefarious power-serving purposes, such as enforcing re-enslavement, and the abhorrent practice of slavery was stitched into their very existence. Yet, simultaneously, they watched over the city in order to protect it through finding and fighting fires, an unambiguous social good in a densely populated urban setting, for nobody wants to burn to death. From this ancient example we can extrapolate that surveillance has long been used by centralized power to defend and extend itself, yet it has also—at times—been connected to a parental impulse to protect children, to watch over them in order to keep them safe from danger. This latter deeply human impulse can become problematic, particularly when shaped by the forces of patriarchy and when abstracted upward from a family to something far larger and more powerful, such as a "Fatherland" where the people—or more often a specific section of the people (the wealthy, the white, etc.)—are designated as kinds of "children" in need of protection from those deemed threatening; such as the thief or the escaped slave. This kind of patriarchy was concisely captured in Anohni's 2016 surveillance song "Watch Me," specifically in her haunting, quavering wails of the word "daddy."

The point is that with surveillance, often protection and domination are bound up with one another, with a kind of constitutive ambivalence that can protect and punish, reward and repress, care and control, albeit in highly uneven ways. This is important to note, as while I subject surveillance to sustained criticism across this book, I want to stress from the beginning that it is not a bad concept in a one-dimensional way. Rather, the task of this book is to take a critical look at surveillance and determine who is being dominated, who is being protected, what they are being protected from, and, crucially, who has the power to decide.

To give a personal example of the ambiguity of surveillance in action, I live in Melbourne, Australia, which like many cities around the world has a number of extreme right-wing groups. In the Australian context these grouplets like to flatter themselves with the self-aggrandizing term "patriot movement." This label attempts to smear a veneer of legitimacy across a membership that is largely composed of violent, paranoid, white supremacists, misogynists, and neo-Nazis. These groups are sometimes subject to police surveillance, whereby their photos are taken, their leadership hierarchies mapped, and their incoherent, semi-literate writings on social media are trawled through. Police also use human intelligence strategies, such as sending undercover officers to infiltrate the groups, as well as grooming deserters and exploiting rival factions. These measures are taken to understand the groups and keep them from getting out of hand, while simultaneously allowing them to function, as opposed to taking the grassroots anti-fascist ("antifa") approach that would not allow anything that virulent and violent to breed. This is significant, as these groups are playing a part in the increasingly reactionary and resurgent race politics that make up a segment of the emergent twenty-first-century remix of right-wing extremism. This new hard right is on the rise around the world, taking root where increasing inequality, ravaged social relations, and stunted capacity for social meaning mix with sensationalist media, and digital echo-chambers, which provide opportunistic leaders with the chance to give vent to a generalized resentment at the rotting social order.[4]

Nevertheless, it was through targeted surveillance that the police in Melbourne were able to preempt and prevent a massacre that was being planned in 2016. An Australian right-wing extremist named Phillip Galea was arrested by the Victorian police and charged with two terrorism-related offenses; planning a lethal bomb attack and attempting to recruit others to help him carry out a massacre. Galea drew inspiration from the atrocities of Anders Breivik, another right-wing extremist who in 2011 slaughtered seventy-seven people in a terror attack in Oslo, Norway.[5] Galea was planning on killing members of various Melbourne-based left-wing, pro-refugee, and anti-racism groups. One of the locations that he considered attacking was Trades Hall, the world's oldest trade union building. At the time, I was working in a small space in one of Trades Hall towers, and hence—should this massacre have gone ahead—I could have potentially been in or around the planned carnage. I cite this as a personal example of a case where surveillance led to an unambiguous social good: the fewer neo-Nazis we have massacring innocent people the better. This attack was prevented by surveillance—a specific and targeted surveillance of a dangerous and deranged person. This style of surveillance is very different from the huge "collect it all" style of surveillance employed by the tech-titans and government spies.[6]

Following this example, it is important to note that while right-wing extremists may sometimes come under surveillance, they are far from the primary targets. In collaboration with corporate forces, the surveillance state's focus is largely on the poor, ethnic minorities, the institutionalized, and political dissidents/activists. First, in richer countries, the poor come into sharp focus of surveillance through welfare institutions, in collaboration with the private poverty industries that pick up outsourced work formerly performed by the state. While these welfare agencies are apparently there to provide much-needed support for the poor, in an age of grossly unequal austerity, these agencies use advanced surveillance techniques to monitor and control an enormous amount of the everyday practices of people receiving welfare as they struggle to subsist. A compelling window into how this type of surveillance manifests in the United Kingdom can be seen in the 2016 film *I, Daniel Blake*, which follows the story of a fifty-nine-year-old widower who, after suffering a heart attack at work, is forced to grind through the demoralizing bureaucracy of the welfare system.[7]

Second, ethnic and religious minorities (and sometimes majorities) are also frequently disproportionally targeted by state surveillance—often in close collaboration with the private spy industries that join in on the outsourcing feast on public money. Examples of targeted groups are rife throughout the world, include Uyghurs in China, Kurds in Turkey and elsewhere, West Papuans in Indonesia, Aboriginals in Australia, Muslims in the United States and Europe, Rohingya in Myanmar, and Palestinians in Israel, the Occupied Territories, and the refugee camps in neighboring Jordon, Lebanon, and Syria. Alas, these examples could go on and on. In light of the above far from exhaustive list of cases, it is important to point out that the "globalization of surveillance is both a global phenomenon that unfolds differently in different countries, so as to produce situations of complex inter-relation."[8] A point to emphasize at the onset is the enduring importance of embodied difference—the variations between our bodies, sexually, racially, abilities, ages, and so forth—and its entanglement with historical lines of imperial power that lead to highly uneven conditions of surveillance.

Third, surveillance is far more acute inside totalizing institutions like factories and prisons. As I discuss below in more detail, this has

long roots going back centuries to the overseeing of slaves on plantations and the drilling of soldiers in modern militaries. These practices
migrated to the factories and the prisons during the industrial revolution and from there have oozed into many other facets of everyday life.
Significantly, the control of totalizing institutions can merge with the
uneven focus on racial minorities mentioned above, as can be seen with
the imprisonment and monitoring around targeted minorities around
the world. For example, Australia operates a number of "immigration
detention facilities," a public relations euphemism for a prison camp
where refugees are held indefinitely for attempting to assert their
legal right to seek asylum. The Australian government outsources
many of their operations to multinational mercenary corporations—
Broadspectrum, G4S, Paladin Group, Serco, and Wilson Security—who
use surveillance and force to keep these injustices operating. A brilliant
first-hand exposé of these prison camps was written by Behrouz Boochani, a Kurdish journalist illegally imprisoned by Australia in a colonial
outpost in Papua New Guinea since 2013. Writing inside the camps on
a smuggled mobile phone, this critically important story speaks of the
calculated oppression, dehumanization, absurd bureaucracy, and colonial madness of these prison camps. It is a story riddled with hunger,
beatings, torment, squalor, suicide, and death, a story that demands
confrontation and justice.[9]

Fourth, political dissidents and activists, predominantly from the
political left, disproportionally fall under the gaze of the surveillance
state. Security officials from the Australian Security Intelligence Organisation (ASIO) have suggested that environmental activists targeting the
burning and export of coal pose greater threats to energy infrastructure
than terrorists.[10] Leaving aside the unmentioned existential threat
that burning coal in vast quantities represents to life as we know it on
planet Earth, this demonstrates the focus of this surveillance is firmly
on those who seek to disrupt "business as usual." Part of the reason
for this focus is because non-violent direct action and civil disobedi-
ence can, in some contexts, be highly effective tactics to generate social
change, and consequently it faces heavy opposition from entrenched
powers. Unevenly around the world, police, spies, and private security
forces have long employed multiple surveillance techniques in their
struggle against activism, with activists finding ways to learn from
this repression and continue their struggles.[11] As I write these words,

police and security forces around the world are focusing surveillance on the children involved in the global "School Strike for the Climate" protests. The ongoing global tragedy of the innumerable activists who have suffered repression in their struggles is powerfully captured in the famous protest song "If They Come in the Morning," by American folksinger Jack Warshaw. Originally written in 1976, the track was updated and expanded in 2018, to include verses such as "The boys in blue are only a few of the everyday cops on their beat / The CID, NSA, Google, and Apple, and spies and eyes in the skies do their job well / And behind them the brains that build systems that collect every word that we breathe / And the ones who decide when it's time to drag you to a cell."[12] So, the poor, the racialized "other," the nationalized, and the dissenter often get far more surveillance attention from state security agents, and their corporate collaborators.

A MAP OF SURVEILLANCE

The word "surveillance" was first used in English in 1799, the year that Napoleon's coup d'état ended the French Revolution. The concept thus appeared at a time when capitalist modernity was gathering steam—literally with the industrial revolution—along with the nationalization of warfare, great concentrations of wealth, and the global projection of power, which were all enabled by the forces of science, capital, and the state coming together in a synthesis.[13] The word surveillance has parallels to the much older word "survey"—*sur* ("over") *veeir* ("to see"). Historically, survey meant to determine the boundaries of private property, to cartographically map something via linear and angular measurements, and, more generally, to look at it from above, from a commanding height, a position of power. Like surveillance, it means to watch over something in order to exert control over it. With these conceptual parallels in mind, it may be insightful to think of surveillance through survey, for the latter seems to have preceded and prefigured the former.

The word "survey" was first used in English in the 1400s and went on to have most of its meanings forged during the "long sixteenth century" (c.1450–1640), the key period where capitalist modernity first emerged as a world-historic social formation. Across these years, feudalism in Europe disintegrated with various forces and practices unfolding: the Spanish and Portuguese empires; the powerful banks of the

Italian city-states; the reinvention of slavery; the rise of witch burning and the subordination of women; new ways of producing food via plantations, and the germination of new knowledge—scientific, technical, and philosophical—all of which led to new ways of relating to nature and one another, and new ways of understanding the world and our place in it. While this phenomenon apparently congealed in Europe, it was part of a thoroughly global process, being driven in large part by the conquest of the Americas, which began after Columbus's in/famous journey in 1492, a venture initially undertaken to reach China to tap into the infinite riches it was believed to possess. Full-scale European conquest soon followed, with immense amounts of looted silver and gold being swiftly extracted and commercialized thorough racialized slave labor.[14] As the continent of the Americas was entirely unmentioned in any holy book or classical philosophy, its "discovery" forced a rethinking of established knowledge. This rethinking was furthered as new elements of classical philosophy entered Europe, updated and redacted by generations of Islamic scholarship. Additionally, intensifying industrial activity, the increasing scale of military engagements and the emergence of capitalist production all came together into the broth of capitalist modernity, a ferment that was always already global.[15]

The pivotal year of 1492 is often held up as the beginning of the modern world, for that was the year that Columbus made his fateful voyage westward.[16] While the world-historic changes that occurred with the conquest of the Americas is undeniable, the dynamics of European expansion were under way well before Columbus was born. The Portuguese prince known as Henry the Navigator (1394–1460) was an enthusiastic patron of nautical expansion, taking an active interest in exploring and plundering Africa, with maps helping to realize these ends. Henry understood that maps were crucial to this process, and he created a law to make them a state monopoly and ban their dissemination.[17] He realized that the knowledge in a map grants power, a realization that prefigured much of the development of capitalist modernity.

To make an accurate map necessitates *surveying* the earth, measuring it and abstracting pertinent details of it onto a representation. Given the infinite complexity of the embodied earth, it is fundamentally not possible to include everything on a map. The earth is composed of interwoven manifolds of processes, relations, and systems, all layered by tangled scales and orders of complexity, and all dynamically transforming. Facing this impossible complexity, mapmakers must be highly selective; they must make decisions about what to include and what to exclude. The surveyor chooses some specific details from the complexity of the embodied earth and represents them. This process necessarily and unavoidably requires making simplifications and distortions, and it is always accompanied by cultural assumptions and social power. Once drawn, maps can possess a real power over the world they represent, shaping the way in which the world is understood and experienced. The process of abstracting the world into a map and viewing the world from the commanding height of survey, grants an organizing power in the hands of the surveyor, or the social formation that they serve.[18]

In many respects, surveillance parallels surveying. Like the embodied earth of which they are a part, human social relations are infinitely complex. For any one social situation to be completely grasped it would require mapping every relationship, the material conditions that enabled it, the symbolic, the unsaid, the unsayable, as well as layer after layer of history, their ecological entanglements, and all the passions, tribulations, and irresolvable dilemmas of the human condition, all of which are caked in irresolvable uncertainty and ambiguity.[19] Plainly, this is an impossible task, particularly for a narrow functionary of power who is tasked with upholding the status quo. To engage in surveillance, like surveying, one must be highly selective, choosing what to focus on and what to ignore. As with mapping, this creates simplifications and distortions according to the cultural assumptions and the nature of the interests being served. The point is not to represent the whole, but rather a limited slice of reality that is deemed relevant to the surveilling agent and the power they serve. This narrow slice can be used to create data that can serve to remake reality, to influence the organization of the world and to advance a certain set of interests. Like surveying a territory, surveillance of people grants a real-world power, giving an organizing power into the hands of the surveilling agent and the interests they serve.

Perhaps an example will make this more concrete. Imagine that a spy contracting for the CIA from a mercenary company is tasked with surveilling a group of environmental activists. They are not likely to be interested in understanding their target's sense of social justice, how it was culturally nourished, and how it relates to the ethics of humanity's relationship with the environment. Rather, the spy is interested in when and where the activists are seeking to block the coal-carrying train in order to crush the direct action, and to make an example of them to discourage other activists. The spy extracts data from the activists, with this being drawn away and filed systematically for analysis, comparison, and action. It may be put into reports and presented to senior bureaucrats; it may be shared with the mining company who may take things into their own hands. Data is drawn from the activists, from their social media communications, their geographic location, who they have met with, when, where, from the facial recognition CCTV system, from their credit records, from their smart devices, and so on. While surveillance thinking is very reliant on visual metaphors and practices—overseeing, supervision, watching over, and so forth—it does not necessarily mean "seeing" as in perceiving with the eyes. Rather, surveillance reduces its subjects to abstract data in order to exert control over them in the name of a centralized power. The techno-social processes that produce data strip "away social context, leaving a disembodied and highly abstract depiction of the world and of what matters in it."[20] This process enables control at a distance and is fundamental to the understanding of surveillance, with the limited, abstracted data set being set to serve the concentration of power and maintenance of a status quo of inequality.

An important contradiction here is that while surveillance tends toward abstraction and the amassing of disembodied data on targets, the human body nevertheless remains as a crucial site of struggle, violence, and contestation. Bodies are monitored—inside and out—by surveillance, from facial recognition algorithms to airport pat downs. Indeed, the relation between the body and disembodiment is a central contradiction in the twenty-first century, with many manifestations from the resurgence of race-politics in the age of disembodied global networks of communication to the new obsession with taking control of bodies through self-surveillance machines, like fitness trackers, that run in parallel with the abstracted, global forms of integration (chapter 4). Each side of this contradiction reinforces the other "in an intimate spiral of externalized desire and an internalized sense of incompleteness."[21] So while surveillance can be very abstract in its function, it often does this by focusing on the flesh. This isn't just a story of techno-ingenuity but also of very blunt and brutal expressions of power, from data centers to beatings in cold rooms.

Indeed, the ominous image of the one-way mirror in the interrogation room remains a potent symbol of surveillance, although one that has attracted far less attention than the watchtower. The "transparent mirror" was first patented in the United States in 1903, featuring a glass coated with a very thin, largely see-through layer of aluminum. Then, when there are uneven levels of lighting, with one side being bright and the other dark, the mirror grants a one-way window for the surveyor in the darkness and grants the light-flooded surveilled a reflection of themselves. In this way, a one-way mirror embodies the power asymmetry at the heart of surveillance: it tries to make the surveilled transparent to power while concealing the surveyor.

SURVEYS OF ENCLOSURE AND EMPIRE

Many of the examples used across this book are taken from different post/colonial contexts, for this is where the forces of empire come into contact with the Other. Colonialism has long tested the occupying power's statecraft, demanding new tactics and techniques for the conquest and pacification of the colony. Furthermore, the practice of empire allowed for experiments in control that would not have been possible within the home country, thus making "empire a crucible for forging new state forms and functions."[22] This process has unfolded on a global scale—for example the British colonial domination of India and subjugation of China; as well as on national and regional scales— for example, India's military occupation of the contested territories of Jammu and Kashmir, and the Chinese repression in Tibet and Xinjiang.

The geography of surveillance is a curious subject, for there seems to be a movement, whereby many of the tactics used to project control over "the Other" have since invaded the everyday. Techniques first used to surveil slaves, natives, workers, and vagrants spread; the gaze turned to the insane, the sick, and the prisoner, as well as the unionist, the "hysteric woman," and the school child before eventually being cast across all of society, albeit with enduring uneven attention. For example, almost everyone who wishes to travel by plane must submit to the regimes of surveillance in an airport: biometric scans, identification documents, bag inspection, and other such techniques historically reserved for those deemed undesirable.[23] Not everyone has the same chance of being singled out for special attention, with ethnicity, religion, class, and political subjectivity playing important and discriminatory roles. At the other end of the spectrum, those with access to private jets entirely evade these surveillance rituals, and those who can afford special treatment can avoid the worst of it. The uneven application of this surveillance can result in the same guard or police officer being viewed by some as employed to protect and others as employed to persecute. This binding up of protection and domination is characteristic of surveillance's contradictory nature.

To understand surveillance, I shall discuss its roots within the practice of "survey," as this is central to understanding that the early processes of globalization set the conditions for contemporary surveillance to emerge. The longer-term study presented here reveals some of the core dynamics that characterize surveillance up to the present. For surveying was not just a way to describe the earth, rather it was a technology to dominate the world. Likewise, surveillance is not just a way to look at the people, rather it is a technology of domination, a way to project power and subject people to control from above. Both work in part through abstraction, through taking a limited slice of reality and representing it in a system, with the insights from this process granting an organizing power that can reshape practice, the ability to project control from above.

The rise of capitalist modernity saw a number of profound transformations begin as the feudal order gave way to the new and increasingly dominant mode of practice. Unevenly across the long sixteenth century, land was commodified: it was transformed into private property that could be bought and sold on the market. Land was abstracted from the complex webs of relations that characterized peasant farmers' indigenous land use systems, to being measured and marked on maps so as to parcel it out in pieces of private property. As has long been recognized, this "primitive accumulation" was crucial to set up the conditions for capitalist expansion.[24]

Historians often refer to this process as the "enclosure of the commons," the ongoing processes in which what was formerly held in common was transformed into private property. Today, it can be difficult for some to imagine the extent of the transformations wrought by the coming of absolute private property, or what the world was like before. It may be particularly difficult for those of us raised in settler-colonial contexts, for the institution of private property was a founding principle of these "new worlds" standing in stark contrast to the preinvasion systems. The enclosure movements began as a kind of internal colonization, with the indigenous peasants of places like England being the first to be dispossessed. The commoners were removed from the commons, thus completely undermining the older ways of being and doing. Enclosure transformed the collective ownership rooted in customary practices, to exclusive rights for individuals and corporate "persons" enforced by legal systems pushed down from above. These processes were often resisted from below, with the peasantry accurately seeing it as an assault on their way of life, both with the rise of bourgeois property owners, reassertions of landed aristocracy, and states eager to extract more tax revenues. In England, there were a series of uprisings that sought to resist the enclosure of the commons, such as the Kett's Rebellion in 1549, where local rebels destroyed the fences erected by the landlords. During these uprisings the defenders of the commons faced off with those who wanted them enclosed, with their struggles echoing on across the entire history of capitalist modernity. Even today, new capitalist enclosure movements are met with calls to defend the commons, drawing on a vision of sharing and solidarity as the foundation of social relations as opposed to desire for power and riches.[25]

An example of this can be seen playing out today in the struggles over the Amazon rainforest, with indigenous peoples protesting to try and keep their customary land intact against the violent confrontation of the logging and cattle industries, newly empowered by the hard-right government of Jair Bolsonaro. This struggle between commons and enclosure has enormous consequences for the world, for cattle grazing in the burned-out ruins of the Amazon comes at terrifying expense with respect to the carbon that they release and the opportunity cost of the destroyed forest. One kilogram of beef protein from the Brazilian Amazon releases 1,250 kilograms of CO_2 emissions, roughly the same as taking a flight from New York to London and back.[26] As Brazil is one of the biggest exporters of beef in the world, such struggles for the commons are crucial if we are to avoid cataclysmic global warming. Over the centuries, enclosure movements have formed a central dynamic of capitalism. This was neatly captured by an anonymous author in the seventeenth century who wrote a protest poem about the enclosure movements, with its first verse reading:

> The law locks up the man or woman
> Who steals the goose from off the common
> But leaves the greater villain loose
> Who steals the common from off the goose.

The "view from above" offered by surveys was a key component of the process of enclosure and hence the formation of capitalism. Through measuring and abstracting land onto maps, it was able to be alienated as a commodity. Cartography was bound up with the violent imposition of state-sponsored private property relations, whereby maps were "tools for the consolidation or extension of power."[27] By providing part of the means to carve up and enclose land, cadastral maps (maps of private property) allow space to be literally "drawn away" into a representation that reconstitutes space on a more abstract level. As the commons were increasingly enclosed, this served to destroy the customary rights and relations that they previously supported. This was necessary to "free" peasants from the land, which is to say give them the freedom to work for masters, to starve, or be incarcerated in workhouses for vagrancy. Beyond England, enclosure movements were common across Europe, in the Nordic nations with their northward expansion, within the German states' internal colonizations, and in France's centralization under absolutist rule. Importantly, while these processes began internally in European countries, they soon began to project enclosure outward.

Maps were used to assert the right of alienated property, as well as a tool for the management and exploitation of privatized estates. "It was only a short step to the wider use of maps as general instruments of state policy and control through more systematic management and exploitation of state lands, in particular state forests."[28] In this way, surveying and enclosure were bound up with important transformations of nature across early capitalist modernity. A telling example can be seen with the rise of forestry, the industrial practice of cultivating trees for commercial purposes. Across the long sixteenth century, there was an increased need for wood—largely for shipbuilding, mining, and as fuel for metallurgy—which put pressure on the dwindling old-growth forests of Europe. In order to extract as much wood as possible, forests had to be reorganized, and surveying was key to this process. Forestry sought to transform an entire forest—all the myriad processes, relations, and systems—replacing it with neat, uniform lines of monocultural trees of the same age spread evenly across a surveyed territory. All the tremendous complexity of the forests—the inorganic minerals, sunlight, and rainfall upon which it is founded, through to the microbes, fungus, and lichen; the plants, from moss to shrubs; the invertebrates, worms through insects; the vertebrates, frogs, lizards, and birds; as well as the long history of human interaction, the foraging, gathering, coppicing, and hunting; the intricate tapestry of cultural practices, symbols, and spiritual significance—were all subordinated to the extractive impulse of capital accumulation. Peasants went on attempting to use the forests in the way they always had, yet their ancient practices were rebranded and criminalized as "poaching." The forests then had to be policed in order to keep the people out, with surveillance following the survey. The commanding height of the surveyor allowed for a power to be exerted over nature, for it to be remade according to abstract lines of power. This enabled a concentration and centralization of power in the hands of the forest master with his (intentional gendering) ability to produce a single commodity that can easily transform into wealth and thus social power. From their origins in central Europe, this model of forestry plantation was projected across the world, with surveying facilitating the violent simplifications that go with monocultural extraction.[29]

After beginning in England, the practices of enclosure soon went "beyond the pale," an expression that referred to the Pale, a part of Ireland centered on Dublin that was under the imperial control of the English since the late Middle Ages. To move beyond the pale was an imperial expression meaning to move beyond the boundaries of civilization and into the realm of savagery. At the beginning of capitalist modernity, the English increasingly imagined Ireland—their first colony—as a primitive and backward place. Through degrading Gaelic cultures, they resurrected the ancient notion of the barbarism of nomadic and pastoral people, fusing it with the modern idea of civilization as corresponding to cultivated fields and land as enclosed parcels of private property. Abstracting land in this way not only allowed for the ease of maintaining a reliable taxation roll, which was necessary to extract as much wealth as possible from the colony, but also it was an attempt to force the Irish to adopt English practices. Simultaneously, the colonization of Virginia proceeded on the same "plantation" model as took place in Ulster. In the Virginian colony, the conquering English were dumbfounded by the natives and their strange, savage ways. The English came from a civilized nation where women were the property of their husbands and fathers; yet Iroquois women could have opinions, participate in community decisions, get divorced, and men did not have the arbitrary right to punish them.[30] Likewise, the colonists could not understand that the land was not commodified and enclosed. Once again, the survey was a key technique of power in this project, for it was through surveying, and the accompanying knowledge of geography and cartography, that the Irish landscape became conceivable as an object that could be known and thus controlled.[31]

As capitalist modernity increased, great enclosure movements projected out of Europe, sweeping the world on a planetary scale, whereby capitalist empire "creates a world after its own image."[32] "The concept of exclusive property in land, as a norm to which other practices must be adjusted, was now extending across the whole globe, like a coinage reducing all things to a common measure."[33] Surveyors, cartographers, and geographers were made to "buckle down, administer empire, map, and plan land use and territorial rights, and gather and analyze useful data for purposes of business and state administration."[34] Prior to the American Revolution George Washington was a colonial surveyor for westward expansion that would necessarily exclude Indigenous land use. This surveying and enclosure was essential for capitalism, for as Adam Smith would go on to argue, private property must be absolute, or it was meaningless. Furthermore, the great theorist of capitalism argued that it was the central role of the state to protect the private property of the rich from the indignation of the poor.[35] This justification for the use of state power to defend and extend private property relations was core to the enclosure movements and their increasingly global reorganizations, with important repercussions for the story of globalization and surveillance.

Going further beyond the pale, when the British began their conquest of India, absolute property rights did not exist on the subcontinent. This is not to suggest that India was an idyllic commons with sharing and caring for all. Rather, most of it was ruled by the Mughal Empire (1526–1858), and they had an elaborate system of property and ownership, with various forms of commons unevenly intersecting with grossly unequal caste relations. As the British increasingly gained control of the hugely diverse subcontinent, they began imposing their own singular system of private property rights and abolishing the various indigenous systems. As with their Irish and American colonies, the British believed that civilization requires fixed borders—marked with fences on the ground and lines on a map—in order to enclose and delineate private property. Hence, one of the tasks of the imperial surveyor in India was to enclose land according to their imported system of private property relations.

A key player in this was the "Survey of India," an engineering agency established in 1767 by the British East India Company and charged with mapping the subcontinent. Initially set up for the purposes of consolidating the company's imperial territories (1767–1858), it went on to be used by the British Raj to enable their imperial domination of the continent (1858–1947) before serving the central government of the independent nation (1947–present). The Survey of India's ability to coordinate the intensive mapping of the colony came directly from the power of the empire: from the political and economic organization of the world that allowed for the concentration of power, from the culture of imperialism that gave it justification, and from the ecological power that came from dominating nature. As the number of ad hoc surveys of privatized property increased, the imperialists felt a need to integrate them into a systematic framework, launching the "Great Trigonometrical Survey" in 1802. This quest sought to measure the entire Indian subcontinent with scientific precision, including mapping the heights of the world's biggest mountains, the tallest of which was named after one of the project's leaders, George Everest. Following this, the survey is frequently remembered in highly romanticized terms, of adventurous men, braving harsh environments and savages for the sake of science and the glorious progress of civilization. That may capture part of the dynamic, but the surveyors were also active agents of empire, plotting points on a map in order for a distant power to dominate and exploit another.[36]

One of the goals of the Great Trigonometrical Survey was to measure arches of longitude. One of their first actions involved following the 80 degree line from Chennai (known then as Madras) in the south to the foothills of the Himalayas, around 1,700 kilometers to the north. This was the world's first accurate measurement of an arch of longitude and a key moment in the long history of mapping the globe.[37] The ambitious survey attempted to map India in order to project an organizing power over it, a power firmly attached to the global hierarchy as devised by the British Empire. In practice, many factors limited the effectiveness of the survey, including lack of funding, technical difficulties, language barriers, local resistance, bureaucratic rigidity, fickle support of ministers, and divided power blocs within the East India Company. As a social practice, surveying is replete with complexities and contingencies, ambiguities and ambivalences. Initially imagined taking five years, the process took nearly seventy, well beyond the Indian Rebellion of 1857 and the end of the company's rule of the subcontinent shortly thereafter.

This is significant, for mapmakers were never just measuring the land in some neutral manner. Rather, through surveying they were methodically abstracting the land, extracting data traces from it—this compass bearing and this angle, taking into account the gravitational influence of mountains and the non-spherical nature of the earth's curve, and so on. All these data traces were quantified and recomposed as a representation that the powerful can use to reorganize space to suit their interests. These processes created something that was highly accurate in a very narrow sense, a vast abstraction—a monstrously simplified version of the actual embodied India that was made to appear as something that could be known and controlled, as an object to be mastered from above.[38] Again, in this sense surveying prefigures and parallels surveillance.

Shortly before the word "surveillance" was first formulated, an English engineer Samuel Bentham (1757–1831) moved to Russia in 1780 to work for Prince Potemkin on his great southern estate, a piece of land that was colonized by the Russians after the defeat of the Ottomans in the 1768–1774 war. As a naval engineer and weapons designer, Bentham was put in charge of the prince's factories and workshops, thus forcing him to supervise a large and sometimes unruly workforce. Experimenting with ways of imposing centralized control, Samuel came upon the kernel of the idea of the "Panopticon," a concept and architectural principle that would be popularized by his more famous big brother, the utilitarian philosopher Jeremy Bentham (1748–1832).[39]

The evocative name, meaning "all visible," echoes back to Argus Panoptes, a giant from Greek mythology said to have had one hundred eyes, a monstrous incarnation of surveillance. The elder Bentham first formalized the panopticon as a model for prison. The structure was to be built in a ring, with each cell opening up inwardly, all focused on a central watchtower. The interior of each cell was visible to the tower, where a single guard could survey all the inmates all the time, without the inmates being aware of whether or not they were under surveillance. The architecture itself sought to motivate the prisoners to internalize the guard's all-pervasive gaze and regulate their behavior accordingly. Over the ensuing centuries, prison panopticons were built, often largely in the colonies and peripheries, with nineteenth century examples including Port Arthur, Tasmania, Australia; and the Old Provost, in South Africa. Twentieth-century examples include Caseros Prison in Argentina; Presidio Modelo in Cuba; Palacio de Lecumberri in Mexico; New Bilibid Prison in the Philippines; and Chí Hòa Prison in Vietnam.

While the idea of the panopticon is often associated with prisons, Bentham imagined it as a much more expansive concept, describing it as a "new mode of obtaining power of mind over mind, in a quantity hitherto without example: and that, to a degree equally without example, secured by whoever chooses to have it so: Such is the engine: such the work that may be done with it."[40] He preached of how this "engine" could be applied to all manner of domineering and totalizing institutions: factories, hospitals, asylums, poorhouses, and schools. Yet in these organizations, the hierarchies are largely explicit, with the overlords, observers, and overseers firmly in control. It was when panoptic principles began to bleed beyond these institutions that the fabric of social life was to be remade by surveillance. In this way, the ancient monster Panoptes was resurrected as an engine, as an all-seeing machine designed to reorganize subjectivity according to the whims of power.[41]

Bentham worked tirelessly to convince world leaders to adopt his ideas, curiously finding some of his most receptive ears outside Europe. For example, he corresponded with Muhammad Ali Pasha (1769–1849), an Albanian-born commander who ended up founding a dynasty that ruled Egypt for over a century, and he sought to transform it into a powerful modern state. The monarch set about thoroughly reorganizing Egyptian society, strengthening and streamlining the economy, training bureaucrats, and modernizing the military. Bentham advised that panoptic principles be applied to the entire body of Egyptian society so as to make it controllable from above. One of his closest friends and collaborators was also a key advisor to Muhammad Ali, and he wrote that introducing European-style military organization into Egypt brought with it "a general system of dependence and subordination, [which] were the needful companions of the new state of things. The transfer of the military power from unruly and undisciplined hordes to a body of troops regularly trained through the various grades of obedience and discipline, was in itself the establishment of a principle of order which spread over the whole surface of society."[42]

This push from above resulted in large-scale reorganization of Egyptian society based not on architectural panopticons, but on panoptic principles of surveillance and control. The country was surveyed, with absolute private-property lines being drawn, thus remaking land into a commodity that enabled increased taxation and processes of capital accumulation. Much of historic Cairo was demolished and rebuilt, with the old maze-like center being replaced by open streets and a grid, simplifying and opening up the great city to policing and centralized control. Surveillance, checkpoints, bureaucratic passes, all served to control and minimize unruly movement. Compulsory schooling sought to train the youth into obedient political subjects, and factories imposed authoritarian labor practices on workers. In a great variety of ways, the panoptic principle of the power of surveillance, of viewing the world from above and exerting control onto social practices, was key to the remaking of Egypt.[43] It should be noted that panoptic control was never a one-dimensional power of total domination, for there are always contradictions and spaces of struggle that present potential openings for forces of resistance.[44] It is not uncommon for anti-colonial movements to have formed within the barracks, hence turning the forces of authoritarian control and indoctrination against the foreign power that set them up. The resultant new regime may well be haunted by the domination of their predecessors in equally contradictory ways.

The kernel of surveillance at the core of the panopticon—the principle of centralized control from above and outside—is crucial. In using the mechanical metaphor of the "engine" for his panopticon, Bentham was keenly aware of its productive power. This power was both subjective and material, it exists within the minds of the observer and the observed, and it is encoded into the architecture and into the organization of matter. In this way, the panoptic principles spread via technologies and techniques for projecting control.

THE NINETEENTH CENTURY'S "INFORMATION REVOLUTION"

As previously noted, the word "surveillance" first appeared in the Napoleonic era, which came to an end in 1815 with the Battle of Waterloo and the defeat of the French military by the united armies of Britain and Prussia. From this point, a kind of *Pax Britannica* came into place, a century of expansion and accumulation, globalization and empire. This 100-year peace "held its sway sometimes by the ominous poise of a heavy ship's cannon, but more frequently it prevailed by the timely pull of a thread in the international monetary network."[45] The forces of empire reorganized the world with a racialized global division of labor taking shape, with people the world over being drawn into a "vortex of change the origins of which were obscure to them," with the "new and tremendous hazards of planetary interdependence" springing into being.[46]

During this period, capitalist modernity literally gathered steam. Propelled by the demands for accumulation and expansion, steam power transformed transportation on land and sea, with both being enabled by the satellite industries of steel production and coal mining, as well as the science of surveying. On the sea the speed of trade increased as steam power came into concert with more accurate navigation techniques and new maps resulting from marine surveys and abstract measurements. Before steam, it took the average sail-powered clipper ship with approximately one thousand tons of cargo between 120 and 130 days to make a journey from China to London. Steamships of the Blue Funnel Line—launched in 1865 with a capacity for three thousand tons of cargo—could do the journey in seventy-seven days. As a consequence, the volume of trade moving around the world via ship increased massively, from 32,000 tons in 1831 to 3.3 million tons in 1876.

Steam-power on land was also big business. The railroad baron Thomas Brassey, for example, sometimes employed up to eighty thousand workers on five continents, launching these "shock troops of industrialization" upon the world. Railroad construction increased from 72,000 kilometers in 1840 (almost entirely in Europe and North America), to more than 367,000 kilometers globally by 1880, with surveys preceding the laying of rail. Powerful international financial institutions funded these expensive projects and the railway lines unfolded according to the demands of imperial markets. Using the "penetration model," designed to connect production areas with seaports, rail networks maximized the extraction of natural resources and cheap labor. The train—perhaps the most important emblem of progress at the time—formed another "decisive part of the cage of dependency" that was tightening its grip on the colonized world. Frequently, as in the west-to-east section of the U.S. transcontinental railway, the work was overseen by white colonizers while the bulk of the heavy work was carried out by racialized and brutalized workforces, in this instance by Chinese laborers.[47]

Another key development ran in tangled parallel to steam. Across the nineteenth century there was a kind of "information revolution," whereby sets of technologies, techniques, and intellectual practices came together to create new ways of communicating, storing, and processing large amounts of data in an unprecedented global information regime. The most famous piece of this was the electric telegraph, which vastly increased the speed of communication. Across capitalist modernity, the speed at which a message could be sent went from the metabolic speed of a messenger on foot or horseback to the mechanical speed of a train or steam engine to the electric speed of pulses along a copper wire. The acceleration in this last step "was not a doubling or tripling of transmission speed; it was a leap of many orders of magnitude. It was like the bursting of a dam whose presence had not even been known." This brought on an era of communication that was without precedent or even possible comparison.[48]

Some consequences of this were observed immediately. In 1875 an English telegraphic engineer claimed, "Distance and time have been so changed in our imaginations that the globe has been practically reduced in magnitude, and there can be no doubt that our conceptions of its dimension is entirely different to that held by our forefathers."[49] For instance, in 1840 it took one hundred days for the news of a dead president to get across the North American continent to the tiny farming settlement that was Los Angeles. After the 1860 transcontinental telegram line was erected, communication was almost instant. This led to multidimensional transformations, with this "time-space compression" being seen as a central part of the globalization process, which resulted in transformations in the material organization and subjective experience of the world.[50] It also served to intensify the possibilities of surveillance. For example, during the American Civil War (1861–1865), President Lincoln granted total control of the nation's telegraph lines to his secretary of war, rerouting the flow of information through the war offices. Information extracted from this arrangement granted insights into the turbulent situation, and allowed for strict controls of the press, with censorship, intimidation, and the extra-judicial arrests of journalists.

The speed at which telegraphs enabled communications to flow contributed to many subjective and material transformations. For example, shortly after the telegram network began to be expanded, people became aware of what the weather was doing much further away than was previously knowable. Some scientists and navy officers—such as Robert FitzRoy, the former captain of the *Beagle*, the ship that bore Charles Darwin around the world—started studying weather reports from distant locals. They began setting up integrated and standardized systems of observation that could be used to predict weather patterns. Their attention was first focused on gale winds, which were dangerous to Britain's ships—so central to the Empire's global projection of power. From these military beginnings, these predictions went public. *The Times* was the first newspaper to print daily weather forecasts, beginning with a prediction that, on August 1, 1861, London would reach 62 degrees Fahrenheit (16.7 degrees Celsius), with a clear, southwesterly wind. Thus, surveillance of the atmosphere through telegrams led to two powerful transformations: firstly, the weather began to be conceived as a global system, not just a local occurrence; and secondly, it could be predicted with far more accuracy than older methods of forecasting.

In addition to the electric telegraph a collection of other marvelous gadgetry came about in the nineteenth century, all with long contested histories but coming to new levels and commercial production. The telegraph, along with the typewriter and telephone, allowed for the transmission of recorded data at tremendous speeds and accuracy. These devices ran across networks consisting of transcontinental and transoceanic telegraph lines, with the former being presided over by monopoly capital and the latter by British naval power. Developments in photography and advanced printmaking techniques enabled the visual to be similarly encoded. The key-driven adding machine, arguably the biggest breakthrough in accounting since double-entry bookkeeping in the long sixteenth century, and updated punch cards allowed for proto-computers to process enormous amounts of data very rapidly. Furthermore, there was the rise of integrated and universalizing systems for the rapid filing and retrieval of large sets of information, such as the decimal classification system used in libraries (e.g., the proprietary Dewey Decimal Classification first published in 1876). Library information systems like this effectively reduced the classification of all textual human knowledge to a code of numbers and letters.[51]

Once this information regime was in place, it "finally represented the means of communication adequate to modern means of production."[52] These transformations dramatically increased the geographic size and speed at which capitalism could function, with an entirely new organization of the world being added to the old and integrated into it in messy, contradicting, and overlapping ways. Investors "developed completely global interests, and international investment grew even more rapidly than world trade." The tremendous amounts of wealth that was extracted from land and produced by labor was optimized by telecommunications, and this was "plowed back into the creation of hierarchies of top and middle managers [who] specialized in monitoring and regulating markets and labor processes," with powerful repercussions for the possibilities of surveillance.[53] Yet this was a hugely uneven global process. While London and New York printed the same newspaper letters on the same day, these newspapers and letters would take half a year to reach colonial outposts in Africa and were highly unreliable in the United States' frontier with/against so-called Indian territory. Thus, the speed of communication was paradoxically created through contrast, "the 'wilderness' of the [white] 'Wild West' and the 'darkness' of the 'dark continent.'"[54]

Curiously, in the late nineteenth century, the steam train and surveillance came together in one of the most important moments in the history of computing-machines. A German-American engineer named Herman Hollerith (1860–1929) was sitting aboard a train inspecting the ticket that he had been issued. The issuing officer had punched holes in the ticket, encoding it with crude biometric data in order to capture someone's appearance. If one was tall with blue eyes and a small nose, then punch, punch, punch into the card and it would be difficult to share this ticket with a short, brown eyed and big-nosed person. These tickets were brought in by inspectors in an effort to minimize fraud—for the practices of ticket sharing and ticket recycling were rampant among the poor of the Gilded Age—and to maximize the profits of the railroad barons. At some point, this routine practice of surveilling and policing the poor inspired Hollerith: perhaps the principle could be applied on a national level. The idea was taken up by the Census Bureau, a federal institution charged with surveying the country's population. The Bureau was aware of the limits of manual methods for it was still processing numbers it had collected eight years earlier in the 1880 census. As with all surveillance, the census was not interested in the complexity of whole people but rather the easily extractable data in order to make them legible from above. Easily extractable data included sex, age, marital status, profession, and race, with the options there being white, black, mulatto, quadroon, octoroon, Chinese, Japanese, or Indian. For the 1890 census, they opted to use electric tabulating machines designed by Hollerith, with the data collected on each person being punched into cards and processed semi-automatically. Using this machine, a clerk working in the Census Bureau could process twenty thousand cards per day. It was regarded as a huge success, with computing-machines being employed in statecraft, business, scientific, and military organizations. Shortly afterwards, Hollerith founded a company that would later be amalgamated to form the corporate behemoth International Business Machines Corporation, better known as IBM.

Along with other technologies and techniques of abstraction, such as the survey, the calendar, and the museum, the census forged part of an emergent "totalizing classificatory grid, which could be applied with endless flexibility to anything under the state's real or contemplated control: peoples, regions, religions, languages, products, monuments, and so forth," with everything rendered countable.[55] Woven with threads of capital, science, and the state, this globalizing enterprise was entwined with the impulse to survey, to surveil, and to control.

Some of the tremendous economic booms that unevenly surged through the nineteenth century's industrial expansion reached an impasse. The United States' railroad expansion, like all such booms, became bloated with speculative capital and overproduction, which combined with shifting global dynamics—such as Germany's unification under an Imperial constitution and later decision to cease minting silver—led to a financial crisis in 1873 that spilled out into the "Long Depression" that carried on unevenly across the world capitalist system until near the end of the century. Production, profits, prices, and interest rates were all depressed, with unemployment rising, strikes, police brutality, and bankruptcies revealing major tensions between national economies and global markets, free trade, and protectionism in the nineteenth-century globalization. This protracted crisis led to many contradictory and complex developments, with two being of particular interest to this narrative, namely, intensifying control of workplaces and the intensification of imperialism, both of which were closely bound to surveillance.

Workplaces have long been a key site of surveillance, from the origins of capitalist production on the slave driven sugar plantations in the long sixteenth century, to the colonial factories that inspired the original panopticon.[56] In the latter part of the nineteenth century, the unfolding crisis mixed with the rationalizations in ways that served to intensify the concentration and centralization of power in production processes. This story is often told by focusing on the industrial foreman turned management theorist Fredrick Winslow Taylor (1856–1915). Disgusted by the inefficiencies he witnessed, Taylor spent decades formulating a system designed to maximize the efficiency of production, formulating the principles he called "Scientific Management," a system that often bore his name, "Taylorism." He advocated that managers need to amass all the traditional knowledge of labor via close surveillance, a process designed to transform the skills embodied in a laborer by "reducing this knowledge to rules, laws, and formulae" controlled by management.[57] This was achieved through time and motion studies that sought to optimize each movement and use wages and bonuses as incentives to push workers harder. Taylorism systematically gathered knowledge from surveillance to strengthen power, with this being "the pivot upon which all modern management turns: the control of work though control over the *decisions that are made in the course of work*."[58] The implementation of Taylorism remade the work of industrial labor, with its workers becoming less skilled and more replaceable, hence cheaper and less able to defend their interests against the owners. Of course, the deskilling and disempowering of workers was not total, for many intellectually trained workers, such as engineers, increased their skills and power, yet they were increasingly more closely aligned with management. Indeed, the empowerment of management was part of a trend whereby "the 'visible hand' of modern corporate organization and management now replaced the 'invisible hand' of Adam Smith's anonymous market."[59]

While this system made little widespread progress during Taylor's lifetime, after the Great War (1914–1918) it took off, merging with other pioneers of mass production, like Henry Ford's assembly lines. Ford took inspiration from a management technique pioneered in a Chicago slaughterhouse. In this death factory, animals would be hung by their hooves on hooks and hacked to pieces by a procession of poorly paid people. In these hellish *dis*assembly lines was the kernel that would go on to make the assembly line, a new technique that greatly accelerated production speed, and hence profit making.[60] One curious impact of Taylor's system was in Russia. In 1914, the activist Vladimir Ilyich Ulyanov (later better known by the pseudonym V. I. Lenin) wrote a short and damning article lampooning Taylor's system under the heading *Man's Enslavement by the Machine*. This is curious, for after the Revolution thrust him to the head of the newly formed Soviet government in 1917, Lenin changed his tone on Scientific Management, proclaiming that Russians needed to "learn to work." In 1918 he wrote that Taylorism, like all capitalist systems—from his perspective—was simultaneously refined bourgeois brutality and the greatest scientific system for control over production: "The Soviet Republic must at all costs adopt all that is valuable in the achievements of science and technology in this field." He argued that the system must be adopted to their purpose of building socialism.[61] This is curious, for it shows how these ideas were globalized, and adopted to different quests, capital accumulation or the construction of state socialism, with surveillance providing centralized control over production in both cases.

Another response to the crises of the late nineteenth century that also intimately involved surveillance was the intensification of imperialism, as if the "concept of unlimited expansion . . . alone can fulfill the hope for unlimited accumulation of capital."[62] The suite of nineteenth-century information technologies discussed above was put into the service of empire by the United States in its late burst for a global expansion (1898–1899). Their quest stretched from the Caribbean—Puerto Rico and Cuba—through to the Panama Canal and across a string of Pacific Islands, including half of Samoa and Guam, all the way to the Philippines at the edge of Asia. The United States conquered the archipelago from Spain, easily kicking over the rotting edifice of the older imperial order first established in 1521. By a curious historical irony, just as U.S. forces took control of Manila, a native revolutionary army surrounded the city walls, ready to throw out any colonial forces. The Philippines became the site of Asia's first national revolution, at the same time that the United States became an imperial power on a global rather than continental scale, imitating but at that point not quite equaling the Spanish circum-global empire, given that the United States had no colonies in Europe, Africa, or the Asian continent. This situation rapidly led to war between the First Philippine Republic and the United States, with the Americans claiming victory on the battlefield, but they were then left with the task of trying to control an unruly colonial population. Drawing on the communication and data extraction/management systems, the Americans found that the key to control in the Philippines was found in surveillance. The following chapter draws this argument into the context of the Cold War and U.S. foreign policy.

Unlike earlier European empires, the United States did not attempt to operate a rigid command style bureaucracy to manage the colony; rather they favored a market model, looking for quick, efficient, and cheap solutions. Also, unlike the British, the Americans did not engage in deep anthropological studies, learn the local languages, or engage in archeological digs. Rather, they sought a very practical solution: how to suppress revolutionary tendencies to maintain control and economic domination. To go about this, they began by surveying the territory, with the United States engaging in large-scale military map-making and cadastral charts to shore up the lines of private property and to make the city legible to the control of the colonial police. The local population was encoded via tabulating machines in a national census, which when combined with photography, helped to make people identifiable to the police. Criminal identification systems, such as fingerprinting—important elements pioneered in colonial India and Argentina—were used to identify and surveil the local people. All the surveillance data was stored in a centralized data management system and connected, via telecommunication links, with lines crossing the Pacific back to the United States. The United States also opened its first covert agency in the Philippines, seeking to locate and crush subversive groups, a pattern that would soon be imported back into the colonizing country, particularly during the first "Red Scare" in the wake of the Russian Revolution. This provides another example of how imperial control in colonies can provide a crucible for power to experiment with forms and functions, to intensify forms of surveillance and control that then spread throughout the world following the uneven development of capitalist globalization.[63]

CONCLUSION

The social processes of surveillance and globalization have been long bound together in mutually constitutive ways. Surveillance has enabled the intensification of social relations across world space-time, and globalization has seen the practices of surveillance spread across the planet. Surveillance, as in the watching over something in order to project control over it, has long been used to defend and extend unequal power relations and to concentrate and centralize power. Like spatial surveys before, surveillance extracts data traces from the infinite complexity of social ecology in order to simplify and make them legible to power. This uneven process has often blossomed through the expansion of empire, with colonialism being a crucible for the formation of new control techniques. The next chapter turns to the twentieth century as it continues to chart the extensive and intensive increases in the interlinked forces of surveillance and globalization.

CHAPTER 2

THE ATOM AND THE WATCHTOWER

CYBERNETICS, WAR, AND THE REORGANIZATION OF THE WORLD

This chapter begins with a world-historic event that occurred in New Mexico on July 16, 1945, at precisely twenty-one seconds past 5:29 a.m. local time. At that moment, the first atomic bomb—graced with the holy name "Trinity"—was detonated in an ancient volcanic basin turned desert. Plutonium atoms were torn apart in a nuclear reaction, releasing an immense amount of energy in the form of heat, light, sound, and radiation, trembling the earth, melting the sand of the desert into green radioactive glass, and sending an ominous mushroom cloud twelve kilometers into the sky. This rigorously calculated incident is a crucial moment in world history. At this point, the techno-scientific forces enabled people to reorganize nature by tearing atoms apart to release immense energy, hence transforming the way in which people relate with the natural world.

Nuclear weapons have been bound up with increased globalization and recognition of global interconnection. Back in 1955 an atomic scientist wrote, "It is no longer a question of two nations, or groups of nations, devastating each other, but of all the future generations of all nations who will forever pay, through disease, malformation, and mental disability, for our folly."[1] Three generations later, the looming prospect of a global nuclear winter, which would tear life, as we know it asunder, by reducing much of the world to radioactive ruins, remains a critically important and acutely dangerous problem. Indeed, that most people believe nuclear war could never happen is a major part of this problem.[2] Nevertheless, the nuclear issue has been central to many twentieth-century protest movements and environmentalism more broadly. The coming of the nuclear era has even featured as a proposed date for the beginning of the "Anthropocene," the so-called Age of Man, in which the human impact on earth is seen as a geological force, leaving traces in the composition of the earth's crust. While this is hotly debated within and beyond geology, this concept speaks to the undeniable enormity of the current ecological catastrophes brought on as a result of the twists and turns of capitalist modernity.[3] At any rate, nuclear weapons are highly engaged with post–World War II globalization, emerging in parallel with computing-machines and, as I show below, long entangled with surveillance.

Before moving on to tell this story, it is worth reflecting on the politics of technology. While it is common to imagine that technology is somehow neutral, this perspective fails to account for how thoroughly social technology is, and how—as with everything people do—it is fundamentally shaped by power relations. That is to say that technologies themselves are inherently political. Consider the atomic bomb as a provocative example. As long as a weapon as outrageously dangerous as a nuclear bomb exists, it demands to be controlled by a centralized organization with a rigidly hierarchical chain of command; indeed, the "internal social system of the bomb must be authoritarian; there is no other way."[4] Furthermore, this also applies to the "civilian" side of atomic power, nuclear energy, which is far more integrated into war industries than its champions suggest.[5] The social system that nurtures the nuclear power justifies itself through keeping the weapons safe and out of dangerous hands, be they terrorists or "rogue" states. This kind of interplay between the social power system and the weapons system—of politics and technology—stands regardless of national context, be it American, British, Chinese, French, Indian, Israeli, North Korean, Pakistani, or Russian. Through all the cultural and political differences between this list of nuclear-armed states, they are all strongly centralized and of various shades of authoritarianism. This kind of social organization is a necessary precursor to the development of the bomb, for constructing the ultimate weapon requires massive techno-scientific war industries and strongly centralized power of the means of destruction. This politics is inherent in the bomb itself. Atomic bombs may be considered an extreme case, but they serve to illustrate the point I make repeatedly throughout this book: technologies are not neutral. Rather through critical inquiry it can be possible to tease out the organization of power and resource, of meaning and matter that necessarily surround technologies. Furthermore, while this book discusses technology at length, it is not the end in itself. Rather, "the real concern is with people, with the social relations which bind and divide them, [and] with the shared dreams and delusions which inspire and blind them. For this is the substrate from which all of our technology emerges, the power and promise which gives it shape and meaning."[6]

This chapter examines the rise of surveillance through warfare, specifically the nuclear bomb and the computing-machine. It focuses on developments in the United States, but always in a properly global context. This is significant, for as the history of globalization has intensified across five centuries of capitalist modernity, various empires have found themselves as world hegemons: the Spanish, Dutch, French, and British, with the latter having its classical liberal world-order torn apart during two world wars resulting in catastrophic economic crises. When the American empire found itself in the position of global hegemony after World War II, it was immediately challenged from the outside by the Soviet model and anti-colonial movements in the global south, as well as from the inside by a strong labor movement. It seemed that it had come to rule over a world that had largely turned against empire, an ironic twist of history and a precursor to the U.S. colonization of the Philippines at the dawn of the first national revolution in Asia (chapter 1).

THE WORLD-MAKING WAR

World War II (1939–1945) was a properly global and utterly catastrophic event. The seeds of destruction sown in the Great War (1914–1918) came to a bitter harvest of over sixty million souls—largely non-combatants—as a deranged rationality tore apart the old European colonial order and violently reconfigured the world. The war can be understood as intensifying globalization processes, through the suturing of various international alliances and organizations, the strengthening of socialism, and the weakening of nationalism. One aspect of this global reconfiguration came in the form of technological advances that came out of the war effort, such as radar, jet engines, and rockets capable of reaching space. Also, from this period came the jewels in the bloody crown of control, the conjoined twins of nuclear weapons and computing-machines.

During the war, the United States mobilized scientists and engineers in state-controlled research facilities. Science was seen as the key to military victory and was hence encouraged and enabled through massive government-sponsored research projects. These were run with a mix of the state's militaristic and civilian arms, with universities being the key institutions of the latter, along with intensive involvement from the forces of capital, with various corporations working in this "military-industrial complex." Emerging simultaneously in both the United States and Nazi Germany—before and during World War II—the military-industrial complex is essentially an alliance between the military, the for-profit defense industry, and intellectuals in universities working in the techno-sciences, all of which became integral parts of the new power system.[7] If the origins of the military-industrial complex could be personified by any one person, the American engineer Vannevar Bush (1890–1974) must be a likely candidate. He was the dean of the university engineering department at the prestigious Massachusetts Institute of Technology (MIT); founder of the military corporation Raytheon; central administrator of the Manhattan Project's scientific effort to construct the atomic bomb; and a key figure in the history of computing-machines. He was, in effect, the first presidential science advisor, writing a report for the U.S. president that used a telling colonial metaphor: *Science, The Endless Frontier*, which sang praise to the glory of the techno-sciences in the service of the state, and implicitly, the capitalist world-system.[8] This combination of power over public policy, university laboratories, and corporate profiteering in war-making epitomizes the military-industrial complex; the fusion of state, science, and capital.

While dedicated to war, the new military-industrial research laboratories provided spaces for intellectual inquiry, allowing for free-wheeling, interdisciplinary, and interinstitutional research, and large-scale collaborations backed by enormous amounts of public money. Despite the rigid bureaucracy of the military, these new research laboratories proved to be surprisingly flexible, entrepreneurial, and individualistic workplaces, which in some ways prefigured the "neoliberal" turn of workplaces decades later. Indeed, these university laboratories were central to a deep transformation that was under way. Through systematically harnessing intellectual energy they shifted the trajectory of technological developments, going from being characterized by the incidental and piecemeal results of individual creativity and practical tinkering—as exemplified by someone like Nikola Tesla (1856–1943)—to institutions designed to take massively abstract ideas and transform them into social practices in the service of power structures. The resultant techno-sciences and their rise was a world-historic development with tremendous implications for the planet.[9]

The rise of the techno-sciences built on the much older "scientific revolution," which originated in the long sixteenth century. A key figure in the early history of this movement was the English statesman and philosopher Francis Bacon (1561–1626). Bacon is credited with many things, being the "father of modern science" for one, as well as being the first to conceive of a research institute, the first to imagine industrial sciences as a source of economic and political power, and the first technocrat. To this frequently cited list, we could add another: he was also a pioneer of the genre of science fiction. His incomplete utopian novel, *New Atlantis*, written in 1624 and published posthumously, imagined the workings of a state-sponsored scientific research institute on a fictitious Pacific Island. There the inhabitants practiced Bacon's scientific method of isolating natural phenomena in controlled and contained settings where they could be subject to instrumental analysis and rational inquiry. Running with Bacon's aphorism-turned-modern maxim "knowledge is power," intellectually trained workers studied nature in order to extract secrets that could lead to prediction and control, in order to establish the "Empire of Man over creation."[10] The quest for knowledge-as-power created enduring connections "with more vulgar forms of conquest, those of the trader, the inventor, the ruthless conquistador, the driving industrialist seeking to displace natural abundance and natural satisfactions with those he could profitably sell."[11] This process was supposed to aid humanity as a whole, and yet in practice its benefits and detriments were very unevenly spread, with Bacon's "Empire of Man over creation" being more accurately stated as: the Empire of some Men over most other Men and all Men over Women and Nature. Here, as elsewhere, "the rhetoric of power all too easily produces an illusion of benevolence when deployed in an imperial setting."[12] The scientists in Bacon's imagination—and then actually existing scientists in subsequent centuries—were informed, in part, by surveillance, broadly understood. They observed phenomena from above—meaning in an abstracted way—so as to strip away the actual existing complexities of nature in order to make predictions, and often to gain control. Confronted with the infinite complexity of the embodied universe, they sought to strip away what was seen as extraneous to the problem in order to simplify and render it controllable. There are strong parallels here to surveillance.

The intellectually trained workers—scientists, engineers, and technicians—poured their energy into this venture, believing that they were contributing to the fight against fascism in Europe and Asia, with some already eyeing their next enemy, their Soviet allies. Many intellectually trained workers wanted to bring about an end to the devastating global war. One of these intellectuals caught up in the war effort was the mathematician-philosopher Norbert Wiener (1894–1964). This former child prodigy was employed by the United States' National Defense Research Committee to work on a top-secret project developing the mathematics of fire-control mechanisms for anti-aircraft guns. Appearing suddenly over the battlefield, the sheer speed of warplanes had rendered prior ballistic mathematics obsolete. The committee's chairman, Vannevar Bush, drolly described the work of scientists like Wiener as "applying corrections to the gun control so that the shell and the target will arrive at the same position at the same time." To arrange this meeting of shell and aircraft requires considering hundreds of factors, from the war plane's speed and direction to the shell's parabolic arc, air temperature, humidity, altitude, and wind speed, among many, many more.[13]

Wiener tackled this intellectual challenge by positing it in terms of an information system. Employing a machine metaphor, he imagined soldiers and anti-aircraft gun as components of the same system: part flesh, part weapon, all machine. Computers, as information processing machines, could be used to draw in data from sensors in real time, to convert phenomena to binary numbers for calculation, to crunch the numbers of the various variables in order to reduce uncertainty by attempting to predict the future and to exert control over it. That is to say that one of the key moments in the history of computers was deeply entangled with *surveillance*, the abstract view from above. Wiener's weapon system used surveillance sensors to reduce the embodied complexity of material reality down to extractable data traces and sets of numbers that could be processed by computing-machines. Made in the service of a centralized hierarchical structure, the system granted the ability to make predictions to gain control and project power—in this case in the form of a heavy three-point-seven-inch anti-aircraft shell.

The "rigorous mathematical basis and the increasing precision of artillery fire made itself a model for the new industrial arts."[14] These words were published in 1934 to describe the changes that gripped the world in the late eighteenth century with the Napoleonic conquests, the nationalization of warfare, the intensification of industrialization, and the role of the sciences in serving the state and capital. Through a curious rhythm of history, this quote can apply verbatim in this new context, in which the same dynamics play out at a much higher level of intensity, for it was through this wartime research on artillery mathematics that a key component of the foundation of the upcoming "information revolution" was laid. Hence it was bound up with the globalization of warfare, and a further intensification of the role of techno-science in service of the state and the expansion of global capitalism.[15]

Extrapolating from the theorizing behind these weapons, Wiener held that social, biological, and physical systems were essentially machines that could be understood using the flow of information. He labeled this emergence science as "cybernetics," which he defined as "control and communication in the animal and the machine." Cybernetics went on to be an extraordinarily important conception, with impacts well beyond the comparatively small, but ambitious, discipline called cybernetics. Seen from a long-term perspective, the development of cybernetics fits firmly into the long-term trajectory of the capitalist modernity's quest for control over the uncertainty and complexities of the natural world, which of course includes humanity. Building on this history, cybernetics has increasingly become entangled with the mode of practice known as global capitalism, producing a profound mutation and intensification in the social formation leading to a qualitative shift into "cybernetic capitalism." The mix of technique, technology, and social power is explored at length across this book as I seek to trace the contours of control.

Wiener was aware that the forces of control would be strengthened by cybernetics and did what he could to resist this pull. Unlike the vast majority of other scientists involved in the war effort, he turned around and urged his colleagues to consider the ethical implications of their work for "irresponsible militarists" and noted how computing-machines could easily escape control and have a malevolent impact on society, strengthening the forces of war and capitalism. In making these prophetic observations, Wiener touched on a central paradox of our times: efforts to gain control can get out of control, a point which we'll return to. Yet through it all, he maintained that computers could be used to serve other ends, potentially enabling a more democratic and egalitarian world order. In this sense, Wiener was a complex and contradictory figure, illustrative of the ambiguities that pervade such phenomena. Nevertheless, he correctly noted the potential impact of computing-machines, stating, "If the seventeenth and the early eighteenth centuries are the age of clocks, the later eighteenth and nineteenth centuries constitute the age of steam engines, the present time is the age of communication and control."[16]

Scientific research laboratories brought forth the conjoined twins of the twentieth century control project: computing-machines and nuclear weapons. They were entangled, with the former being needed to crunch the vast number tables for the Manhattan Project in order to bring about the latter. As stressed at the beginning of this chapter, the first nuclear explosion was a truly world-historic moment. Something of the gravity of this was stunningly captured in popular culture in the eighth episode of *Twin Peaks: The Return* (2017). In frightful and surreal detail, the episode depicts the blast over four grueling minutes to the soundtrack of Krzysztof Penderecki's *Threnody to the Victims of Hiroshima*. A mere twenty-three days after the Trinity blast, the United States decided to use their terrible weapons on the people of Japan. In the first attack, three warplanes were sent to Hiroshima: the *Enola Gay, The Great Artiste,* and a nameless aircraft, retrospectively called *Neces-*

sary Evil in an effort to rationalize the unrationalizable rationalization. The first carried the payload—the atomic weapon "Little Boy"—the second was filled with scientists operating various instruments and sensors to measure the blast, and the third was there to photograph the event. Hence surveillance literally flanked both sides of the world-historic atomic bombing mission. Upon returning from their field trip, the scientists surveyed the surveillance data, feeding numbers into computing-machines and making calculations about the success of their experiment on unsuspecting human beings.

After the mushroom clouds dissipated into the atmosphere, an uneasy *pax Americana* ensued, yet the triumphant superpower was metaphorically poisoned by its own weapons. There is another cruel paradox at the core of their control: while extremely rational on one level, this control can be characterized by utter irrationality on another. The utter rationality needed to theorize and create a machine powerful enough to split atoms was simultaneously gripped by a deep "institutionalized madness." The apocalyptic absurdity of this is evident to Daniel Ellsberg, who worked for the Pentagon and RAND Corporation as a strategic analyst of nuclear command and control from 1958 to 1969. He noted that the official estimates for the total toll of a U.S. first strike at the Soviet Union, China, and Warsaw Pact satellites would be around six hundred million deaths: "A hundred Holocausts." Ellsberg writes, "That expected outcome exposed a dizzying irrationality, madness, insanity, at the heart and soul of our nuclear planning and apparatus."[17] Thus, as soon as the project of control intensified to the point where it could reach into atoms, it simultaneously went out of control, casting the very real threat of death on a titanic scale across the planet.

THE NEW HEGEMON

After the nineteenth century imperial expansions into Mexico and with overseas annexations of Hawaii, Puerto Rico, and the Philippines, the United States turned comparatively inward and isolationist. It voiced mild opposition to British and French colonialism, and Woodrow Wilson's Fourteen Points (1918) advanced the rights for national self-determination. As a result, some early twentieth-century anti-colonial nationalists imagined that the United States might be a potential ally in the struggle against the older empires of Britain, France, and the other

European powers. In the wake of World War II, when the United States assumed the mantle of world hegemon, this new superpower took a different course, becoming rapidly reactionary. In 1947 the United States passed the National Security Act, which was a major restructuring of the military and intelligence powers, with developments that included changing the aptly named Department of War into the Orwellian "Department of Defense," along with the establishment of the National Security Council, and the CIA. This was done as part of their obsession with "containing" communism, a dubious project that involved crushing internal dissent, sponsoring right-wing dictatorships, and toppling independent governments in the Third World, while also touting an insanely belligerent nuclear policy. All of this was given a veneer of pseudo-science legitimation by "rational choice theory" formulated by RAND Corporation scientists and seemingly backed up by tremendous developments in the techno-sciences. RAND is another compelling example of the military-industrial complex, sitting at the intersection of capital and science in the service of the state, with an enormous influence on the U.S. commitment to construct a rationally managed technocratic society in order to manage democracy in such a way that gave the appearance of inclusions while helping to centralize elite decision-making power and to prevent alternatives. At the same time, simplistic views of Good-versus-Evil reigned as the severe rationality and binary morality served to mask a deep anxiety, a kind of desperation that comes from trying to master and control an uncontrollable world. Some of these contradictions come from the fact that as the United States became world hegemon, it did so from a simultaneous position of immense strength and attendant paranoia.[18]

Emerging out of World War II largely unscathed, the United States was enormously empowered by the global conflict. One figure gives a sense of this shift: in 1939 the U.S. economy was only about half the size of the key belligerents in Europe, plus the Soviet Union and Japan; yet, in 1946 its economy was bigger than all of these countries combined.[19] By contrast, the Soviet Union, the secondary superpower, suffered the most deaths of any nation in World War I when it was the Russian Empire, before another seven to twelve million people perished in the Civil War following the Revolution, and then they suffered the highest death count in World War II, with approximately one-third of all deaths of the deadliest military conflict in human history. With

Europe and Japan devastated and the majority of the world left with crumbling empires, the United States possessed by far most of the world's industrial, military, and financial power. Never before had world history seen such an extreme concentration of productive power. In the decades that have followed, the United States has used its dominant position to project power around the world. As of 2017, U.S. Special Operations forces, including Navy SEALs and Army Green Berets, are actively deployed in 149 countries, or around 75 percent of the planet's nations. Additionally, the United States gathers intelligence on a truly global scale, has its navy patrol all oceans and seas, and maintains around eight hundred military garrisons in other countries.[20]

The decades that followed World War II became a so-called golden age of U.S. capitalism as the American economy expanded dramatically. Indeed, the twenty-three-year period from the beginning of the Korean War until the end of the Vietnam War was one of "the most sustained and profitable period of economic growth in the history of world capitalism." Underpinned by the industrialization of agriculture and cheap oil prices, this tremendous growth period also related to a set of policies brought in by President Roosevelt's administration in 1933 to deal with the Great Depression. This compromise between sections of the elite and workers movements resulted in the New Deal, a series of enormous public works projects, along with social security reforms and the regulation of Wall Street. Much of the industrialization of the West Coast of the United States was enacted as a taxpayer funded Federal policy designed not only to increase employment but to build up defenses against a potential Japanese invasion. After World War II, the military spending continued in what some have called "military Keynesianism," with a long boom in productivity going until the crisis period of the 1970s (discussed below).[21]

The United States' strength post-war was readily apparent, yet perhaps more elusive was its weakness, largely because celebratory American histories have since suppressed this side of the story in order to paint the triumph of global capitalism as inevitable. Yet there was nothing triumphant about the predominant public mood in the wake of the brutalities of World War I, the 1929 Wall Street Crash and the following Great Depression, and the even more horrific World War II; the result was a creeping sense of dismay that pervaded the United States and Western Europe—all while the Soviet Union went through a period of extremely rapid industrialization and growth. Many believed that liberal capitalism was doomed to fail, to be replaced by either socialism to the left or fascism to the right. Many of the sharpest pro-capitalist intellectuals, such as Joseph Schumpeter, Friedrich Hayek, and Karl Popper, voiced their fears that their preferred model of liberalism was in grave danger.[22] The defeat of fascism in World War II did little to appease these fears, with escalating problems in the United States and around the world.

Concerns about the strength of the United States' position lingered after World War II, for all supreme violence of the atomic bombs, the war was already largely won by the time of the experiment. Perhaps the decisive turning point was the Soviet victory over the Nazis in Stalingrad—the largest and bloodiest battle in the history of warfare. Riding the turned tides of war, the Soviets proceeded, at tremendous human cost, to grind toward Germany, only to plant the hammer-and-sickle flag into the roof of the Reichstag in Berlin and sift through Hitler's burnt remains in search of his teeth. Thereafter, the bulk of the Soviet army crossed Siberia and began crushing the weakened and overextended Japanese Empire in the East. The United States sought to slow the Soviets and to take Japan and half of Korea, with this being the first part of their global project of containing communism—conducted as they were technically allied with "Uncle Joe," to use the U.S. media's friendly name for Stalin.

Just four years later, the Soviets constructed their own nuclear weapon, hence following the path of techno-scientific control. For the test, the Soviets built a pseudo town on the Kazakh steppes, with buildings, houses, aircraft, military hardware, pits of various depths, a bridge over nothing, and a train on a track going from nowhere to nowhere. Fifteen hundred animals populated this strange sacrificial spectacle; cows, pigs, dogs, and such were tied up, waiting. Center stage, atop a wooden tower, sat "First Lightning," a replica of the American bomb that annihilated Nagasaki, and almost certainly the result of espionage. At 7 a.m. on August 29, 1949, the plutonium atoms split, devastating the hastily constructed animal town. The Soviets sought to keep their breakthrough a secret; yet traces of the blast were detected a month later by an American Air Force plane that flew on a reconnaissance mission from Japan to Alaska with a device to measure radioactive debris in the atmosphere, specifically testing for signs of atomic activity. So to the Soviets surprise, the Americans announced their secret to the world, with a double act of surveillance serving to intensify the fledgling Cold War. The utter rationality and utter madness of nuclear weapons claimed a second servant, the Soviet Union, and with this the prospect of a global holocaust—from the Greek *hólos,* "whole" and *kaustós,* "burnt"—began to become apparent.

Thus as World War I left the seeds of World War II, World War II left the seeds for what could well be called "World War Three." For much of the world, it was not a "Cold War" for napalm burns at 1,000 degrees Celsius and the United States dropped over thirty thousand tons of it on Korea in 1950–1953, not to mention the six hundred thousand tons of bombs—more than was dropped in the entire Pacific campaign of World War II. The United States embarked on this brutal aerial campaign after their embarrassing defeat on the ground at the hands of Chinese soldiers. This vicious war had profoundly twisted both North and South Korea, as well as the key proxy belligerents, the United States and the newly established People's Republic of [Communist] China.[23] Despite the brutality of this and subsequent hot moments of the Cold War, one paradox was that neither the United States nor especially the weaker USSR wanted direct confrontation with the other. Despite their respective rhetorical posturing each was relatively content with the status quo division of the world. The insane doctrine of "mutually assured destruction," known by the appropriate acronym MAD, was a large factor in this, thus making the Cold War a thoroughly twisted "Cold Peace." China under Mao was in some ways another matter. The Red Helmsman once told the leader of the Italian Communist Party that in the event of nuclear war "three hundred million Chinese will be left, and that will be enough for the human race to continue." That he envisioned fighting and surviving nuclear war as a way to end capitalism dumbfounded his comrades around the world.[24] Despite the superpowers' unwillingness to engage in direct conflict, a global alphabet of countries was dragged into the fray—from Afghanistan to Zaire—with the Cold War serving to intensify globalization processes, albeit in uneven and contradictory ways. These conflicts came from the decay of the old order of European colonialism, which largely collapsed after World War II in quite messy ways, for example, in Malaya, Vietnam, Algeria, Palestine, and so on. Part of the contradictory position that the United States found itself in was that as it became world hegemon, the majority of the world was more committed than ever to not be ruled by foreign powers, with anti-colonial movements and insurgencies attempting to cast aside the ruins of old empires. They did not want to be subordinate to new superpowers.

Cybernetics was also bound up with the dynamics of global war, with its emergence first occurring in the laboratories of the United States, in collaboration with their allies in the UK, but resulting from thoroughly global processes. The forces of techno-scientific control, brought to new heights in the military-industrial complex, were themselves globalized. When the concept of cybernetics first entered the Soviet Union, it was dismissed as a reactionary bourgeois idea replacing the potentially revolutionary human with subservient machines designed to carry out the will of the capitalist-imperialist-militarist. Yet as the sciences began to de-Stalinize themselves, the predominant view on cybernetics shifted dramatically, with the analogy of machine and organism becoming less offensive. By 1961 the Soviet Academy of Sciences published a volume with the intriguing title *Cybernetics: To the Service of Communism*. The book outlined the great potential of applying the computing-machine to a wide range of fields, including production, transportation, and central economic planning, all in service of the Communist Party. As with cybernetics everywhere, these goals were all entangled with surveillance in order to track production, monitor transportation, and pull traces of these activities to where they could be viewed from above. In this way, the goal of control through cybernetics was put into the service of the Soviet state.[25]

If this Soviet proposal was formulated "from above" to aid the centralized state power's ability to formulate large-scale plans, a more "from below" proposal emerged a decade later with Project Cybersyn. This computer network began in Chile under the left-wing political alliance Popular Unity, led by Salvador Allende (1908–1973). This project sought to use cybernetic systems to facilitate economic coordination and decision making within a socialist worker democracy. This system may have resulted in the more hopeful sort of technological practice whereby it could help to extend a more egalitarian, democratic order by allowing worker-controlled workplaces to use computing-machines to coordinate their actions on larger scales. The system involved surveillance, yet differently, for the model of worker democracy allowed the workers surveilled control over the data, access to the power granted by it, and more involvement with the decision making across the process. These never-completed experiments in the Soviet Union and Chile are important as they stem from the Second and Third World respectively and hence run against the grain of the usual U.S.-centered narrative. It is also significant to note that the CIA had a task force to counter the Soviet experiment and in 1973 supported a full-blown right-wing military coup that violently ended the Chilean democratic experiment leading to the violent death of Allende in the Presidential Palace. The United States was instrumental in replacing Allende's democratically elected government with the dictatorial regime of Augusto Pinochet, who violently imposed "free market" reforms. Hence in both cases the world hegemon sought to crush attempts to have cybernetics serve goals that varied from the order of global capitalism.[26]

Another important threat to the post-war U.S. hegemony was found, not in the threat of the Soviets or a recalcitrant Third World, but in internal labor movements. During World War II, the enormous demand for production saw a major expansion of industry, with many new workers—often women and blacks—entering the industrial work-force. Over the war years, wages were frozen while the cost of living rose around forty-five percent, making it difficult for many workers to get by. Over the same period, corporate profits rose by 250 percent; a fact that did not go unnoticed by organized labor. At the same time, industrial relations were in a poor state, with no collective bargaining rights, the forcing of (often unsuccessful) non-strike pledges, and working conditions being determined by compulsory arbitration from the War Labor Board. Excluding the interests of workers from production led to increasingly dangerous workplaces. Between 1940 and 1945, over eighty-five thousand workers were killed and another eleven million were injured in workplace accidents. This is *eleven times* the total number of casualties the United States had in World War II. In the year after the atomic bombs fell, some of the largest waves of strikes in history played out in the United States, with over forty-three thousand strikes involving over twenty-seven million workers. The severity and militancy of these strikes frightened capitalists, the government, and liberal and conservative intelligentsia alike, with many factions of the elite seeking various ways to pacify the workers: anti-communist repression, intensifying the supervision, and automation of workplaces, all of which involved increasing surveillance.[27]

Some right-wing forces saw the Cold War as an opportunity to defeat the organized labor movement, with a "home front" of the global conflict opening up in the factories in the United States. In this second "Red Scare"—built on the sordid legacy of the first Red Scare that occurred in the wake of the Russian Revolution in 1917—unionist workers and left-leaning intellectuals and artists were identified as "communists" and aligned with the external enemy, thus justifying repression and the invasive surveillance deemed necessary to uncover subversives and to defend the status quo. This dynamic ran in tangled parallel with other countries on the capitalist side of the Cold War, often taking far more violent forms than played out in the United States. This globalizing dynamic was very pronounced in the Indonesian archipelago in the wake of a right-wing military coup in 1965, which ended the government of democratically elected President Sukarno who had led the country through its struggle for independence from the Netherlands and into the Non-Aligned Movement. The new military dictatorship rapidly unleashed large-scale slaughter upon those deemed to be political enemies, targeting communists, alleged communists, communist sympathizers, and alleged communist sympathizers, infidels, and ethnic Chinese, often regardless of their political or religious orientation, resulting in the murder of at least five hundred thousand people. Most of the actual killings were done by paramilitary death squads. These squads were informed by haphazard surveillance in collaboration with the military government, which in turn had the tactical support of the United States and UK governments, both of which assisted the army's coordinated campaign, provided material support, and maintained official silence amid mounting violence, while also providing justifications on the global stage. The violent destruction of the political left in Indonesia saw power tip toward the military and the Islamists, while foreign policy went from the pro–Third World Non-Aligned Movement to one that was very open toward the West, who tactically allow decades of brutal Indonesian oppression and occupation of East Timor, as well as the continuing violent occupation of West Papua. A fascinating and shocking insight into an aspect of this situation is presented in the documentaries *The Act of Killing* (2012) and *The Look of Silence* (2014).[28]

Surveillance of production was also central in the United States' containment of the post-war labor unrest. The previous chapter noted the enduring and intensifying connection between the surveillance of labor forces and capitalist modernity, from the panopticon's origins in factories to the rise of scientific management (chapter 1). "Information, surveillance, efficiency: the very principles of Taylorism become intensified, extended, and automated through the application of new communications and information technologies. One fundamental aspect of the 'communications revolution' has been to refine the planning and control of consumer behaviour that was already inherent in the early philosophy of scientific management."[29] These developments intensified during the post–World War II period, as new cybernetic possibilities, the specter of labor unrest, international competition, and the pressures of capital accumulation came together to increase automation in the workplace. New production machines were introduced that could be operated by low-paid, low-skilled workers who could, without ingenuity, produce goods in high quantities. This was distinct from the old machinists, who skillfully used their devices to enhance their own ability to act in production, thus showing that technological developments could be used to serve workers, not replace them.[30] Nevertheless, spilling from the military, military-industrial corporations, and the military-sponsored intellectual community, automation was "promoted by an army of technical enthusiasts, peddled by the vendors of war-born gadgetry, subsidized by the military in the name of performance, command, and national security, legitimized as technical necessity, and celebrated as progress."[31] Managers of large industrial firms soon caught on, with automation becoming fashionable, patriotic, prestigious, and highly profitable. In this context it was also "coupled both to the traditional belief that superior efficiency resulted from work simplification, the substitution of capital for labor, and the concentration of management control over production, and to the postwar preoccupation with controlling labor as an end in itself in order to safeguard and extend management 'rights.'"[32]

CYBERNETIC REORGANIZATIONS

Using the intersection of war and surveillance, I shall consider how cybernetic transformations took shape across the crisis decades, which came after decades of strong growth gave way to a multidimensional crisis of accumulation in the 1970s. Owing to massive protest movements, increased union militancy, emergent environmentalism, high oil prices, stagnant production, inflation, market instability, and an increasingly independent Third World movement, the global capitalism faced a threat. If the conditions of accumulation were not restarted, capitalism would have collapsed. The response from above to this crisis is often called "neoliberalism." Finance was unleashed with an explosion of debt relations within and between countries, a roll back of public interest regulations, the crushing of unions, privatization of public assets, waves of outsourcing and offshoring, tax breaks for the rich, and austerity for the poor. As a result of these transformations, inequalities have greatly intensified globally. Furthermore, the crisis is bound up with capitalism's insatiable desire for infinite growth within finite nature, one of the central contradictions of this mode of practice. This impossible demand has a multiplicity of ramifications, one of which can be seen in capitalism's tendency toward overproduction as a result of improved technologies and more intensive use of labor and resources, a tendency that leads to expansion of debt and monumental amounts of waste. Furthermore, overproduction is always accompanied by its grim shadow of underconsumption, the phenomena of "poverty in the midst of plenty," to use Mahatma Gandhi's phrase. Next, I shall focus on the cybernetic reconstitution of capitalism that began during the crisis of the 1970s and has since increased extensively and intensively in the decades since.[33]

As the crisis in global capitalism began to unfold, a key development was under way at the apex of the military-industrial complex, the Pentagon's peak research body, the Advanced Research Projects Agency (ARPA, and since 1972 DARPA, with "Defense" being put at the beginning of the acronym). This agency has been responsible for funding research on emerging technologies for the sake of war and the projection of control, having involvement in many influential technologies from graphical user interfaces to the computer mouse to Google (chapter 3). On October 29, 1969, the first data traveled between two nodes of ARPANET (Advanced Research Projects Agency Network), the Pentagon created genealogical ancestor of the Internet, perhaps the most consequential of ARPA's projects. This first communication followed from a history of such moments. Back in 1844 Samuel Morse quoted the Bible as he tapped the world's first interstate telegram message: "What hath God wrought." Then, at the dawn of the twentieth century, Guglielmo Marconi transmitted radio waves across the Atlantic, sending not a Biblical quote but a single pulse, a sign of modern minimalism. Then, to return to 1969, the Pentagon engineers sent just two letters, "LO." The system crashed before they could continue to type: "LOGIN." Nevertheless, this half-failed thoroughly utilitarian signal marked a key first moment in the history of communications. As is well known, the Pentagon's computing-machines became networked in order to survive a possible nuclear attack and to coordinate counterstrikes, likely resulting in an apocalyptic nuclear winter. Again, the twins of a twentieth-century control project—computing-machines and atomic weapons—grew in tangled parallel. The networking of computing-machines began as an effort to control uncertainty, to project power onto the unpredictable world. From its origin within Pentagon-funded research laboratories, the net expanded outward seemingly exponentially, going on to enmesh more and more of the world leading to the emergence of an uneven yet global "society of control."[34] Indeed, one can make a provocative case that the Internet itself "is a *war machine*."[35]

These militaristic origins of the Internet are well known, yet it is not often emphasized just how deep they run or how persistent they are (chapter 3). A very different take on the story began unfolding on the other side of the Pacific during the American invasion of Vietnam. After the French failed to re-colonize Vietnam, the imperial baton was passed to the United States The Vietnam War—called the American War in Vietnam—was a thoroughly global affair, with the world hegemon fighting to demonstrate its power and to "contain communism" by devastating a poor country. The conflict involved the First, Second, and Third Worlds, with its roots in the old European imperial order, and its effect extended well beyond Vietnam's borders, with bloody consequences in Laos and Cambodia, and there were ramifications stretching back to the nations of the invaders, with the United States and its allies being transformed by the war.[36]

Part of these dynamics can be seen the United States' use of defoliants in Vietnam, a key surveillance technology. Defoliants are toxic substances that when sprayed onto plants make them drop their foliage, which is to say, die. The Americans took their inspiration from the British who fought against an anti-colonial insurgency in Malaya that sought to cast out the crumbling empire post–World War II. This became the "Malayan Emergency," a preposterous name that came as a result of the owners of the rubber plantations and tin mines not wanting to call it a "war," for then any losses would not be covered by insurance. Regardless, the conflict was in many ways like a small-scale precursor to the Vietnam War. The British pioneered the use of spraying defoliants onto jungle, farms, and rural areas in order to expose insurgents to surveillance, to starve them through crop loss, and to displace a supportive peasantry.

The United States took this vile practice and proceeded to greatly intensify it in Vietnam. Their powerful military-industrial complex had teams of DARPA-funded scientists research defoliants in collaboration with major corporations, such as Dow Chemical. Together, they cooked up a collection of highly toxic substances known as the "Rainbow Herbicides," of which Agent Orange is the most famous. It was joined by Agents Green, Pink, Purple, Blue, White, and extended in Agent Orange II, III, and Super Orange. These poisons were used to kill forests and to ruin crops, hence destroying the very foundations of the peasant way of life, forcing millions of people to abandon the land and flee to the U.S.-dominated cities, from where they would be unable to support the insurgents. This is one extreme case where wartime surveillance forced a transformation in a mode of practice with very long roots, severing the peasants' relationship with their land. This is highly significant; for most of history the majority of people lived in localized place-based communities characterized by intergenerational kinship relations. They lived as part of the natural world in which they were embedded. Colonialism, capitalism, war, and the techno-sciences came together to force millions of Vietnamese peasants—and countless others around the world—from their ancestral land, thus tearing asunder the very social and ecological fabric on which their being depended.

Since 1966, resolutions were put through the United Nations charging the United States with violations of the Geneva Convention prohibition on the use of chemical and biological weapons. The United States wormed its way out by claiming that the substances sprayed were for surveillance purposes and not "poisons" or "weapons" designed to harm human beings. These weasel words aside, great harm has indeed occurred and on a massive scale. In South Vietnam alone, over ten million hectares of agricultural land was ruined. The toxins have caused a legion of ailments—genetic defects, leukemia, spina bifida, bandied legs, missing limbs, extra fingers, neural tubes defects, cancers, still births, twisted spines, and mental disabilities—all of which have caused an enormous amount of human suffering. The Red Cross gives the conservative estimate that there are currently one million people suffering birth defects or illness from exposure to the toxins. The war museum in Ho Chi Minh City gives a devastating account of this, one that culminates in the display of several pickled human fetuses, grossly deformed, and twisted by this toxic method of surveillance. It should also be noted that despite all the power of the American war machine, all the ingenious surveillance techniques and killing devices, their effort ultimately failed. Saigon fell and the Americans fled.[37] Thus, over the course of thirty bloody years of war, the extraordinarily resilient Vietnamese insurgents managed to defeat both the French and the Americans. While having lost the war, the American military learned much about surveillance and cybernetics from the colonial crucible that the invasion provided.

The image reproduced on the lower half of the front cover of this book was chosen as it is bound up with militaristic surveillance technology. The photograph, called "Safe from Harm," depicts a member of Mai-Mai Yakutumba, a community-based militia group, posing with his camouflage headdress and weapon near Fizi, South Kivu, Democratic Republic of the Congo. Appearing as part of Richard Mosse's striking installation *The Enclave*, the photograph was captured on obsolete military film designed in World War II as a surveillance technology that could reveal camouflaged installations hidden in forested landscapes. The film functions by registering invisible infrared light, rendering the familiar greens of plant life in surreal hues of pink, purple, crimson, and lavender, while leaving other colors, such as skin tone, unaffected to surreal effect. Mosse's repurposing of this technology reveals the "invisible" catastrophe that has been unfolding in the Congo for the last twenty years: a sprawling and complex war that has claimed more than five million lives. The photograph is a stunning example of art recuperating a war technology and using it as a call for justice. It can also be seen as symbolic of this book's work to illuminate the power relations of surveillance and globalizations.

Another major surveillance experiment conducted by the United States in Vietnam was called "Operation Igloo White." This multi-billion-dollar project used electronic sensors, airborne communication relays, and state-of-the-art computing-machines in an attempt to automate the killing of communists. Taking off from a secret air force based in Thailand, branches of the United States Air Force dropped over twenty thousand radio-operated surveillance devices out of warplanes and into the jungles of Laos and Vietnam in search of the illusive Ho Chi Minh Trail. These surveillance devices included microphones, heat and urine detectors, motion and seismic sensors, and they were disguised as sticks, plants, and animal poo to blend in. Should one of these surveillance devices register something deemed suspicious, it could relay a radio signal via airborne communication planes to a centralized computer system housed in the "Infiltration Surveillance Centre." When it was built near Nakhon Phanom, Thailand, in 1968, it was the biggest building in South East Asia. Inside this enormous windowless structure, many American military technicians sat in air-conditioned comfort before glowing screens. Powerful IBM 360/65 computing-machines awaited signals from the surveillance devices. Upon receiving surveillance data, the system would show the results on a grid map of the theater of war. It would then calculate the direction and the rate of movement before sending the attack coordinates to a bomber already airborne over the area. Responding in as little as five minutes, the machine could even trigger the release of the air strike bombs, with the human pilot following its orders to bomb the seemingly arbitrary part of forest. Frequently, the target was not the target. Insurgents quickly figured out about some of these high-tech tricks and they worked out ingenious ways to jam the system. Viet Cong with bags of piss had the surveilling war machine call in a strike to an empty patch of jungle while convoys of anti-colonial insurgents and equipment wove their way safely through the forest far from the danger zone. The extraordinarily expensive project Operation Igloo White was broadly considered a failure. Part of the problem was the overwhelming amount of surveillance data sent back and the inability to properly sort through it all because their computer systems were not sophisticated enough. A key lesson was learned: large-scale surveillance needs powerful computing-machines to sift through data and draw out patterns in order to project control.[38]

Another global arch of the narrative of the crisis involves developments in East Asia, particularly South Korea and Taiwan, for these countries became world leaders in the manufacturing of computing-machines and as a consequence they are important to the story of globalization and surveillance. These two authoritarian states were propped up by U.S. hegemony and they proceeded to create "economic miracles" in the form of extremely rapid growth. A key example of this can be seen in Samsung, a company that began dealing with dried fish. After the military dictatorship of Park Chung-Hee, which began in 1961, Samsung was one of several companies selected for special treatment in the country's drive toward rapid industrialization. The selected firms were provided with strong government support in the forms of tariffs, subsidies, guaranteed loans, research, and shelter from direct foreign investment, as well as strategic encouragement to reverse engineer patents—which is to say, pirate. These, among other factors, resulted in the company and the country embarking on a period of tremendous economic growth.

This growth was later exalted by the World Bank in a report called *The East Asian Miracle* that described the developments by praising the glory of free-market enterprise. This emphasis was highly disingenuous, for the Korean approach was very different from the "free market" orthodoxy of the Washington Consensus, a policy package that exemplified the neoliberal approach.[39] In contrast to this "free market" approach, the Korean government held absolute power over foreign exchange, with violations of foreign exchange controls possibly resulting in the death penalty. The World Bank report also totally overlooked the repressive military police regime and the parallel gangster violence that was needed to coerce working people into accepting such a high degree of exploitation, as well as the surveillance that enabled these dominating practices. It also ignored the harsh gender inequalities— with women being paid only half of what men would get for the same work—while also being expected to do the vast majority of reproductive labor in the home. Some of this hideous underbelly of "economic miracles" is captured in the South Korean documentary *Factory Complex* (2015). As it does with patriarchy's grim shadow, the World Bank's report also smiles blankly past the tremendous ecological consequences of breakneck industrialization and the toxification of bodies and landscapes that goes with it.[40]

Nevertheless, Samsung took its special treatment from the South Korean state and invested heavily in research and produced their first color TV set in 1977. In 1983 Samsung announced it would be moving into semi-conductors, a key component of computing-machines. They proceeded to build manufacturing plants in other countries, including Portugal, England, Japan, China, and the United States. Indeed, Samsung invested $13 billion in its semi-conductor factory in Austin, Texas. This was one of the United States' largest foreign investments, hence it is a good example to illustrate the twists and turns in the globalization process in the cybernetic age. The success of non-U.S. firms in Asia, like Samsung—as well as Japan's Sony and Taiwan's Foxconn among others—as well as European firms, like Sweden's Ericsson, the Netherlands' Philips, Finland's Nokia, and Germany's Siemens put U.S. producers under increasing international competition. That a company like Samsung could scatter its productive processes across a series of factories around the world is part of a larger pattern of outsourcing, off-shoring, and foreign direct investment. These actions were all enabled by, among other things, the extension of the increasingly networked twentieth century from the communication network that enmeshed the world in cables and satellites, a tightening transport system, shipping containerization, and increasingly elaborate financial mechanisms. All of these systems built on older modes of communication and transport yet were taken to new levels of intensity by the extensive involvement of computing-machines, thus illustrating the transformative power of cybernetic capitalism.

As surveillance proved to be a powerful tool for organizing workplaces, as discussed in chapter 1, it also proved important in logistics. The role of shipping containers in facilitating and intensifying global trade is well known. Coming out of the United States' military organizational developments of World War II, via more wars in Korea and Vietnam, the core of the "container revolution" was solidified between 1968 and 1972 in a series of International Maritime Organization standardization practices that saw a more consistent method of loading, moving, and transporting goods. These standardized boxes are part of an ensemble of cybernetic technologies, techniques, and practices that enable this highly rationalized system of global trade, a system that spreads out much further into global supply chains that have resulted in wide-reaching transformation of social practice. All containers are issued unique numbers and are tracked via computerized systems to make the processes as automated as possible. This is to say that the containerization of shipping was enabled by cybernetic surveillance. Data-traces were drawn away from reality in order to impose a simplified order of control. The logistical business software that facilitates these processes are as significant as the containers themselves, hence making this cybernetic moment crucial in the study of political economy. Computers, and the vessel planning workers who operate them, "determine the order in which the containers are to be discharged, to speed the process without destabilizing the ship," with all of the actions of the container cranes and other shipyard equipment being programed in advance.[41] Surveillance thus underpins the logistical transformations that have enabled global capitalism to reorganize itself into the more abstract form of cybernetic capitalism.[42]

Shipping containers, and the surveillance that enables them, have contributed to the intensification of globalization's processes by greatly lowering the price of transporting goods, and thus contributing to the flow of more trade and the spread of overproduction across the planet. In 2008, BBC News shone a light into this little-considered world of logistics by attaching a surveillance device to a specific shipping container bearing the name "NYKU-8210-506," renaming it *The Box*. The BBC rented the standard forty-foot shipping container from Nippon Yusen Kabushiki Kalsha (NYK Line), one of the world's oldest and largest shipping companies, first founded in Japan by the Tosa clan back in 1870. In its maiden voyage as *The Box*, the container traveled from Southampton in England up to Scotland where it was filled with 15,120 bottles of Chivas Regal Scotch Whisky. After leaving the UK, the container went through the Suez Canal in Egypt, across the Indian Ocean to be reloaded in Singapore, before reaching Shanghai, where the contents were destined to be drunk by wealthy Chinese consumers. In place of the Scotch, the container was loaded with tape measures, cosmetics, and gardening products made on factory lines, whereupon it traveled east, via Japan, to the Port of Los Angeles, then by rail to New Jersey and road to Pennsylvania. The Chinese products were unloaded and American ones loaded—ink, spearmint flavoring, additives, and polyester fiber—before *The Box* left New York on a ship headed south to Santos, Brazil, where it was loaded with monosodium glutamate (MSG) and auto parts, before crossing the Atlantic, around the southern tip of Africa, through Singapore and Hong Kong, to Yokohama, Japan. Thereafter the container went to Thailand, then back to the UK bearing a load of 95,940 tins of cat food. Upon arriving in Southampton again, it was loaded by the same operator who put it on when it left the port in 2008, hence demonstrating the tiny size of the port staff. After this, the GPS surveillance device in *The Box* failed somewhere off Mauritius, where-upon *The Box* spent almost half a year unused in Yokohama owing to a drop in demand triggered by the Global Financial Crisis. The journey of this one shipping container points to the vast logistical web of transportation that is a key aspect of contemporary globalization, one enabled and intensified by the surveillance afforded by computing-machines.[43]

Some of the militaristic dynamics that powered the cybernetic make-over of shipping also occurred in the logistical system that governs the sky. The automatic anti-aircraft weapon system that Wiener imagined (discussed above) came to fruition in the late 1950s in the form of the Semi-Automatic Ground Environment, known by the inappropriate acronym SAGE, a synonym for wisdom. At the heart of this extraordinarily expensive system lay the largest computing-machine ever built, the AN/FSQ-7 Combat Direction Central, affectionately known as Q7. Weighing in at over 5,448 tons and spread over almost two thousand square meters, Q7 could use surveillance data drawn from multiple radar to monitor an enormous space, tracking hundreds of planes simultaneously using one of the largest computer programs ever made, the product of the intellectual labor of seven thousand IBM engineers. As a cybernetic surveillance system, SAGE drew in data traces from around the world in order to make predictions, gain control, and project power. Q7 could launch supersonic surface-to-air missiles, made by military-industrial giant Boeing, and guide them toward their aerial target with real-time homing drives. It even had the capacity to launch missiles armed with nuclear warheads, a particularly deranged idea when one remembers that this system was apparently for defensive purposes, hence shooting down an enemy aircraft with a nuke as it flew over American soil could kill the people on the ground that it was supposed to be protecting. The system's headquarters, NORAD, became an archetype of the Cold War imaginary. Nestled deep in a bunker bored into a mountain, behind heavy nuclear blast doors, sat groups of uniformed military engineers—virtually all middle-aged white men—with enormous screens before them, and walls of buttons and dials, computers with ashtrays and cigarette lighters built into their interfaces. It was from chambers like this that such men "rationally" risked the balance of life on Earth, as we know it, calculating the specter of nuclear annihilation.

There was however, one tremendous problem with SAGE's surveil-lance system: it was vulnerable to radar-jamming technologies. Radar jamming was common; all advanced bombers used such techniques during World War II, and despite SAGE's technological marvels it simply could not deal with this problem. In all public demonstrations and propaganda about the system, radar jamming was never mentioned. The Soviet Union surely knew about this fundamental weakness and could have exploited it, yet there is no historical evidence that they were ever considering a full-scale confrontation with the United States. Despite this lack of threat and the dire shortcoming of the system—which was of course known to the scientists working on the system and their military supervisors—it was hidden from the public and SAGE ran for twenty-five years costing the U.S. government hundreds of billions of dollars. This raises an important point: if this surveillance system was unable to serve its ostensible defensive purpose, what function did it serve? While useless to counter contemporary radar jamming, the complex system was extremely profitable for the military-industrial complex. All the big contractors involved—AT&T, Boeing, General Electric, IBM, Lockheed, and MITRE Corporation—profited on this fraudulent feast of public money.[44]

Leaving aside these major contradictions, the SAGE system was very effective at tracking aircraft that did not use jamming, which means commercial aircraft, and this was a booming industry in the post–World War II era. Bookings for airlines were all processed manually using adding machines, telephones, and paper filing systems. This pre-digital system was effective, but it had difficulty scaling to meet the surging demand and the sprawling size of airline corporations, which meant that planes would sometimes be over- or underbooked. Either way this created problems of profitability to the company. This was a hole that SAGE could fill, with its essential technology being rebranded SABRE, the Semi-Automated Business Research Environment. According to SABRE's official story, the president of American Airlines met a senior sales representative from IBM by chance on a flight and apparently cooked up a plan to automate airline booking. By 1960 an experimental system was online; in the 1970s it had expanded beyond American Airlines to allow travel agents to use the system; in the 1980s it expanded to allow other airlines to use their system; and in the 1990s they launched a public-facing airline booking website, Travelocity, before spinning off entirely from American Airlines to become an independent corporation in the year 2000. They then expanded into hotel bookings, car rental, tour operators, and other tourism-related services. In this way a "kernel of computational Cold War paranoia sites at the heart of billions of journeys made every year."[45] It is possible to get a sense of the cybernetic power of SABRE's surveillance system by viewing a publicly accessible plane-tracking website such as FlightRadar24.com. In combination with Google Maps, it shows the real-time locations of the approximately ten thousand commercial aircraft that are flying around the world at any given time. Taken as a whole, the surveillance of planes or shipping containers described here can serve as a way to imagine the systems of control and communication that have converged, thus enabling the quantitative and qualitative intensification in globalization that has occurred under the dominance of cybernetic capitalism.

THE DRONE OF THE DRONES

On October 7, 2001, the United States invaded Afghanistan. The government of Afghanistan had the insolence to ask the hegemon for evidence of Osama Bin Laden's involvement in the 9/11 attacks in 2001, stating that they required evidence before they would be prepared to arrest him and pass him onto a neutral country for a fair trial. Still reeling from the attacks in New York and Washington, DC, the U.S. administration found this totally unacceptable, with George W. Bush saying, "There's no need to discuss innocence or guilt. We know he's guilty," and ordered the invasion of the impoverished nation.[46] That afternoon, an Air Force pilot named Captain Scott Swanson sat in a dark trailer parked behind the CIA's headquarters in Virginia in front of a control panel. From there, he remotely operated a Predator drone flying some eleven thousand kilometers away above Kandahar, Afghanistan, feeding back grainy surveillance footage. After an order was passed down the military's hierarchy, Swanson clicked a button on a joystick, thus releasing a missile on the other side of the world, and, in the dead of the night, it exploded into a truck supposed to be hiding the commander of the Taliban. The commander was nowhere near, but the attack succeeded in killing two unidentified men that the Pentagon claimed were his bodyguards without substantiation. These two mistargeted and unknown men—their deaths written-off as "collateral damage"—became the first in the history of warfare to have been killed by remote control.[47]

Drone warfare is a compelling example of contemporary surveillance and globalization on several levels. These war machines literally watch over people in order to exert control over them—control over their lives and deaths. Surveillance is integral to the very function of hunter-killer drones. They are at the cutting edge of this technology as it tears into the social fabric of poor communities in distant parts of the globe. Like a flying, invisible watchtower and executioner-machine, drones are terrifying. While they cannot be seen, those unfortunate enough to live below them can hear a constant hum of their engines—the drone of the drones—that echoes ominously 24/7 across the land, as a constant, and intimidating reminder that death could come at any second. With the press of a button on the other side of the planet, these terminators are poised to rain down death from above—via a $117,000-a-shot Lockheed Martin hellfire missile—which can reduce a wedding procession to a gory blast of burnt flesh and shards of bone, mutilation, and suffering. As I write these words, war drones are circling in the air above various "theatres of war." At present, war drones are actively deployed by the U.S. military in seven Muslim majority countries: Afghanistan, Iraq, Libya, Pakistan, Somalia, Syria, and Yemen, where they inflict great terror on whole populations. The U.S. military is very aware of terror they promote, with it being reflected in, for example, the official badge of the U.S. Air Force's Reaper Drone Unit. This morbid badge depicts the Grim Reaper, the skeletal personification of death, looking forward with hell-fire eyes, dead smile, and a blood-dripping gore scythe, all poised above the unfurling slogan: "That others may die."

Beginning under the G. W. Bush regime's invasion of Afghanistan, drone assassination increased sharply under the Nobel Peace Prize–winning U.S. President Barack Obama, who ordered 1,878 drone strikes during his eight years in office in a bizarre ritual called "Terror Tuesdays," when he would personally go and tick off faces from a "kill list." As drone warfare began with the death of "missed" targets, so it has continued to be notoriously inaccurate. In Pakistan alone, between 2004 and 2015, there have been an estimated 3,341 deaths by U.S. drones. From that total, only fifty-two of these deaths were of "high profile" targets. To make up for the shocking inaccuracies, the Obama administration ruled that all males aged sixteen and over who were killed by a drone strike were automatically counted as "combatants" regardless of evidence. Then, after Trump took office, his first two years have seen 2,243 drone strikes, approximately ten times as many and in a quarter the time as under Obama. In 2019 the Trump administration revoked a policy that required intelligence agencies like the CIA to publish the number of civilians who were killed by drone strikes outside of war zones in places like Pakistan. The Trump administration claimed that this rule was "superfluous" and distracting, hence it is now increasingly difficult to see just who is being murdered by the drones.[48]

Atop all of this, the production and use of drones is becoming increasingly globalized. For example, in 2015 Pakistan became the ninth state in the world to develop its own war drones, and the fourth military in the world to actively utilize their lethal effects in a "field test" (following Israel, the United States, and the UK). Developed by the National Engineering and Scientific Commission, producing fleets of the "Burraq" drones, it has emboldened Pakistan's military in its conflicts, both internally with insurgencies in the northwest and the southwest, and externally, both with respect to war-torn Afghanistan, and its fraught relationship with India. In response to this development, India has announced that it is intensifying its own production of war drones, as well as purchasing drones from Israel Aerospace Industries.[49] As of 2016, there were at least thirty-eight types of drones operating in Iraq and Syria, with thirty-two of them having been identified, with them being made by six different nations—China, Iran, Israel, Russia, Turkey, and the United States.[50] In all cases, these machines are produced by corporations who profit from the sale of arms and war. For example, one of the most widely used military drones in the world is the "Elbit Hermes 450" produced by the Israeli war company, Elbit System. This multibillion-dollar corporation has profited from selling these terminators to the militaries of Botswana, Brazil, Colombia, Georgia, Israel, Mexico, Philippines, Singapore, Thailand, the UK, the United States, and Zambia.[51]

Drone warfare is best understood as a continuation of the colonial wars—such as the French bombing of Algeria, the British in Malaya, or America in Vietnam—with even greater layers of technological abstraction. This abstraction has removed the possibility of direct retaliation, with this important shift marking a key transformation from combat—where two contestants engage one another—to hunting. Asymmetrical warfare becomes utterly unilateral. As those targeted by drones cannot fight back against them directly, in that they cannot kill their distant operators, it forces retaliations in the form of civil war—regarded since

Roman times as one of the worst forms of war. Furthermore, drones make spreading war much easier. It does not involve sending in flesh-and-blood soldiers that have repeatedly proven controversial. Drones allow strikes to occur in secret, in countries where there are no declared conflicts, and with no responsibility of providing evidence or fair trials, these automated executioners intensify an uneven spread of "global civil war." Civil war is becoming unevenly globalized, with massacres in nightclubs and mosques from Paris to Baghdad, from Colombo to Christchurch, a descent into a wretched state of "war of all against all." As a key component of the cycles of terror, drones are both a tactical response to this state of global civil war and a keen driver of these grim dynamics. All up, drones as death-dealing surveillance-engines change the possibility of violence, the nature of war, and, ultimately, what it means to be human.[52]

Furthermore, there is much effort in the military-industrial complex, particularly within its "artificial intelligence" wing, to try and bring about "lethal autonomous robots," computing-machines that can act independent of a human operator and slaughter people without a human in the loop. Current drones still require an operator to sit in an air-conditioned bunker somewhere and guide the semi-automated system toward committing summary executions. Future drones seek to automate away the human, thus putting patchy software in charge of death dealing. While there have been talks in Geneva of preemptively banning such ghastly machines, international law is limited when the most powerful countries have fully embraced the logic of the drone.[53] One does not need to be a science fiction writer to imagine a very grim future extending from these developments, particularly in an age where massive toxification of the planet's ecosystem and the destruction of local economies is set to displace hundreds of millions of people in the near future. Furthermore, considering the historical connections between the conjoined twins of control—computing machines and nuclear weapons—the push to modernize nuclear arsenals could see these horrific weapons become increasingly automated and autonomous, thus raising this frightful question: could robot wars go nuclear?

Building on these militaristic developments of technologies of control and communication, the next chapter continues the tale of globalization and surveillance by discussing Google and looking at how the emergent dynamics of cybernetic capitalism have increasingly been woven into everyday life.

Chapter 3

Welcome to the Machine

Google's Commodification Engines and the Web of Power

This chapter begins with another precisely dated anecdote. On August 16, 2013, at 3:51 p.m. local time in California, between 50 and 70 percent of all requests to Google's services received error signals. Many of these services were restored one minute later and the entire website had fully recovered after four minutes. According to web-analytics firms, Google's four-minute stagger directly resulted in a phenomenal 40 percent dip in global internet traffic. Other than these skeletal facts, little else is known about the causes and effects of this Google "flash crash," as the corporation refused to comment or to answer any questions on the disruption. Nevertheless, it is possible to speculate on the impacts of this sharp 40 percent dip in web traffic, which likely had ramifications around the world. Google—who has thoroughly internalized Benjamin Franklin's maxim "time is money"—had an average revenue of US$113,831 per minute in 2013—and so the glitch would have cost them at least half a million in advertising dollars, to say nothing of the companies who rely on their Google advertisements.[1]

In describing Google, one must deploy a series of very large numbers. For instance, in 2013, the year of the Google flash-crash, the tech firm was conducting over 177 billion searches per month, a number far higher than any competitor—well over 100 billion higher in fact.[2] In the same year, over one billion people—that is about one-sixth of humanity—used their products, giving the company a 77 percent share of Internet search business. This concentration is even more extreme in the global mobile-device market, where, at the beginning of 2017, Google had a 95 percent share of the market. In addition to these very large numbers, another set—conspicuously starting with a dollar symbol—are needed to convey the size of this cybernetic institution. As of April 2019, Alphabet Inc., Google's holding company, had a market capitalization of $893 billion for its GOOG stocks. To put this into some perspective, this figure is approximately the same as the World Bank's estimates of the gross domestic product (GDP) of nation-states like Turkey or the Netherlands, both in the top twenty countries. Alternatively put, Google's market capitalization is more than the world's poorest ninety-three countries combined. At this time, Alphabet had the third highest market capitalization of any corporation in the world; behind Apple and Amazon, and above Microsoft and Facebook. That the top five slots are occupied by American tech-titans is a fact of world-historic importance. Likewise, slots number six and eight are occupied by two Chinese tech-titans, Alibaba and Tencent Holdings, who feature in the next chapter. These figures serve to show just how powerful and profitable the vanguard of cybernetic capitalism has become in the early twenty-first century.

The above Google glitch episode demonstrates just how important the corporation has become. As the world's number-one website, the tech-titan has become a central institution of global communication and control, exerting an organizing force across cyberspace and the patterns of social practice that are entwined with this abstract layer. With its origin in the military-industrial research laboratories of World War II (chapter 2), cybernetic capitalism has gone on to become one of the dominant forces in the world today, with companies like Google being its most visible face. Cybernetic capitalism affects patterns of production, communication, exchange, organization, and inquiry; ways of organizing the natural world and ways of being in the world. They profoundly affect globalization as we understand it in the early twenty-first century. Google's products and services acutely affect the way in which a vast number of people, unevenly scattered around the world act, create, relate, and make meaning. Furthermore, Google is significant to the narrative of this book because it is an exemplar of surveillance. The story of how this came to be is worth recounting, as it shows how the quest for accumulation and control has increased sharply since the rise of cybernetic computing-machines.

THE RISE OF GOOGLE

After having met as PhD students at Stanford University, Larry Page and Sergey Brin registered the domain Google.com on September 15, 1997 and discontinued their studies to pursue the dream of creating their own company, a dream shared by many others in Silicon Valley during the inflation of the dot.com bubble at the end of the twentieth century. The initial research that led the pair to this decision began a couple of years before, following their meeting at Stanford University, and laid the foundations for what would become Google—with the search-engine's original URL being "google.stanford.edu." Through Stanford's very well-connected computer science department, the pair had access to funding provided by various U.S. government bodies, some of which was directly connected to the military-industrial complex. Their co-authored article acknowledges funds drawn from the Defense Advanced Research Projects Agency (DARPA), the jewel in the crown of the military-industrial complex. In another early article, the team acknowledge the funds from the Digital Library Initiative, a program aimed at supporting research on data mining based on money provided by the National Science Foundation, NASA, and DARPA.[3]

More than merely receiving funds passively, investigative journalism has revealed that the co-founder's connections with the military ran much deeper. While at Stanford, Brin regularly reported his research findings directly to "senior US intelligence representatives including a CIA official [who] oversaw the evolution of Google in this pre-launch phase, all the way until the company was ready to be officially founded." The journalist concludes, "Google was incubated, nurtured, and financed by interests that were directly affiliated or closely aligned with the US military-intelligence community." This is not to suggest that Google was particularly militaristic or that these connections were unusual. Rather it is to serve as a reminder that cybernetic capitalism as a whole remains highly intermeshed with the military, as well as academic institutions.[4] Indeed, as the previous chapter noted, it was the combination of militaries, universities, and capital that came together to create the conditions for the cybernetic reconstitution of capitalism after World War II. While the term "military-industrial complex" may today evoke olive-drab generals and Eisenhower's famous speech, it has not gone away but rather expanded greatly. A comprehensive if clunky update of this term could see it rebranded as the "new military-industrial-technological-entertainment-academic-scientific-media-intelligence-homeland security-surveillance-national security-corporate complex."[5] While this monstrous term is unusable—with an equally ugly initialism, the "NMITEASMIHSSNSC" complex—it is an important reminder as to how much the military-industrial complex has sprawled across society and globalized across the world, with its cybernetically reconstitutions intensifying surveillance and projecting control.

Using these military-industrial funds and support, Brin and Page created the foundation of their search-engine. They introduced Google in an article, describing it as "a prototype of a large-scale search engine which makes heavy use of the structure present in hypertext. Google is designed to crawl and index the Web efficiently and produce much more satisfying search results than existing systems." This article also introduced PageRank, an algorithm that maps hyperlinks in an attempt to "bring order to the web." They described it as "an objective measure of its citation importance that corresponds well with people's subjective idea of importance." The co-founders had, in Brin's words, "converted the entire web into a big equation with several hundred million variables, which are the PageRanks of all the webpages, and billions of terms, which are all the links."[6]

Drawing inspiration from how academic texts reference one another, the co-founders imagined that a similar process could be used to navigate the web. To this end, they created "PageRank," an algorithm named after Larry. This algorithm sort to determine the nature of relationships between websites in order to judge their relative importance. It does this by counting the number of links to a page, with the underlying assumption being that more important websites have more hyper-links pointing toward them than less important websites. This system proved superior to the fledgling company's competition, which were all based largely on keyword relevance indexes and web directories, and were maintained by humans. The PageRank algorithm was a more abstract step: it avoided the need to have teams of humans to organize data into categories of a directory. They went a step further than simply looking at the content (as a keyword search does) and looked at which websites point to it, lending a degree of legitimization to it that drew from the architecture of the World Wide Web. This development was profoundly cybernetic, with PageRank constituting the introduction of a kind of second-order surveillance; the algorithm surveys other web-sites, thus automatically observing other observers. This served to in-corporate the structure and content of the web into a dynamic feedback loop that fed into generating search results. In effect, this led to more and better results, hence the rapid explosion of Google's popularity.[7]

The Google search-engine involves a complicated and abstracted conjunction of processes that are central to how the cyber-capitalist firm began to draw everyday life into its circuits. Before Google can conduct a search, they must make an index of the World Wide Web. The company launches waves of software spiders that figuratively crawl across cyberspace, surveying the abstracted territory and weaving a data map as they go. Their current data map is truly vast, exceeding one hundred million gigabytes and indexing over sixty trillion pages. The survey of cyberspace is a necessary precursor to conducting a search, and hence Google's spiders are constantly crawl-ing and updating their map. This is yet another instance of surveying preceding surveillance, as I argued in chapter 1, with the corporation using the map of the web as a way to "enclose" the commons into the circuits of their profit-seeking algorithms.

The next step involves a search query being entered. For example, if I type the word "dachshund" into Google, the keyboard allows me to interface with my computer by registering the physical strokes of my fingers and translating them into digital information. This information is organized by my computer's operating system, which runs a browser that can navigate the Web. Then, via an active Internet connection, let-ter by letter, the request is sent from my location in Melbourne—via a network of world-spanning fiber-optic cables and through multiple regimes of protocols, standardization, and interoperability—to Google in the United States. Upon arriving, the request is processed by around a thousand computing-machines in several of Google massive data centers, intense infrastructure systems sometimes known by the lofty euphemism "the cloud."[8] The search request is resolved against content that has been previously indexed and ranked by Google's incessant mining and recombining of data. According to the company, the collection of algorithms used to deliver a search query result draws on over two hundred factors including "user context" and "safe search." What's more, these search algorithms are revised as often as six hundred times a year hence they are in a state of constant flux. The amalgam of algorithms retrieves what it deems to be the "best suited answer" to my query. The results are given within one-eighth of a second and are blasted back around the globe to my computer, which translates the abstract code into words, images, advertisements, and hyperlinks relating to sausage dogs. This, in a highly simplified nutshell, is how their search-engine works.[9]

It is crucially important to note that the above processes are simultaneously very abstract and yet the whole thing is also totally material.[10] Each component of the cybernetic network is composed of minerals and petrochemicals that have been mined and recombined across complex supply chains, much of which is characterized by degrading working conditions for the people who toil to create the machines "we just can't live without." Furthermore, the whole thing is powered by vast quantities of electricity—largely produced by the burning of fossil fuels—with data centers alone consuming more energy than major countries like Argentina, Iran, or Thailand. Put differently, the carbon emissions of computing-machines are about equal to the global aviation industry, a far more visible polluter. What's more, energy usage from this sector is expanding massively, set to reach an alarming 20 percent of global electricity by 2030.[11] While a compelling case can be made to drastically reduce energy consumption in order to minimize the ecological crisis, the expansion of computing is pointing in exactly the opposite direction; with more connected devices, faster speeds, more "on demand" services, and bigger data flows all adding up to intensify the toxification of everything. The "cloud" then is more than a vaporous metaphor for computing-machine infrastructure; it is also a major contributor to the real and metaphoric clouds that are darkening the prospects of life as we know it on Planet Earth. Driven by cybernetic capitalism's desperate need for infinite growth within finite nature, the facts that stem from this vicious contradiction seldom enter into public discussions about computing.[12]

Google's search algorithm delivered results, and this made the website extremely popular—however, it did not make them any money. The fledgling company received funds from DARPA-linked angel investor Andy Bechtolsheim and then, after incorporation, they received a "Series A" round of funding—to use the start-up lingo—from venture capitalist firms Sequoia Capital and Kleiner Perkins Caufield & Byers (KPCB). These two firms have been instrumental in investing in many high-profile companies, including KPCB in AOL, Amazon.com, Genetech, Netscape, and Sun Microsystems; and Sequoia in Apple, Instagram, Oracle, PayPal, and YouTube. Likewise, both investors have many strong links to the Department of Defense and the CIA, thus making them a part of the military-industrial complex. Illustrating this connection, in the aftermath of the World Trade Center attacks, a member of Sequoia arranged to have a meeting with defense secretary Donald Rumsfeld, his senior lieutenants, and a handful of tech-industry players, including Page and Brin. This meeting at the Pentagon "kicked off a classified project to match military needs with emerging technologies from startups—and gave [them a] view of what venture capitalists could achieve working with an unfettered government."[13]

THE GROWTH CURVE

After Bechtolsheim's funding in 1998, plus Sequoia and KPCB's in 1999, the venture-capitalist firms applied increasing pressure on the start-up to generate return on their investments. This intensified after the peak of the dot.com bubble in 2000, and more so after 2001 when the bubble began to hiss and spit as capitalism entered another cyclic semi-meltdown. Steven Levy, who wrote a quasi-official biography of the company, describes Google's tack out of the doldrums with a sense of melodrama: "Then came a development that was sudden, transforming, decisive, and, for Google's investors and employees, glorious. Google launched the most successful scheme for making money on the internet that the world has ever seen." As the story is often told, Google's incredible financial success was founded on the accidental discovery that simple text advertisements mixed in with search-engine results generated tremendous profit, thus allowing the company's incredible expansion. "More than a decade after its launch, this 'accident' is nowhere near being matched by any competitor. It became the lifeblood of Google, funding every new idea and innovation the company conceived thereafter."[14] While capturing some of the dynamics, this leaves out a crucially important aspect of the narrative. We may ask, just why were these plain text advertisements so effective? In a word: *surveillance*.

In the early days of Google, the search-engine collected data on the people who used their website, and the company's engineers groomed over the process in order to improve the results. Afterwards, this data was treated as waste and deleted. Then, in an effort to turn a profit, the company began to use data-gathering in combination with their analytic capabilities to target advertisements to specific people. This surveillance-driven advertising now accounts for around 85 percent of Google's total revenue. Thus the surveillance-commodification complex is at the core of what enabled Google to become one of the fastest growing companies in history, enabling them to grow from garage project to global institution in under a decade.[15]

The exponential expansion is evident in table 3.1, laid out in five-year increments to demonstrate Google's sharp rise in searches, revenue, and market capitalization. Fascinatingly, of the billions of searches that Google conducts daily, a whopping 15 percent of them have never been conducted before. This fact points toward the massive creativity of collective subjectivity, the curiosity, and diversity that emanates from the people whose everyday lives have become entangled in the Web. People are becoming more sophisticated and complex with how they navigate the web, with search query length increasing nearly 5 percent annually. Through its cybernetic survey and surveillance, Google draws on the collective creativity of people around the world, pulling it into their quest for accumulation and control.

Table 3.1. Google's Search, Revenue, and Growth in Five-Year Intervals

Year	Searches per Day	Revenue	Market Capitalization
1998	9,800	$0	(private)
2003	250,000,000	$1.5 billion	(private)
2008	1,745,000,000	$21.8 billion	$180 billion
2013	5,922,000,000	$59.83 billion	$304 billion
2018	Unknown outside Google	$136.82 billion	$866 billion

THE ADVERTISING ALGORITHMS

Growing from a useful online navigation device, Google's use of surveillance enabled its advertisements to be particularly effective, allowing the corporation to seize a monopoly position for itself and to embark on a massive commodification project. Commodification has long been central to the long history of capitalism, beginning with the enclosure movements transforming land into private property and slavery transforming people into commodities to be bought and sold in markets (chapter 1). Since the beginnings of these processes in the long sixteenth century, commodification has increased intensively and extensively, with a tendency to become more abstract as it went along. As advertisers provide Google with 85 percent of the revenue that funds their operations, it is crucially important to understand how this process of profit extraction works, for it is at the core of the reproduction and augmentation of Google's cybernetic accumulation strategy. The patterns of this process can be seen in virtually everything the firm does.

Google launched AdWords in October 2000. Beginning with just 350 customers, the service could be activated with a credit card and it enabled an advertiser to target keywords and access performance feedback. Since then it has expanded massively, with likely millions of advertisers getting on board, although the exact numbers are unknown outside Google. Whenever someone enters a word into one of Google's services—be it search, maps, and so on—AdWords launches an automated global auction. This auction enables advertisers to make bids on words that they want their brand to be associated with. Any word—security, sensibility, salad, or Schumpeter—entered into Google can lead to a bid in this global linguistic market. Or, to be more accurate, not quite any word. Google prohibits a number of keywords in various countries to comply with national laws. For example, one cannot use alcohol keywords in Thailand or "abortion" in Ukraine. Most strikingly, Google has put a worldwide ban on adult-related services or products worldwide as of 2014. Hence, typing "porn" into Google will not lead to an AdWords auction; despite the tremendous potential for profit from tapping into the Web's libido, the company's moral concerns prevail. Nevertheless, Google's CEO for a decade Eric Schmidt said, "We run many more auctions than anyone else on the planet because we run them in real time, we run one auction per ad per page, and that's multiplied by the numbers of ads per page. It's a phenomenal number."

The winners of the auction appear above or among the search results as "sponsored links." These text advertisements are very short; they consist of one headline of a maximum twenty-five characters, followed by two additional text lines of up to thirty-five characters each.

Not all AdWords are created equal. For example, if I put the words "Don Quixote" into Google, I get the novel's Wikipedia page, various summaries, and the Imperial Russian Ballet Company. There are no advertisements. However, if I type "Don Quixote buy" into Google, the top of my results page is filled with "sponsored links" to buy a copy of the book from a diversity of sources, including Amazon, Book-Depository (owned by Amazon), and AbeBooks (owned by Amazon). Paid search listings beat "organic"—read unpaid—links by a margin of nearly 2:1 for keywords with high commercial intent in the United States. There seems to be a mixed awareness about how Google manipulates searches. According to a couple of recent surveys, 50 percent of adults using the Web were unable to recognize advertisements in Google's search results. While contestable, this figure is huge.[16]

It is significant also because Google can target advertisements to specific people. Using their surveillance-engines they can target ads to specific kinds of people within specific geographic localities, on specific days of the week, hours in the day, or relative to the device used. For instance, an advertiser could specifically aim to have their advertisement appear to someone conducting a search on a Friday at 7:30 p.m. from a smart-phone near the restaurant district on Lygon Street, Melbourne. Advertisers are even given the possibility to increase their bid according to the specific location of a person using Google; hence they could bid higher if a person was within a certain radius of their store. In this way, AdWords, and its shadow of surveillance, merges seamlessly with their cartographic machine, Google Maps.

Should I click on one of these "sponsored links" to buy a copy of *Don Quixote*, then Amazon automatically pays Google a fee. The open, ascending price auction system allows the cost of the advertisement to be determined by how competitive the keyword in question is and hence prices vary massively while also allowing for the efficient allocation of resources. Some uncompetitive words and phrases are very cheap. To take some actual examples from early 2018, in U.S. dollars, advertisers can pay $0.07 to place an ad on searches for "cut and paste," $0.02 for "coolest car in the world," or for the lower-than-low price, one can pay only $0.01 to bid on "the stuff." Plainly, these keywords don't tend to generate big sales. At the other end of the spectrum, Google's auctions can extract a remarkably high fee for a single click. Advertisers will pay $26.75 for an ad on "does laser hair removal hurt," $112.07 for "online business degree," $130.31 for "alcoholic," and a whopping $389.25 for "truck accident lawyer." Building on this, if I wanted to learn about, say, "climate change," then I may type these words into Google's search-engine. The company uses this search to extract data about me, which is compiled with other information already amassed about me in a digitalized dossier. In this way, the company appropriates my actions and transforms them into commodities to be literally sold to the highest bidder. When I conducted this search, the first four results that Google displayed from my "climate change" search were advertisements. Hence my desire to learn about the toxification of the atmosphere, and the broader existential crisis of which it is entangled, is abstracted and re-combined as a commodity in the circuits of cybernetic capitalism.

Through controlling key components of this energy-intensive infrastructure, Google has gained significant power. It uses this power to extend its advertising abilities through a series of acquisitions, thus fortifying its monopolistic position. For instance, AdWords was extended through AdSense, a program developed by Applied Semantics and acquired by Google in 2003. AdSense allows website publishers in their network to put automated advertisements—text, visual, video, or interactive—on their websites, and to target them to a specific audience. Even if one does not use Google search, any participating websites can display a Google-enabled advertisement. In this way, the company pushes consumerism outside the bounds of its own websites and onto the broader Web, thus facilitating the extension of advertising into more parts of everyday life.

The fact that advertisers provide the vast majority of Google's revenue is crucial to understanding the tech-titan. This is what enables Google to roll out the majority of their services for "free." This apparent free-ness is a key way that the corporation simultaneously extends itself into everyday life, whilst simultaneously legitimizing its practices. While one can access many of Google's services without hitting a paywall, one cannot use them without paying a hidden cost. Without going into the full complexity of theorizing how Google accumulates capital, one aspect of this phenomenon can be understood by using the audience-as-commodity theory that was formulated a generation ago. A succinct expression of this theory follows: in capitalism, if you're not paying for a commercial product, then you're not the customer—you're the product being sold. Built into the logic of commercial broadcasting, the audience-commodity concept has been abstracted and expanded massively by Google.[17] Surveillance allows data traces to be automatically extracted from everyday life, traces that are fed into the furnace of accumulation and expansion, vast cybernetic systems that through feedback loops seek to manipulate people's everyday practices in accordance with the whims of those who can pay top dollar. One can argue that we "are not Google's customers: we are its product. We—our fancies, fetishes, predilections, and preferences—are what Google sells to advertisers. When we use Google to find out things on the Web, Google uses our Web searches to find out things about us. Therefore, we need to understand Google and how it influences what we know and believe."[18] A senior vice president at Google put the matter very frankly: "We don't monetize the thing we create. We monetize the people that use it. The more people that use our products, the more opportunity we have to advertise to them." When Android was released for "free," Schmidt gloated: "You get a billion people doing something, there's lots of ways to make money. Absolutely, trust me. We'll get lots of money for it." Curiously, a similar point was raised in a radically different context by William Burroughs in his grueling 1959 beatnik-era novel *Naked Lunch*: "The junk merchant doesn't sell his product to the consumer, he sells the consumer to his product."[19]

The surveillance-commodification complex can also explain why Google promotes the image of free-ness. The logic of this model runs thus: the more people that use the web, the more they will use its number one website, and therefore the more Google can survey and appropriate their actions. This allows more commodification opportunities, selling the audience to advertisers. More precisely targeted advertisements lead to an increasing number of engagements with AdWords, hence an intensifying stream of revenue for Google. As with other big companies, part of this vast revenue stream is scraped off as profit for the company's shareholding owners, and part of it is capitalized—being reinvested in more hardware, research, acquisitions, and political power in a calculated attempt to further their monopolistic grip and quest for infinite accumulation. Also, by pulling as many people as possible into their proprietorial system, fewer opportunities will exist for others in the arena of high-tech monopolistic competition. Highlighting the importance of monopoly power is essential to understand capitalism, for the popularly spread imaginary of heroic little-guy upstarts battling it out in a competitive free market is illusion in today's world. The reality is of tremendous market concentrations in virtually all domains of economic activity, with a corporation like Google controlling upwards of 90 percent in multiple markets—search, maps, browsers, mobile operating systems, and so on—with this giving them the ability to control huge systems of infrastructure, extract huge amounts of data and money from billions of people, and altogether have an immense influence over society. Such material power is not readily replicable by some upstarts in a garage, with many startups not attempting the near impossible task of replacing the tech-titans and instead working to get bought up by one of the tech-titans whose main innovations now come through acquisitions.[20]

All of this is standard corporate practice, for not only are corporations structurally pressured to maximize their profits, they are entangled in a web of endless accumulation. There is a structural necessity for them to grow, to expand, and to deliver increasing returns on investments—a necessity that is deeply problematic within a finite nature, including finite human nature. Nevertheless, twenty-first-century cybernetic capitalism has intensified to the point where, through automated surveillance, "world, self and body are reduced to the permanent status of *objects* as they disappear into the bloodstream of a titanic new conception of markets. His washing machine, her car's accelerator, and your intestinal flora are collapsed into a single dimension of equivalency as information assets that can be disaggregated, reconstituted, indexed, browsed, manipulated, analyzed, reaggregated, predicted, productized, bought, and sold: anywhere, anytime."[21]

The imperatives of a market-driven society mean that *"Members of the society of consumers are themselves consumer commodities,* and it is the quality of being a consumer commodity that makes them bona fide members of that society."[22] As advertising extends, it draws more of life into the circuits of consumerism and capital accumulation, with Google being an exemplar of this trend, along with many others, such as Baidu and Facebook, engaging in similar practices. Furthermore, it is worth pointing out that Google's systematic prioritization of advertising, consumerism, and commercial interests comes at the direct expense of economic and political democracy.[23] For instance, one can only imagine the different world that would be produced if the enormous amount of resources and intellectual labor that goes into commercial indoctrination were to be instead invested into promoting critical thinking as a way toward self-governance. Furthermore, advertising cannot be written off as a peripheral phenomenon, for it plays an integral and structural role in capitalism. Across the twentieth century, capitalists discovered that creating products that fulfilled needs or realized aspirations simply wasn't profitable enough, for a satisfied consumer wouldn't keep spending. This was a major problem for overproducing companies desperately attempting to achieve infinite profit within finite nature. Along with the invention of planned obsolescence, one of the major responses to this was to turn to advertising in an effort to remake people's subjectivities. Since its "scientific" turn in the early twentieth century, advertising has become a set of enormously powerful techniques for the mass manipulation of practice. Advertising sought to promote subjectivities of consumerism into members of the working classes of wealthier nations so that they could absorb the excessive products produced and keep the cycles of accumulation spinning. This process intensified greatly as advertising went fully cybernetic in the early twenty-first century, with companies like Google participating in attempts to reorganize consciousness in more profitable and wasteful ways.[24]

THE SMARTENING DEVICES

Since the rise of computing-machines, these devices have been bound up with the creation of an increasingly abstract world, one drawn away from embodied reality and overlaid by esoteric apparatuses and arcane algorithms. Companies like Google, and the other tech-titans, are part of the cutting edge of the abstract blade that slices deep into the flesh of the world, reorganizing the way people think, act, and organize. One of the most illustrative examples of this creeping, colonizing abstraction can be seen in the ways that everyday life is reorganized by the extension of a network of mobile computing-machines called "smart-phones." Despite the deceptively simple name, these are not a single technology, rather a bundle of technologies: computer, screen, cameras, various networking antenna, a GPS chip, a suite of sensors, a speaker, and a microphone, all enclosed in a sleek palm-sized box of polycarbonate. Each of these components spills beyond the unit itself into an abstract ecosystem of techniques and technologies: from satellites, cables, and data centers; to bureaucratic administrators and financial institutions; to protocols, machine language, and interoperability standards; mining operations, mineral refinement, sweatshop labor, toxic by-products, and enormous amounts of energy. These devices are a complex mix of negotiations and compromise, competition and monopoly, power and control, clever tweaks and unintended consequences. Among other things, smart-phones are powerful surveillance devices. Taken as a whole, smart-phones, and other "smart" products, can be seen as the teeth of the abstract saw blade of cybernetics as it is drawn through everyday life.[25]

Over the last decade, Google, along with Apple, Facebook, Huawei, and Samsung among others, have been among the most powerful corporations pushing the wide adoption of smart-phones. In Google's case, their product Android controls an 88 percent global market share of the operating systems that run smart-phones. Some people in wealthy English-speaking countries may be surprised by that statistic, for iPhones take around 50 percent or more of the market there, a figure very much in line with Apple's commercial strategy but out of step with the majority of the world. Apple's enormously profitable accumulation model consists of selling expensive goods to rich people and then locking them into a system of staunch end-to-end vertical integration. This differs from Google's also enormously profitable accumulation model, which is more open-ended and founded on surveillance.

At present, convincing arguments can be made that the smart-phone may well represent the fastest technology take-up in history. Certainly, use of these mobile computing-machines has increased dramatically over the last decade, going from an extremely limited ownership to ubiquitous. This is not reducible to corporations pushing them onto people, for many, many people plainly want and/or need these devices to function in our increasingly technologically mediated world.[26] These machines have been bound up with great changes in daily practices and habits. In rich countries, it is estimated that people spend around *four hours per day* on their smart-phones. Put differently, this means that people spend around one quarter of their waking hours flicking between corporate apps on their devices. Research has shown that people consistently and significantly underestimate how much time they spend on their phones, and when presented with measurements, they are usually shocked but seldom alter their practices. It is not just the total time that is problematic but also the disruptive, compulsive behavior that accompanies it, with people checking their phones on average every twelve minutes of the waking day, frequently unlocking the screens for no purpose whatsoever. These kinds of pathological actions invade many other forms of social practices, with people irresistibly checking their machines while speaking face-to-face with friends, in class, at work, on a date, on holiday, while practicing a religion, while attending a funeral. It is the first thing most people reach for in the morning, and the last thing they put down at night. Indeed, a disturbing number of people—between 7 percent to 20 percent depending on age and specific study—admit to having checked their phones during sexual intercourse. Nothing in the social sphere seems to escape the desperate grasp of these attention-demanding distraction devices.[27]

Corporations like Google have a vested interest in encouraging these kinds of obsessive practices, for the more time people pour into their devices, the more opportunities there are to extract data via surveillance. From this perspective, it matters less the specifics of what people are doing online—which may be variously enjoyable or educational, helpful or hateful, mindless or meaningful—rather that they can have data extracted from their actions and are encouraged to adopt certain profitable practices. This data is then processed seeking insights that might give an organizational power, such as finding new and more sophisticated ways to coax people into being more consumeristic, hence allowing for more wealth to be extracted and more power projected by the cyber-capitalist. At present, the tech-titan is expanding into new surveillance-fueled methods to make generated "suggestions" automatically as to where people should go, what they should buy, what news they should read, what they should search for, and, more broadly, what they should think. In each and every case, companies like Google systematically promote commercial possibilities above other considerations, putting structural pressure on people to adopt specific sets of practices—practices defined by the peculiar norms of the elite engineers who build the systems. These norms fetishize "convenience" above all other considerations, specifically high-tech solutions that facilitate corporate wealth extraction and surveillance. Want a lift? Uber.

Want a meal delivered? Uber Eats. Want accommodations? Airbnb. And the list goes on. Spilling out of Silicon Valley's elite engineer sector, these become default options of an increasingly large number of people who, as they adopt these technological mediated practices into their everyday lives, become more and more reliant on the corporations and less able to function without them. This breeds a persuasive dependency, one characterized by constant technological upgrade, subscription-based services, constant consumption, and, of course, profound asymmetries in power. In making these critiques, it is important to stress that much of this is a result of how cyber-technologies have been thoroughly constituted by capitalism and its desperate need for infinite growth of profits.

These days, people are using smart-phones to mediate an enormously large and increasing range of activities. People think, learn, speak, flirt, buy, listen, watch, and play with their mobile machines. Indeed, they are central to how much meaning-making takes place, with complex sets of possibilities and limitations stemming from the devices. In many cases, people are directly *outsourcing parts of their mind to corporations* with significant implications on subjectivity and society. For example, Google Maps can largely replace the need to be spatially aware of one's surroundings or to socially engage with someone through asking for directions. Google Maps achieves this spatial cognitive outsourcing through a suite of sensors within the phone itself, its connection to abstract global cybernetic systems, and layer upon layer of software. For example, the GPS chip receives pings from satellites orbiting the earth twenty thousand kilometers overhead and uses them to triangulate its geographic location. This works in combination with other sensors, such as the magnetometer, which detects magnetic fields and, like a compass, can determine north; a barometer, which measures air pressure thus enabling it to calculate altitude; and an accelerometer, which monitors stress that appears in the sensitive structures of crystals as a proxy for surveilling how fast the device is moving and in what direction, thus allowing it to track acceleration. All the data extracted by these sensors is processed by algorithms in software systems that ultimately come together to represent a person as a little blue blob moving along the map's abstract terrain. These incredibly complex systems allow for incredible powers of navigation, and make huge transformations in how people have historically moved across space.[28]

As we move through space with a smart-phone, or other such sur-veillance devices, an enormous amount of data traces are extracted from the process. Sensors capture this data, which is then analyzed and stored by multiple parties—including the phone's operating system developer, the app developer, and the phone's service provider—many of whom on-sell this lucrative data to other even more removed agents in order to profile people and provide targeted advertisement and auto-matically customize information. To be sure, digital maps like Google's are powerful machines; they can allow one to go to a new city and navigate it with confidence, yet these abilities come with many hid-den costs, including profound dependencies on the corporate provider and on the resource intensive material infrastructure that enables them to do what they do. This arrangement gives systematic power to the company through their ability to draw in surveillance data, and project control onto the person. In Google Maps' case, it determines what is represented in its image of the world, a representation regularly ac-cessed by around two billion people. There is enormous power in this, as hinted at by the idiom "put on the map," meaning to make well known or noteworthy, whereas "wipe off the map" means to annihilate. These mirrored idioms speak of the power of maps and their ability to create meaning and influence space. Google Maps shapes the way billions of people imagine the world around them and to practically navigate their way through it. This is not to suggest that people are passive cogs—far from it, we are creative social beings—rather, I sug-gest that these simplifying machines exert structuring forces into social practices, reorganizing it around one particular set of possibilities and limitations: those of the social formation of cybernetic capitalism.[29]

It is not an exaggeration to suggest that the widespread adoption of smart-phones, and the tangled system of corporate abstractions that they embody, is transforming the structures of human consciousness itself. As corporations like Google and Facebook make the majority of their money from profitable distractions in the so-called attention economy, they design their systems to be as addictive and compulsive as possible. This involves exploiting psychological susceptibilities, ranging from our deep desire for social connection, through to shallow impulses for instant gratification. Much like with the design of gam-bling machines found in casinos, this is a purposeful project pushed by powerful corporations who use surveillance, research, and engineering to increase people's usage of the machines and thus their own profits.[30] On a far grander scale than any casino, the engineering of addiction through software is currently having major and unknown effects on a huge number of people around the global laboratory. For instance, if, on average, people are checking their phones every twelve minutes of the waking day, then this is going to structurally limit their ability to focus deeply on a task. Studies have shown that students who do not use phones in class take more detailed notes, recall more details from their classes, and score a full letter grade and a half higher in comparison to their fellow students who actively used their phones.[31] Another study found that the mere presence of one's smart-phone may well reduce cognitive capacity.[32] Research like this points toward an enormous contradiction, for on some levels these devices greatly increase one's ability to think and engage, and yet on other levels, they appear to undermine these very activities: again the contradiction of control arises; it is simultaneously gained and lost. One of the reasons for this contradiction comes from a clash between the interests of ordinary people and the tech-titans. Of course, ordinarily people have an incredibly diverse and complex array of interests, needs, motives, and desires, and in comparison to this, the tech-titans are very simple: the structures of cybernetic capitalism demand that they achieve infinite growth. From this perspective, they design computing-machine technology that seeks to promote specific forms of consciousness: ones characterized by a mix of a disembodied dream state with a dash of dementia, simultaneously intoxicated and infantilized. There is an effort to promote structurally shallow thinking for it may well be the most profitable and the most susceptible to control from above.[33]

This elite driven adoption of surveillance apparatuses gets even more invasive with the rise of "wearables," tiny computing-machines designed to be worn on and monitor the body, most famously the so-called smart-watches. This is a cutting-edge area of expansion, with many start-ups and tech-titans seeking to dominate the market. Google's "Wear OS" is a version of their Android system designed to power the inner workings of such machines. As with their smart-phone OS, it runs on devices built by other corporations, such as Samsung Gear Live and LG G Watch, with Google getting to syphon off all the data extracted. These devices compete with products from other Silicon Valley companies, such as "Fitbit" and "Jawbone," as well as the current leader of the market, the Apple Watch. That Apple's famously expensive product dominates the smart-watch market says something about the affluence of the people adopting it, with again the elite engineering sector being overly represented and their fetishes being generalized.

Wearables are surveillance apparatus that use sensors to extract data traces from the human host. They can surveil a person's heart rate, the number of steps taken, stairs climbed, calories burned, and monitor their quality of sleep. All of this extracted biometric data is compiled in large data banks where it is analyzed for profitable exploitation in ways that can be potentially problematic, especially as health insurance is often involved. The newest Apple Watch sells itself as "part guardian, part guru," touting an app for automated mindfulness that claims to keep "you centered by taking you through a series of calming breaths." It tracks this mindfulness with machine precision, allowing one to see exactly how many minutes per day the wearer has spent being mindful in order to optimize it. The machine also sports a yoga app, thus reducing thousands of years of spiritual practice to the thinnest possible on-demand service mediated by a multinational corporation. This striving for embodiment through disembodiment is one of many contradictions of cybernetic capitalism. Through automated alerts and coaching apps, wearables can tell their host to drink more water, exercise more, and give various other automatically generated tips. Apple Watch's sales team states, "All new. For a better you." In this context, the corporation claims that a "better you" is one that is more measured, more exposed to surveillance, more quantified and optimized so as to be more productive, both on a personal level and through producing more surveillance data for extraction. It is a kind of automated Taylorism of the self (chapter 2).

Wearables are largely promoted because of their alleged health benefits. Many corporations have taken up promoting these surveillance devices to their staff in an effort to promote "corporate wellness," based on the human resource management idea that fit and healthy employees are more productive and hence more profitable. Market-leading fitness trackers, like Fitbit and Jawbone, offer discounts to corporations, encouraging them to buy their product in bulk to monitor their workforce en masse by subscribing to data aggregation software to analyze the surveillance data. Fitbit's promotional material encourages companies to "Step towards success like BP," noting that they have recorded employees of the carbon-combustion-giant taking twenty-three billion steps into the rapidly warming future. Oscar Health, a new insurance company founded in 2012 and propelled with funds from Google's venture capitalist arm no less, announced to their members that they would provide a free fitness-tracking bracelet. Once minimum activity goals are set, the system automatically rewards its members with a $1 per day reward, to a maximum of $240 per year, which is paid in the form of an Amazon gift voucher. Apart from the gamified corporate enticement, this device specifically allows health insurance companies to surveil the bodies of their clients, and thus automatically micromanage client payments, minimize risk, and maximize profit.[34]

Amazon—and other online-shopping logistical retailers like Alibaba—are at the cutting edge of this new cybernetic Taylorism, which uses automated surveillance to push workers to greater levels of effort to produce profits for others. Their workers are forced to carry a device that directs them from product to product as they move around the vast warehouses known by the eerie name "fulfillment centers." The goods in these warehouses are ordered algorithmically, with no discernible pattern to the workers, hence the map is necessary to direct them through the abstract maze, a map that constantly surveils their movements. The workers must scan the barcodes, place the goods in the trolley, and a timer is constantly ticking, measuring in seconds how long each movement takes. Another variation of this work sees shelves brought to the workers by robots, which leave the worker standing there, retrieving and packing one item every nine seconds for ten-and-a-half-hours-a-day. On top of this, Amazon has just introduced a newly patented wristband that allows them to automatically surveil every movement of their workers' hands in order to optimize their service to profit-making enterprises. Technology has been used to reduce workers to operative functions of algorithms, meat components of a cybernetic system governed by the desperate need to extract profit, centralize control, and expand. This goes hand in glove with Amazon paying their workers so little that many also receive food stamps to aid their survival. This can be understood as another kind of state subsidy that Amazon receives and should be added to the major public subsidy they get from paying no tax at all, despite tremendous profits. This is a striking example of how the state props up corporate profits.[35]

The Pentagon has also been swept up into the corporate wellness logic, actively encouraging their troops to wear fitness trackers in an

effort to combat obesity in the armed forces. In early 2018 GPS tracking company Stava produced the Global Heat Map. The map plotted
the movements of subscribers to their fitness services over a two-year
period (2015–2017), condensing accumulated information to a layer
on a world map. Around twenty-seven million people use Strava's
services, including everyone with a Fitbit or Jawbone, among other
surveillance devices. Data traces are extracted from people and then
projected onto a world map, itself an abstraction created through surveying and representing the world via the abstract view from above.
The aggregated routes on the map present an image of uneven development: Europe is ablaze with light, contrasting vividly to the "dark
continent" beneath it. The Middle East is likewise very dark, save the
glowing Gulf cities and Israel, along with its colonies in illegally occupied Palestinian territories. Curiously, suspicious pimples of light
punctuate the darkness of the deserts of Iraq and Syria. Zooming in
on these inadvertently revealed the precise locations of U.S. military
bases in the region and beyond, both those publicly known as well as
the secret and illegal black sites. The map's light lines show what we
can assume to be patrol routes and supply lines, sometimes patterns
made by troops forced to run around in circles. That an institution as
security conscious as the Pentagon accidentally revealed this information to the world tells us something about the state of surveillance and
globalization. It is the result of layers of state, science, and capital in-
terweaving in complex patterns of control and accumulation that can
create tensions and contradictions. In this example, we have troops
wearing Fitbits, running Strava's software through the Pentagon's GPS
system, projecting the data onto the web, thus resulting in revealing
something that the powerful wanted hidden.[36]

THE MANAGEMENT OF DEMOCRACY

"The development of powerful new means of communication has
coincided, historically, with the extension of democracy and with
the attempts, by many kinds of ruling groups, to control and manage democracy."[37] These words, written back in 1962, referred to the
rise of printing in the long sixteenth century through to newspapers
in the nineteenth century, and radio and television in the twentieth
century. This point readily applies to the rise of the Internet and the

technological mediatization of everyday life. A recent example of this dynamic was captured neatly in the 2018 Facebook-Cambridge Analytica scandal, which showed how degraded democracy has become in the early twenty-first century. Indeed, in this section when I refer to "democracy," I am specifically referring to representative democracy, a form at the shallow, bureaucratic end of the realm of democratic possibility and one contradicted by being nested within the non-negotiable capitalist system. Nevertheless, an important reflection on this flawed and increasingly endangered system was very concisely captured in the title of a recent book: *Democracy May Not Exist, but We'll Miss It When It's Gone.*[38]

Cambridge Analytica, a British political consulting and data firm, gained access to data extracted from 87 million people via Facebook; the vast majority were from the United States. To do this, Cambridge Analytica used a false academic inquiry mixed with the practically never-read terms and conditions of an app that gave access to a person and their friends' data. Through this, the firm proceeded to, in 2016, subject this data to analytic processes in order to automatically generate psycho-geographic profiles of the people whose data had been breached, leading to the creation of customized political-marketing campaigns. Broadly, this followed the same pattern of surveillance and commodification that was at the core of Google's rise described above. This data was then used to create fake news and targeted advertisements to promote Donald Trump's presidential campaign in the United States, and the Leave.EU campaign in the UK. In addition to these most famous cases, Cambridge Analytica also sold its services to political parties in India, Kenya, Malta, and Mexico in an effort to help them better manipulate voters.[39] On top of this large-scale political manipulation tactic, Cambridge Analytica also added layers of political scandal making, including hiring prostitutes to defame politicians, using bribery sting operations, and setting honey traps, as was gloated about by the CEO Alexander Nix. After this experiment became public, the firm closed its operations (with many members shifting to another arm of the company, Emerdata), Facebook was subjected to Congressional inquiry and an ongoing criminal investigation on both sides of the Atlantic. This resulted in Facebook's breaking records by losing around $120 billion worth of stock in a day, dropping from a market capitalization of around $630 billion to $510 billion. This is the equivalent of subtracting the entire stock market value of powerful companies like General Electric or McDonald's.

There is a curious and seldom told backstory and parallel story to the high-profile Cambridge Analytica scandal, one that reveals the notorious firm to seem like the tip of the democracy sinking iceberg. Back in 2008, during the first election campaign for Obama, his team employed a number of big data companies to make their campaign "data driven," a euphemism for powered by surveillance-engines. Thus began a pattern that would intensify over the coming decade, whereby for-profit companies began working as liberal election engineers, a group strongly aligned with establishment Democrats and a pro-corporate agenda. An example of this can be seen with the firm Catalist, founded in 2006 with money from George Soros and co-founded by Harold Ickes, Bill Clinton's assistant to the president, a deputy chief of staff, and the architect of his 1996 reelection campaign. In their own words, "Catalist compiles, enhances, stores, and dynamically updates data on over 240 million unique voting-age individuals across all fifty states and the District of Columbia. Working with Catalist can help you build membership, target persuasive messaging, engage activists, drive an issue agenda, and mobilize voters."[40]

After the success of the 2008 election, this data-driven streak intensified dramatically in the lead-up to the 2012 campaign. Obama's team assembled a huge data analytic team, consisting of over fifty people—or ten times the size of Romney's—which included social scientists and psychologists. In the lead-up to the election, the analytics team's first task was to rationalize and centralize all the data collected in the 2008 campaign into a single system with organized individualized profiles running through it. This project was given the fanciful name "Narwhal."[41] When the new analytics team came to it, the existing data structures were a mess, with the go-and-vote list not being integrated with the donors list and so on. Over eighteen months, technicians worked on this process of data centralization, creating a system that held data on millions of Americans, each person linked to a unique seven-digit identifier that would follow them across space and time. Hundreds of layers of commercial and private data layers were amassed on Americans, including data scraped from social media, people's mobile contracts, poll responses, fundraising notes, voting record, information purchased from consumer databases, magazine subscriptions, student loans, Twitter handles, marital status, demographic details—age, sex, race, neighborhood, and so forth—and other surveillance data, all with special attention paid to states that could swing Democratic. This allowed them to run a national campaign in a way that was automatically customized to individualized voters imagined as data aggregates.[42]

Obama's 2012 campaign specifically made use of Facebook data, much as Cambridge Analytica did for Trump in 2016—as well as the companies working for Clinton mentioned below. Obama's team encouraged their supporters to download his official Facebook app, which once activated, the almost never-read terms and conditions tick in and—low and behold—access to their data, and their friend's data was granted to the campaigners. This was, in short, the essence of the trick Cambridge Analytica would perform four years later. More than one million Obama supporters downloaded the app, giving access to their friends list. This had a much larger reach than Cambridge Analytica's "This Is Your Digital Life" app, which had a total of 270,000 people grant access to their private data. The digital director of Obama's campaign said, "People don't trust campaigns. They don't even trust media organizations. Who do they trust? Their friends." This cynical move gave them the ability to automatically customize their campaigning and to cloak advertisements as messages from friends. A key difference between Cambridge Analytica and Obama's app was that the former claimed that the information would only be used for academic purposes, whereas the latter explicitly said that it would be used by the campaign for political purposes, making the former undoubtably more deceitful. Yet, once the terms and conditions were clicked, they were functionally very similar. In both cases, the majority of people whose data was accumulated and analyzed had no idea that this was happening. Nevertheless, after the success of the 2012 campaign, Obama's data analytic team was much lauded, with, for instance, MIT's *Technology Review* devoting an entire issue under the title "Big Data Will Save Politics," with Bono's black-and-white face gracing the front cover. The same issue ran another article claiming that such surveillance-based advertising had "restored the soul of politics." A celebratory 2012 article published in *Time* concluded with this line: "By 2016, this sort of campaign-driven sharing over social networks is almost certain to be the norm. Tell your friends."[43] After it was discovered that Cambridge Analytica had helped get Trump elected, the reactions in the media were somewhat less enthusiastic.

Jump to the 2016 U.S. election and some eerie parallels can be seen between a comparison of Cambridge Analytica and another surveillance firm called Civis Analytics. Cambridge Analytica was partially owned and heavily influenced by Robert Mercer, a billionaire sitting at the intersection of finance, cybernetics, and hard-right-wing politics. Civis Analytics was entirely owned and heavily influenced by Eric Schmidt, another billionaire sitting at the intersection of finance, cybernetics, and Clinton's brand of hawkish, imperial market politics. Both are at the forefront of devising new ways that the superrich can shape the political sphere according to their preferred vision. Looking into these two figures and their companies is also revealing of aspects of the current historical moment more generally.

Robert Mercer studied physics and mathematics before turning to computer science, where he did a stint at the United States' Air Force Weapons Laboratory before joining IMB Research to work on pattern recognition technologies for two decades. In 1993 he accepted a request to join the hedge fund Renaissance Technologies, a company that specializes in using quantitative mathematical models to predict and capitalize upon market behavior. The corporation ran an employee-only fund that received an average return rate of 71.8 percent for the twenty years beginning in 1994. This tremendous growth rate made Mercer—and the hedge fund's other core employees—outrageously rich. Since 2010, when the Citizen United decision allowed corporations to pour even more money into politics, Mercer and his family have lavished at least $36 million on Republican candidates and the political action committees (Super PACs) that support them, including $25 million on the 2016 election. This must be understood in the wake of a 2010 Supreme Court ruling that forbid the government from restricting the expenses of political communications issues by corporations and other legal entities, thus granting even more power for capital to shape political processes in their interests. Mercer's key political advisor was Steve Bannon, an important figure of the "alt-right"—a euphemism for the twenty-first-century remix of right-wing extremism—in the United States and more globally. Bannon managed the Mercer-funded news media empire of Breitbart, a commentary website steeped in a ferment of misogyny and racism and peppered with outright misinformation and climate change denialism. Bannon was also the vice president of the board of Cambridge Analytica, helping the organization work to have Trump elected.

After the success of this effort, Bannon was awarded with the position of Trump's first national security advisor, with this "Hand of the King" position embodying Mercer's behind-the-scenes power. When not using his fortune to undermine democracy, the notoriously secretive billionaire goes between his $75 million high-tech luxury superyacht, *Sea Owl*, and his Long Island mansion, Owl's Nest, where he can play with the $2.7 million model train set he keeps in his basement.[44]

Like Mercer, Eric Schmidt also came from computer science, before passing through a series of key institution in the history of computers, including Bell Labs and Xerox's Palo Alto Research Center, before climbing the ranks of Sun Microsystems and becoming the CEO of Novell. Additionally, he also taught a course at Stanford Business School called "Entrepreneurship and Venture Capital." He was brought in as the "adult supervision" of Google and was CEO from 2001 to 2015 and executive chairman until late 2017. After his appointment as Google's CEO, Schmidt became a member of Obama's Office of Science and Technology Policy, and he led the Defense Innovation Advisory Board, which provides the Pentagon with advice from a Silicon Valley perspective. He is an active participant in numerous über-elite organizations, such as the Bilderberg Group, Trilateral Commission, and World Economic Forum. Worth more than $13.5 billion, Schmidt has his own venture capitalist firm, TomorrowVentures and Innovative Endeavors. He co-founded Google's geopolitical arm "Jigsaw," is a large player in the development-industry philanthropy, and is involved in numerous "think-tanks" and advocacy groups. When not using his fortune to undermine democracy, Schmidt can play on his collection of superyachts, going between the $72 million *Oasis*, the custom-built $38 million luxury sailing boat *Elfje*, or the speedy $25 million *Gladiator*.

While favoring different candidates, both Mercer and Schmidt poured tremendous amounts of their money into the U.S. presidential campaign and the broader political sphere. Also, both were, at least in part, backed up by their respective deep-pocketed companies, Renaissance Technologies and Google. Both actively organized to use surveillance, data analytics, and micro-targeted control in an attempt to manage democracy in the favor of their own elite interests. The below looks less at Mercer and Cambridge Analytica, as this has received sustained attention over 2018. Rather, I will focus on the lesser-known developments on the other side of the narrow American political spectrum.

Civis Analytics is big-data start-up spun out of the revolving door between Google and corporate Democrat electioneering. Dan Wagner worked on both of Obama's election campaigns, going from being the "Targeting Lead" for the Great Lakes region, to the targeting and analytics director of the Democratic National Committee, before becoming the chief analytics officer for Obama for America. A child math prodigy who entered college at age thirteen, Wagner ran "the Cave," the big-data war room of the 2012 Obama campaign. The Cave would produce daily reports with detailed run downs of the presidential race and insights extracted from the thousands of nightly computer simulations of potential ways the election could unfold. After the election, Wagner founded Civis Analytics, a start-up composed of Democrat campaigners and initially entirely funded by Google's Schmidt. After correctly predicting the outcome of a 2012 Massachusetts election, Wagner was approached by Schmidt, who after a conversation offered a personal loan, followed by an undisclosed amount of seed funding in 2013, a figure that was rumored by associates to be in an eight-digit sum. Schmidt apparently immediately saw the commercial potential of what the analytics team had developed, foreseeing ways that this kind of surveillance could be used to benefit the private sector beyond political campaigning. For corporate Democrats, there were no contradictions here: in their limited imaginations, profit-maximizing firms, opinion engineering, and democratic politics are part of a virtuous circle. Civis now sells their services to Fortune 500 companies like Verizon, tech-titans like Airbnb, and prominent development industry nonprofits, like the Bill and Melinda Gates Foundation. Schmidt's seed funding took them through to 2018, when they recently received $22 million in a Series A funding from a combination of venture capitalists, including Drive Capital, Verizon Ventures, WPP (a British advertising company and PR firm), and, of course, Eric Schmidt.[45] Civis's mission statement is "to democratize data science so organizations can stop guessing and make decisions based on numbers and scientific fact."[46] Yet, despite this claim, data science is not being *democratized* in any meaningful way; rather it would be more accurate to call it *commercialized*. The insights that may come from their tactics of surveillance and targeted advertising are made available to those who can afford to pay for it. Again, this crucial distinction is lost on corporate Democrats.

During the 2016 U.S. election cycle, Civis Analytics sold its services to the Clinton campaign, with the company receiving $5.1 million—comparable to the $5.9 million the Trump campaign spent on Cambridge Analytica.[47] Furthermore, Civis Analytics was far from the only surveillance corporation working to manipulate voters. They were joined by Timsehl and the Groupwork (both funded by Schmidt), Bluelabs, Precision Strategies, Precision Network, Analytics Media Group, and the Targeted Platform Media, to name a few. Suffice to say, surveillance, data analytics, and customized manipulation through advertising is a far larger problem than Cambridge Analytica. Indeed, managing democracy according to elite interests has become a booming industry.

Of course, all this surveillance and technological modeling that Clinton marshalled in her election ultimately failed; she was defeated by the second least-popular candidate in the history of American electoral politics. The surveillance-based polling methods developed by her analytics team drastically misread the electorate across multiple states and on multiple issues. Sophisticated targeted marketing could not make up for her campaign's lack of vision, her perceived sense of entitlement, fawning to high finance, neglect of serious structural problems, and sheer meaninglessness of her rhetoric. This was perhaps unsurprising, as her public campaign began with a speech that featured many lines drawn straight from the void: "And you know what? America can't succeed unless you succeed. That is why I am running for president of the United States of America." Of course, none of the above should be read as celebrating the rise of Trump. Rather, if we are to proceed into the climatically unstable future with our common humanity intact then there is an urgent need to defend and extend democracy. A fundamental part of this struggle involves an increasingly urgent need to actively resist the corrupting power of big money in politics, as well as the high-tech ways of managing society according to elite interests. The existential crisis that democracy finds itself in demands more searching critiques and, most importantly, concrete political action.

THE LURKING STATE

At least since the fantasies of Jeremy Bentham, surveillance has been attempting to control the behavior of the surveyed. In Google's case, it seeks to alter people's behavior in ways that make them more likely to engage with advertisements that have been automatically targeted at them. This is firmly encoded in the company's philosophy, which states, "We've found that text ads that are relevant to the person reading them draw much higher click-through rates than ads appearing randomly. Any advertiser, whether small or large, can take advantage of this highly targeted medium."[48]

The scope of Google's surveillance powers is truly vast. The firm has the capacity to continuously monitor a very large amount of people's online activity. This includes search terms and web-browsing history, which browser and operating system one uses, their IP address, as well as the time of day and approximate or exact geographic location. In this way, Google's apparatus has the power to pull data traces from a huge amount of everyday life into their commercial circuits. Their ability to collect data on people is heightened within their own monopolistic domains, including Gmail, YouTube, and Maps. The comprehensiveness of Google's surveillance engines has led to posturing by some of the company's elite. Eric Schmidt boasted to the *Washington Post* that because of the information that Google collects, "we know roughly who you are, roughly what you care about, roughly who your friends are." While still CEO, Schmidt encouraged people to "give us more information about you, about your friends, and we can improve the quality of our searches. We don't need you to type at all. We know where you are. We know where you've been. We can more or less know what you're thinking about." When questioned about the implications of this on privacy, the ever-provocative Schmidt also told a CNBC interviewer, "If you have something that you don't want anyone to know, maybe you shouldn't be doing it in the first place."[49]

This kind of flamboyant rhetoric has been strategically suppressed by Google after Edward Snowden's 2013 leaks of National Security Agency (NSA) material showed how major cybernetic capitalist firms, including Google, actively collaborated with the state spy agency in its truly massive surveillance efforts. The Snowden leaks showed more evidence as to how the military-intelligence agencies of the "Five Eyes" nations—Australia, Canada, New Zealand, UK, and United States—have access to the data extracted by Google and other major tech-companies thanks to the NSA's secret programs such as PRISM and MUSCULAR.[50] Indeed, Google's shift in rhetoric is one of the most decisive shifts in the wake of the leaks. Six years after these leaks made headlines around the world, it is staggering to note how little has changed. The spy agencies continue their mass surveillance programs, as do the tech-titans, and beyond public relations posturing, there is no reason to think that their collaboration has ended.[51]

Google's relationship to the NSA started at least three years before the Snowden leaks. Back in 2010, Google approached the NSA in the name of cyber security and formed an unprecedented public-private partnership with the spy agency. Supporters of these developments argue that corporate intellectual property rights trump individual privacy concerns, with one academic writing, "All users of the Internet should be supportive of the fledgling partnership between private industry and the public sector as they work toward the strongest possible security solution to secure cyberspace for the benefit of all Americans."[52] Expressed like this, the author makes an imperial elision, conflating the networked communication of humanity with the United States' security concerns. Close collaboration between the spy agencies and tech-titans like, but far from limited to, Google was attracting little or no public attention until the shocking disclosures of the Snowden leaks catapulted surveillance into the public eye. Just days after the first of the leaks surfaced, Google's co-founder Larry Page claimed, "For me, it's tremendously disappointing that the government secretly did all these things and didn't tell us." This was a typical response from the top executives of the tech-titans, who all publicly expressed their outrage at the NSA's supposed raiding of their data. However, when we consider the following fragments that journalists have worked hard to drag into the light, Page's declaration of the big bad government seems, as best, like disingenuous public relations posturing.[53]

Some of these details came out in a letter declassified by a Freedom of Information Act request by a journalist working for *Al Jazeera America*. General Keith Alexander, the director of the NSA wrote to Google's CEO Eric Schmidt on June 28, 2012, inviting him to attend a top-secret meeting between the U.S. Defense Department, Homeland Security, and the NSA. Eighteen other CEOs from U.S. tech corporations were also invited to participate in the "Enduring Security Framework" (ESF), a highly shadowy operation. Some months before, the NSA director emailed Sergey Brin to thank him and his team for their participation in the ESF. The spy chief wrote to the Google co-founder to say, "Your insights, as a key member of the Defense Industrial Base, are valuable to ensure that ESF's efforts have a measurable impact." General Alexander also invited members of the tech-titans—this time mostly Google, Apple, and Microsoft—to help establish "a set of core security principles." The spymaster added, "Google's participation in refinement, engineering and deployment of the solutions will be essential." These revelations show Page's claim of his company being an uninformed victim of the government intrusion to be untrue and smacking of self-serving libertarian hypocrisy.[54]

After the Snowden leaks, perhaps one of the biggest changes at Google was that Eric Schmidt abruptly ceased making provocative statements mocking privacy. Now companies like Google were "working hard to protect our privacy," or so the PR rhetoric goes. Hollow slogans aside, the cyber-capitalist corporation continues to work closely with the intelligence wing of the American military-industrial complex, actively collaborating in a manifold of ways. Should this trajectory continue, "some dark day in the future, when considered versus the Google Caliphate, the NSA may even come to be seen by some as the 'public option.' 'At least it is accountable in principle to *some* parliamentary limits,' they will say, 'rather than merely stockholder avarice and flimsy user agreements.'"[55]

It is naïve to imagine that Google would willingly stop their surveillance-engine, indeed it cannot lest it sacrifice its primary method of capital accumulation. As I have noted above, their entire business model is fundamentally dependent on the surveillance and monetization of people's personal data, hence it is incompatible with meaningful notions of privacy; or to frame it differently, they are compelled to snoop and pry, extract and spy on us, much as they're compelled to manipulate us, to structurally promote consumerism. Vint Cerf, one of the "founding fathers" of the Internet, to use that gross expression, and a current Google employee, acknowledged this incompatibility. Cerf was also named by General Alexander as a participant in the NSA's talks. While taking part in a panel discussion at the Internet Governance Forum, Cerf was pressed by a privacy activist into saying, "We couldn't run our system if everything in it were encrypted because then we wouldn't know which ads to show you. So this is a system that was designed around a particular business model." Google attempts to spin the entire surveillance affair under the banner of "improving user experience."[56]

Google's corporate attitude was concisely summarized by their head privacy engineer who concisely said, "What's good for the consumer is good for the advertiser." Again, that claim was from Google's *head privacy engineer*. One has to admire how totally she manages to subsume the complex public interest of billions of people into the narrow, profit-maximizing, consumerism-promoting interests of corporations and their wealthy shareholders.[57] Many accounts of Google's rise are written in a celebratory, congratulatory tone, making claims that it was people's private "data that took Google search to the next level. The search behavior of users, captured and encapsulated in the logs that could be analyzed and mined, would make Google the ultimate learning machine."[58] Or, perhaps more accurately, it would make it the ultimate for-profit surveillance-engine, a panoptic control-machine on a truly global scale. This is part of a larger trend in cybernetic capitalism, where power no longer resides in having the most visitor traffic to a particular website; rather it has shifted to those who extract as much surveillance data, mine it for patterns, and then make money from selling the control that comes from this abstract process.

Curiously, both advertising and surveillance were completely absent from Google's initial model when the co-founders—who were originally motivated by the respectable challenge of creating an elegant system—expressed outright hostility toward advertising. Indeed, part of Google's success had to do with their *not* indulging in the online arms race of irritating, flashing, pop-up ads that push their consumerist messages. Prophetically, Brin and Page themselves wrote, "We expect that advertising funded search-engines will be inherently biased towards the advertisers and away from the needs of the consumers." After noting the insidious nature of search-engine bias, the cofounders concluded, "We believe the issue of advertising causes enough mixed incentives that it is crucial to have a competitive search-engine that is transparent and in the academic realm."[59]

Under pressure from the venture capitalists, these concerns were dropped once advertising began pumping tremendous sums of money into the fledgling company. There's nothing like exorbitant riches to encourage some swift ideological acrobatics. Of course, it is not only about shifts in individual morality, for the cybernetic capitalist system in which they operated put pressure on the possible directions the co-founders could take. To justify this drastic change of tune, Google ran a few "experiments" on the people using their website. They discovered that the control group—who received ads on their results—conducted more searches than the group who were given ad-free results. Google considered the issue settled, drawing the preposterous conclusion that "ads made people happy." This crudely ideological "experiment" served to give a thin, greasy veneer of pseudo-scientific legitimacy to this deeply dubious decision. Years later, Schmidt and Rosenberg attempted to rewrite the firm's history in their best-selling book *How Google Works*: "The Google founders knew that they would make money from advertising. Initially they didn't know exactly how, and they were biding their time while scaling their platform, but they were very clear about the general revenue model." Despite these disingenuous attempts at justification and historical revisionism, the concerns that the cofounders expressed in 1998 ring truer than ever.[60]

CONCLUSION

It is hard to find a more telling example of globalization and surveillance in the early twenty-first century than the colorful corporation commonly known as Google. Billions of people unevenly spread around the world use this company's services on a daily basis, and it has a tremendous influence over the Web and the practices that are increasingly entangled within this abstract layer of control. Through its surveillance-driven accumulation strategy, Google systematically promotes consumerism while extracting wealth and power, concentrating it in the monopolistic upper echelons of cybernetic capitalism. Growing from dorm-room project to global institution in the blink of the historical eye, the corporation is now one of a small handful of tech-titans that project a powerful organizing force across the world. These clusters of overlapping technological and bureaucratic extraction apparatuses are used to project social control on a global scale. As a colorful thread helping to stitch this Dr. Frankenstein's monster together, Google's technological structure encourages the massive concentration and centralization of power. The combination of capital, science, and the state come together in a project of control through abstraction, the drive to control the world from above. Indeed, an ex-Google strategist accurately described his former industry as the "largest, most standardized and most centralized form of attentional control in human history."[61]

As a U.S. headquartered corporation, Google is bound up with the concept of American-style capitalism. This model rhetorically promotes the concept of "free markets," yet many industries are functionally highly monopolistic as the system prescribes but the ideology hides. The high-tech sector is an excellent example of this, with a handful of tech-titans dominating the world market. While there are highly competitive edges, and many unpredictable disruptions, the status quo they seek to uphold is undoubtedly one of monopoly. In the American model, the state lurks in the background, funding developments via military research and contracts; inserting their spy machines via corporations, into people's everyday practices; and generally making a world fit for the ongoing process of capital accumulation. While currently dominant, this American model is in no way permanent, with many structural forces and systemic crises currently converging in ways in which the outcomes are inherently unpredictable. In such times of turmoil, it is important to look at other ways in which cybernetic capitalism is manifesting itself, specifically a more openly authoritarian version of the control project is rising in the East.

CHAPTER 4

THE OVERLORDS OF AUTOMATED DEBT

CHINA, USURY, AND THE FINANCIALIZATION OF THE SOUTH

PRELUDE: THE DOOMSDAY BOOK

It was Christmas day 1066 when William the Conqueror received the crown of the freshly defeated Anglo-Saxon Kingdom of England. A bastard from Normandy, who ascended to Dukedom at age eight, the new king looked out across the foreign land and wanted to know, precisely, what he had conquered: "How many hundreds of hides were in the shire, what land the king himself had, and what stock upon the land; or, what dues he ought to have by the year from the shire." To these ends, he ordered a vast survey to amass and centralize knowledge of the land into a single book; an account of the territory, an enumeration and reckoning of the land so as to wield power over it. It was conducted to legitimize the new order and to see how many productive resources were in the kingdom for the purposes of squeezing as much money as possible from the territory; and for the military purpose of securing the state from external threats, and more importantly, from internal rebellions. In this light, it was an early and exemplary example of surveillance: an effort of power to watch over something for the purpose of exerting control over it.

While this ambitious project and the resultant manuscript did not have a formal title, some of those subjected to the survey called it the *Domesday Book*, the Middle English spelling of "Doomsday." It was so labeled because it functioned as a kind of Book of Judgment and because the decisions made by the agents of the new king were final and beyond appeal. Unlike the surveys from early capitalist modernity (chapter 1), the Domesday survey did not involve making maps, rather places were coded quantitatively in Roman numerals that were woven through Latin sentences. To give a random example, the agents of the 1066 survey determined that the village of Wicken in north-west Essex had twenty-three households, a total of five plow teams, ten acres of meadows, thirty pigs, fifty sheep, and thirty-six goats, which gave it a total tax asset of 3.1 units—thus giving it a value to the lord of £7.[1] Indeed, the *Domesday Book* was the most thorough survey of England for the next eight hundred years. Looking at the great wealth of data drawn into the survey, many perplexities and problems rapidly arose. Even excluding the countless errors, the document is plagued with omissions, ambiguities, and conflicting systems of encoding data. All up, there is an unbridgeable void between the data presented in the *Domesday Book* and the actual historic and geographic reality of the lands and people surveyed. The people and places were tremendously complex in comparison to the massively simplified surveillance data, with these simplifications being used to organize the world and project power through centralized knowledge extraction.

CYBERNETIC CAPITALIST WITH CHINESE CHARACTERISTICS

For the purposes of this chapter, the *Domesday Book* serves as a curious precursor to surveillance in the present. While plainly from a radically different historic context, it nevertheless shows the abstracting power of surveillance to centralize knowledge and control, along with the limitations of such attempts. In the early twenty-first century, perhaps the most ambitious attempt by a contemporary state to create a "Domesday Book" can be seen in China through the proposed "Social Credit System." The first public mention of this proposal came in 2007, when the State Council, the chief administrative authority of the People's Republic of China, issued its intention.[2] This document centered on the concept of "supervision," a word sometimes repeated three times in a single sentence. Supervision, it must be noted, is a synonym for surveillance with broadly the same root meaning: the view from above that seeks to project control (chapter 1). A much more detailed policy document came out of the State Council in mid-2014, called the "Planning Outline for the Construction of a Social Credit System (2014–2020)."[3] There the State Council proposed the creation of a vast system of surveillance in which every citizen would be given a numerical score that indicated their trustworthiness. This system would be based on wide-reaching surveillance of online and offline actions, with data traces of everyday life ending up in centralized databases where they can be groomed over by algorithms looking to extract patterns and launch automated control processes. These patterns would then be interpreted in a strongly moral rather than merely commercial way. Taken together, the algorithms settle on a single number: the "Citizen Score." This score has massive impacts on people's lives through punishment and reward once the system becomes operational. The State Council wants to make the Social Credit System compulsory for all 1.3 billion citizens by 2020.

Here's how the State Council puts it:

> Accelerating the construction of a Social Credit System is an important basis for comprehensively implementing the scientific development view and building a harmonious Socialist society, it is an important method to perfect the Socialist market economy system, accelerating and innovating social governance, and it has an important significance for strengthening the sincerity consciousness of the members of society, forging a desirable credit environment, raising the overall competitiveness of the country and stimulating the development of society and the progress of civilization.[4]

Sincerity and socialism, competition and civilization, morality and markets: all mediated by cybernetic computing-machines. The Social Credit System represents a remix of cybernetic capitalism, described in the last two chapters, but with "Chinese characteristics." I have adapted this phrase from Deng Xiaoping, the "Paramount Leader" of China between 1978 and 1992. Taking over from Mao, Deng sought to modernize China through sweeping reforms in agriculture, industry, techno-science, and the military. He created Special Economic Zones to attract foreign direct investment, selectively encouraging free enterprise, and market liberalization in order to increase exports. Deng justified these changes by describing them as "Socialism with Chinese Characteristics." These transformations increased across the 1990s and 2000s, with China forging a very powerful form of authoritarian state capitalism. With the rise of Xi Jinping, the nation's current Paramount Leader, China's system has increasingly turned cybernetic, leading to what I am calling "cybernetic capitalism with Chinese characteristics."

Over the last quarter century China has sustained massive economic growth on a truly world-historic scale. Between 1994 and 2017, China maintained an average GDP growth rate of 9.41 percent; this breakneck curve saw it become the second biggest economy on earth. As a point of comparison, over this same period the world's number one economy, the United States, had an average growth rate of 2.48 percent. Wages in China quadrupled, whereas they have been functionally stagnant in the United States since the 1970s. The vast modernization project that this growth allowed has resulted in significant improvements in resources available to the country's 1.4 billion people, thus providing a major source of legitimacy to the Party at the helm of this great transformation. To zoom in on one famous fact that captures something of the scale of this growth, between 2011 and 2013, China consumed more cement than the United States did during the entire twentieth century. Like the United States' boom in the postwar years (chapter 2), this position of strength runs in contradictory parallel with a pervasive weakness, for this frantic building spree came as an attempt to deal with the crisis dynamics of capitalism that convulsed the world in the aftermath of the Global Financial Crisis.[5] As with other earlier "economic miracles" in places like South Korea, this tremendous growth came at incalculable expenses, leaving countless ruined lives, ravaged landscapes, and layer upon layer of toxification, from smog-sieged cities to a rapidly warming world. Again, to zoom in on one grisly fact that can stand in for the hideous price paid, a study by the Shanghai Academy for Social Sciences found that in the Pearl River Delta region—one of the key nodes of China's high-tech sector—factory workers lose or break around forty thousand fingers each year.[6] Other windows into aspects of this transformation have been captured in film, with Jia Zhangke's *24 City* (2008) and Lixin Fan's *Last Train Home* (2009).[7]

This broader context of tremendous upheaval and unsettling, growth and waste, strength and weakness, is an essential background to understanding the ambitious surveillance project under way in China. Of course, as I will show across this chapter, the vast surveillance system that will underpin the Social Credit System is not unique—the financial wizards of Wall Street, the tech-titans of Silicon Valley, and the spies of the military-intelligence complex have been developing its basic processes for decades. Indeed, such systems are central to their ability to extract profit and project power on a world scale. A key difference in China is the active involvement of the State Council in taking centralized control of the system and assembling it according to a stated plan in collaboration with technology corporations. This mix of power manifests differently to the corporate-led U.S. model, where the state looms in the background behind various corporate enterprises, as well as being different from the European Union model of attempts of greater regulation. It is significant to note at the beginning of this discussion that, at the time of writing, China's Social Credit System is not yet fully unified and centralized. Rather it has advanced over the last few years in a piecemeal fashion, with components being wheeled out by various competing and collaborating corporations and local governments, with each wanting its pilot scheme to become the national standard. How, or even if, it comes together into a single system is yet to be determined; however, it is important to keep in mind that this is explicitly the goal of the State Council's project.[8]

FINANCE, USURY, AND DEBT

"Credit" is a curious concept in China, with the word—*xinyong*—being central to the traditional Confucian ethics formulated four centuries BCE. Traditionally, it was a moral concept that referred to one's trustworthiness, the honesty of one's character. Since China began its post-Mao market metamorphosis, the concept has been extended into the lofty spheres of finance. One core aim of the Social Credit System is to get more people to be able to borrow money, with the Citizen Score being a key factor in determining someone's ability to access credit. Or, to say the same thing differently, their ability to get into debt.[9] This inversion is significant, for it helps to tease out the shifting power relations at play. When someone gets into debt, they make a promise to devote part of their future to repaying this debt, with interest. The other side of this relationship is the creditor, who gets a guaranteed extraction of wealth via interest, with this being one of the core components of all financial profit. It could provocatively be called the "Social Debt System."

Indeed, the word "finance" first appeared in English during the beginning of the capitalist world-system in the long sixteenth century. Coming from the French, it originally meant "to pay ransom," and was soon extended to encompass both state taxation and what we still call a "fine," as in a state-imposed penalty, backed up if needed by police, courts, and prisons. Finance only came to mean "manage money" toward the end of the eighteenth century. This is a curious etymology, for it not only shows finance's long-term dependence on the state, but also its necessary underpinning on forms of violence, as it can hold one to ransom. This goes against common ideological fables of the market as a place where self-interested individuals are imagined coming into harmonious contractual relationships with one another in order to exchange commodities and maximize profits. This classic liberal vision leaves the state outside its framework; however, this only tells part of the story. The ability to enforce debts, and private property relations more generally, must rest on structures of organized violence that are intrinsic to capitalism. The state, as has been famously noted, claims the "*monopoly of the legitimate use of physical force* within a given territory."[10] In practice, this means that the official agents of the state—or the private, mercenary entities they have long contracted to do their biddings—can employ violence to enforce their social order. Without at least the threat of state-imposed violence, debtors may not repay their loans, property could be stolen, intellectual property pirated, all of which corrode or forbid the process of capital accumulation. In this light, "debt is just the perversion of a promise . . . corrupted by both math and violence."[11]

Consider what would happen if one fails to service debt on a mortgage (another financial word with a morbid etymology, it comes from Old French meaning literally "death pledge"). Sooner or later, the crediting bank will send the police to come knocking (or a sheriff, bailiff, or another kind of armed bureaucrat, depending on the country). As police have become increasingly militarized, the officers knocking on the door may carry beating sticks, guns, handcuffs, and chemical weapons, known by the euphemism "pepper spray." It is likely that these weapons will not be used, but nevertheless, they can be employed to enforce the state's system of capitalist private property and debt relations. The door-knocking officers will inform the debtor to pay their debt or suffer the consequences, which could include fines, eviction, community service, beatings or imprisonment depending on one's perceived level of vulnerability. In other settings, a creditor may send debt collectors, goons, gangsters, or mercenaries to enforce this relation. Police evictions have been the grim fate of a tremendous number of families in the United States and Europe in the extended aftermath of the Global Financial Crisis. In the United States in 2016 alone, an estimated 2.3 million people were evicted. Furthermore, this enormous number is a significant underestimate, for it only includes official court-ordered evictions, not common and unofficial landlord evictions where a tenant may be paid to leave, illegally locked out, or be thrown out of their home by intimidation, threat, and violence. Being fundamentally driven by rising inequality, this constant cascade of evictions creates a tremendous amount of human suffering and what should properly be regarded as a full-blown social catastrophe, with many suicides resulting, and a reminder of the dangers of financial crisis and debt relations.[12]

The practice of lending money at interest—long known as "usury"—has a protracted, complex, and often grisly history. Usury has long been seen as morally corrupt, with some of the earliest condemnations of usury coming from Vedic texts of India, which were first committed to paper around 3,500 years ago. The practice of usury has been similarly damned by the major universalizing religions, Buddhism, Christianity, and Islam, as well as various states and empires, with long histories of attempts being made to limit the depredations of the moneylenders. Indeed, it has consistently ranked among one of the most universally despised practices. Hebrew prophet Ezekiel described it as an abomination, among the gravest of sins, down there with murder and rape (18:10–13). In *Politics*, Aristotle denounced usury as a vile, unnatural practice, the "breeding of money"—using money to make money without producing anything. These traditional views dominated, until the rise of capitalism in the long sixteenth century, whereupon the "breeding of money" became a central organizing principle of society.[13]

Like all money-using societies, China has a long history of usury waxing and waning and attempts made to limit the depredations of the moneylenders. One of the reasons that states have sought to limit usury is because it can sow seeds of revolt. A similar story echoes across history: after a spate of bad luck, a peasant family is forced to borrow money and falls into the hands of a moneylender. A little more bad luck, plus a few missed payments, and the moneylender seizes the peasant's property and proceeds to extract rent from them. If such situations multiplied, rural discontent could easily spill out into a peasant insurrection. Occasionally these insurrections have transformed into revolutionary forces that have toppled governments. Indeed, many of China's great dynasties began as peasant insurrections: the Han, Tang, Sung, and Ming—as well as the Maoist revolution that originated the current regime. It was also a factor in the failed Taiping Rebellion (1850–1864), possibly the bloodiest civil war in history, with tens of millions of deaths coming as Hong Xiuquan, the rebellions leader and self-proclaimed brother of Jesus Christ, attempted to reconstitute the state along a syncretic version of Christianity.[14]

In the first half of the twentieth century, usury was common in China, being the province of landlords and merchants, frequently with connections to violent gangs to enforce their predatory debt collection. This was captured in *The White-Haired Girl* (1945), a famous story with many versions, being performed as revolutionary opera, ballet, and films. Set in the 1920s/1930s, it is based on the real-life experiences of various women and captures the deprivations of usury. The story's strong propaganda potential saw it enshrined as one of the Eight Model Plays. The practices of usury were crushed following the 1949 revolution, with cheap credit cooperatives providing public loans to peasants. These practices shifted following China's market metamorphosis that began in 1978, with a revision to the constitution in 1982 made so as to reestablish absolute private property relations. Tremendous growth grew symbolically with spiraling inequality, thus setting the conditions for the return of usury.[15]

China's Social Credit/Debt System belongs to the trajectory of using state power to back-up capitalist relations, thus facilitating usury and the breeding of money. In part, the system is being imposed because the State Council worries that their country's consumer economy is underfinanced, and it is looking to prop up spending via the extension of debt in an attempt to counter the slowing of growth of their enormous economy. This can be understood as part of a global pattern of capital accumulation in the early twenty-first century demanding tremendous amounts of debt-fueled consumption in order to deal with the consequences of overproduction, all in an attempt achieve infinite growth within finite nature. To make up for this structural problem, overconsumption is pushed by powerful forces across society, including technologies designed with built-in obsolescence and compulsory upgrade cycles, huge advertising industries designed to manufacture desires that can never be fulfilled, and debt industries that can unproductively extract rent.

There are some parallels between the situation in China now and the massive increase in debt following the large-scale use of credit cards in the United States in the 1980s. Wages in the United States have been functionally stagnant since the mid-1970s—all the while corporate productivity and profitability boomed dramatically increasing the levels of inequality. Nevertheless, wages paid to workers provided the money needed to buy goods from companies, hence representing a major contradiction in capitalism. Credit cards became a techno-market-solution to the social problem, allowing people to spend money they do not have. It must also be noted that credit cards leave data trails ripe for surveillance, with all of the advantages to the concentration and centralization of power that come with it. Credit cards contribute to the spiraling of personal debt in the United States, which grew an average 30 percent during the 1980s. For a time, this effectively served to cover stagnating wages, however it did this by introducing new contradictions into the economy, contradictions that would only intensify with each new crisis that hit the United States—Black Monday (1987), early nineties recession (1990–1991), the dot.com bubble burst (2000–2002), the Global Financial Crisis (2007–2008). The total amount of consumer debt in the United States was past the $4 trillion line for the first time in early 2019.[16] Included in this tremendous number is debt on credit cards, auto loans, personal loans, and student loans, but notably not on mortgages on property—which comes to around $10 trillion of debt, just shy of the all-time peak before the Global Financial Crisis.[17] One quarter of the consumer credit debt is in the form of credit cards. The interest on these has never being higher, sitting at 17.41 percent at the time of writing in 2019, a twenty-five year high.[18] Putting this together, it means that Americans owe more than 26 percent of their annual income to debt, with repayments absorbing about 10 percent of their monthly incomes. This debt can be seen as a kind of tax, not issued by the government but by financial capital; which, unlike a government, does not have any pretenses of redistributing this money through social services. This reveals a vicious contradiction, for one can imagine how angry many Americans would get if the state were to take this wealth, yet finance gets away with it, extracting enormous sums of money from people without any contributions to collective good or without producing any tangible products—except inequality.[19]

One of the main stated purposes of the Social Credit/Debt System is to facilitate more of China's 1.4 billion people to borrow money. From the perspective of the moneylender, before they hand out a loan, they want to be sure that the borrower has the means to service the interest and potentially repay the debt in order for this to be a profitable venture. This is where credit-rating systems come in, for they work by analyzing people's social practices in order to predict their ability to repay a debt, be it their credit-card bill, a mortgage, a loan app, or otherwise. In this sense, credit-rating requires a system of surveillance to abstract data from material reality in order to grant the center of power the ability to make predictions about a person's ability to repay a debt. Going far beyond narrow concerns with payment histories, credit rating through cybernetic surveillance draws in data traces of a vast array of social practices which are extracted, processed, and sorted by the networked computing-machines that increasingly mediate and financialize everyday life. The issuers of credit ratings believe that "all data is credit data," seeking to find ways to stitch these incommensurable big data sets together using risk-assessment algorithms. Ultimately, all factors are drawn into an equation geared toward the narrow interests of the creditor, the simple dictate at the heart of finance's extractive processes: will the debtor repay the loan and service the interest? If the prediction comes in positive, the loan proceeds, hence enabling the creditor to extract rent from the debtor, hence granting themselves a position of social power over them.

The State Council is keenly aware that the majority of people in China have limited or no credit history, hence it is difficult for them to get a loan, assuming they want one. This is seen as a problem because it limits their ability to spend money that they do not have and hence may slow economic growth, the sacred cow of all capitalist states, of particular importance to China, as it is a major source of legitimacy for the Party's authoritarian rule. In order to lend money to those without credit ratings, surveillance transforms people into data sets to be processed by the rent seekers. Curiously, there are parallels between this movement today and the enclosures of the commons that initiated capitalist modernity. As discussed in chapter 1, states and capital needed to survey and simplify the world in order to facilitate the concentration and centralization of power, as well as their ability to project control. Today, states and capital are likewise seeking to reduce the social complexity in order to project control over it, with multidimensional, living beings being reduced to a simple number. It seems that "seeing like a state" and "seeing like a bank" are parallel processes, with the Social Credit/Debt System serving as an exemplary example of how the two are being reorganized and merged in the age of cybernetic capitalism.[20] China is not unique here, indeed most of the world's population lacks formalized credit-rating histories, which is often framed as a problem by elites. A lack of formal credit histories not only pervades poorer nations, but it is also in the world's richest and most unequal nations, such as the United States where 45 million people do not have a credit score because they lack a credit history, a situation far more common with impoverished and minority communities.

Despite their uneven application, credit-rating systems are entrenched in rich nations. In the United States the origins of credit rating surveillance goes back to the 1830s when New York merchants Arthur and Lewis Tappan sought to increase their market share and profits while supplying goods to booming frontier towns that were continuing their colonial expansion further into indigenous country. The precarious yet profitable supply chains—shot through with possibilities of fraud and theft—pushed goods from the Eastern cities in exchange for raw commodities from the Western and Southern frontiers, with most of these trades happening via credit arrangements. The Tappan brothers wanted to shore up their investment, so Lewis questioned each credit applicant personally, writing down details in a ledger, which acted as a kind of risk-analysis database. Other merchants began requesting access to the Tappan's intelligence files, which, for a fee, the brothers allowed, and quickly transformed their private dossiers into the first national credit-rating service, the Mercantile Agency. Their ledgers consisted of thousands of pages of notes written in longhand and bound in sheepskin, hence having a very different materiality to the computing-machine databases of today.[21]

Growing from these origins, credit rating has remained the domain of for-profit corporations, with around 95 percent of the field being dominated by three American firms: Standard & Poor's, Moody's, and the Fitch Group. In addition to making money for their overseeing shareholders, these companies have been given a special status by the U.S. government. They are "national recognized statistical rating organizations" (NRSRO), by the Securities and Exchange Commission, a branch of government set up during the Depression in the 1930s whose explicit purpose was to protect investors, facilitate capital formation, and maintain efficient markets.[22] The credit-rating business is monopolistic by its nature, with very high barriers to entry and huge profitability. These companies have tremendous control over the lives of ordinary people, in the United States and around the world.

Credit-rating agencies, and the bureaucratic surveillance that underpins them, is not generally seen as controversial in rich nations—except when their fraudulent practices trigger disastrous economic consequences. Perhaps the most dramatic instance of that was when Standard & Poor gave AAA credit ratings to high-risk loans on collateralized debt obligations. Upon the inevitable bubble burst, the collapse of these supposedly solid loans triggered the Global Financial Crisis and its subsequent devastation of poor communities unevenly scattered around the world, with tsunamis of evictions and job losses—while the architects of the crisis gave themselves exorbitant bonuses at the expense of U.S. taxpayers. Nevertheless, credit rating generally goes on in the background; it is just another layer of bureaucratic administration that enables financial capitalism to extract profit.

The lack of credit-ratings systems in the poorer nations is seen as a profitable area of expansion for financial-technology firms (so-called fin-tech) from rich nations. An example of this can be seen in the Entrepreneurial Finance Lab (EFL), a fin-tech firm that claims to specialize in behavioral science and psychometrics—literally meaning "mind measuring"—in an effort to create individualized credit-rating scores for people without a credit history by using a digital personality test. EFL began as a research project in Harvard University's Center for International Development in 2006, and after receiving a major grant from Google, no less, it was launched and went on to become a profit-maximizing corporation in 2010. EFL is not alone here; other fin-tech companies are scrambling to get into this lucrative market, with First Access and CreditInfo being two other notable competitors. Through online quizzes, EFL uses 150 yes/no and multiple-choice questions to put people into neat little personality boxes in order to determine their credit-rating expressed as a number usually between 300 and 500. The quiz claims to test for business skills, ethics, honesty, attitudes, and beliefs, as well as providing a psychological profile. Questions include the following: "Other people's opinions are not important: True/False"; "A big part of success is luck: True/False"; "Remember this number for five seconds, then repeat it: 823460: Right/Wrong." By asking people for their preferred drink, whether they take the same route to work each day, and whether they would be excited to join a mission to Mars apparently gives the apparatus the ability to algorithmically pry into the soul. The quiz runs surveillance software to monitor mouse movement in an attempt to detect apparent indecision, which it flags as a potential lie. The assumption is that the uncreditworthy will lie to get a loan, but they will do so in ways that can be rendered predictable and controllable by surveillance software.[23]

EFL promotes itself thus: "Holistic, Scientific, Universal: Our products quantify individual character—for all financial institutions across any culture." This is problematic for a number of reasons, in part because surveillance deals with categories, not characters; indeed, this was one of the deep suspicions that English peasants had of the *Domesday Book*. The fin-tech firm markets itself to creditors with promises of reduced risk, increased lending, boot efficiency, and increased profitability: "Fortify your competitive advantage by utilizing predictive information." As for 2018, EFL's psychometric software has been translated into twenty languages and was employed in fifteen nations—as different as Ecuador and Zimbabwe—issuing over one million assessments and resulting in the lending of over $1.5 billion. In Indonesia, combining psychometrics with their existing customer data saw loan default rates to small business decrease by 45 percent. EFL dreams of a glorious future where psychometrics software underpins all debt relations, cross-referencing them with other databases of surveillance data, from social media, increasingly ubiquitous mobile phones, and such, in an effort to ensure that creditors can better extract money without engaging in productive activity or even taking much risk.[24] In 2017, EFL merged with Lenddo, its main competitor credit-rater with a focus on the South, to create LenddoEFL, who launched a project called #include1billion.[25] Here and elsewhere across the financialized development industry, the concept of "inclusion" is automatically assumed to be a good in and off itself, without questioning what they are being included into. Thinking these matters through the concepts of surveillance and debt should give some pause to consider more critically and to question the assumptions and power relations that lurk in the background.

The extension of loans to the poor has also appeared in the rich world, with a shining example being the British payday loan provider Wonga.com. Founded in 2006, the website, via an app, provided instant, short-term loans without requiring collateral. The fin-tech firm used "fully automated risk processing technology" that began the second someone opened their webpage. Wonga claimed to check between six thousand and eight thousand "data points," most pulled from the Internet, ranging from price estimates of one's house, genealogy database, and Web searches of the person's name plus "fired" and "redundant." This surveillance data is fed into their algorithmic-engines and automatically processed to determine someone's credit worthiness. Assuming it comes up clear, the money is deposited into one's bank account within fifteen minutes. With advertising campaigns that targeted the vulnerable, Wonga at one point charged interest rates as high as 5,853 percent before being capped by government ministers in 2018 to a still outrageous 1,509 percent. This move by regulators was the beginning of the end for this specific usury business which proceeded to collapse in mid-2018. Wonga's rise and fall has been mired in controversy, becoming a symbol of Britain's exploding household debt crisis, which by 2018 had ballooned to £200 billion, not including mortgages. While this one firm may have become marred by scandal, there is plainly a big market in the increasingly unequal rich world, with much more money to be made from usury.[26]

While Wonga is more at the loan-shark end of the spectrum, it is among other companies, like LenddoEFL, which make up a high-tech layer being added over the history of "microcredit," a phenomenon most commonly associated with Bangladesh and the founding of Grameen Bank in 1983, an institution that, along with its founder

Muhammad Yunus, received a joint Nobel Peace Prize for their efforts in 2006. Yunus drew on older models of village and sector-based cooperatives that attempted to provide non-profit alternatives to loan sharks and their predatory usury. The idea of microcredit is to provide poor people with small loans without requiring collateral in the hope that they could invest money in business, thus simulating the economy and alleviating poverty. Being propelled by profit-seeking corporations, development industry NGOs, wealthy philanthropy organizations—and championed by a chorus of rock stars, celebrities, and royals—microcredit has transformed the way that many think about the relationship between credit and development. The direction that microcredit went was strongly influenced by the Harvard Institute for International Development, a pro-market think tank founded in 1974 that went on to be highly influential over the coming decades before coming undone in the 1990s. Its demise was bound up with it taking a leading role in implementing the catastrophic "shock therapy" privatization of the former Soviet states, where high levels of mismanagement, conflicts of interest, and structural corruption saw the institute ingloriously implode and be dissolved, only to be resurrected as Harvard University's Center for International Development, which went on to spawn EFL and its psychometric surveillance regime.[27]

Microcredit flourished in the wake of "Structural Adjustment," the International Monetary Fund's (IMF) euphemism for austerity measures, which spread rapidly across the poorer world in the 1980s following the uneven contours of the Third World Debt Crisis. In short, poor countries were hit by increasing interest rates from Northern banks that demanded payment on loans that were so high as to be unpayable. Latin America is often held up as the classic example of these depredations; in 1983, 50 percent of the entire continent's gross domestic product went to servicing debt to commercial banks. This impossible situation forced these states to approach the IMF in order to get more loans to service their debt.

The IMF then offered loans, but with harsh and largely non-negotiable conditions that forced austerity measures. These typically demanded large-scale privatization, deregulation (meaning the dismantling of public interest regulations so as to replace them with new regulations that favored powerful private interests), along with the reduction of barriers to trade, the opening of domestic stock markets, allowing foreign direct investment, and a focus on resource extraction. These brutal austerity programs typically demand that public sector jobs are cut, health and education budgets slashed, food or agricultural subsidies ended, and wages cut. All these measures allow the rich, both nationally and globally, to dramatically increase their profits at the direct expense of the poor. Furthermore, all nations accepting IMF loans were forced to open themselves to surveillance to ensure that they were meeting the criteria. For example, Kenya has had a permanent IMF monitoring official sitting in their central bank since 1975, an unelected foreign bureaucrat who gets to oversee the government budgetary decisions. The IMF uses "economic surveillance" as a means of monitoring the economic policies of its 189-member countries. In their words, "the IMF highlights possible risks to stability and advises on the necessary policy adjustments. In this way, it helps the international monetary system serve its essential purpose of facilitating the exchange of goods, services, and capital among countries, thereby sustaining sound economic growth." As with all surveillance, the utterly undemocratic global bureaucracy known as the IMF sits above and outside that which it monitors, seeking to impose control for the benefit of the powerful.[28]

Microcredit fully embraces the market model that was imposed on poor states via the IMF austerity measures, with its implementation coinciding with the major rollback of welfare and a lowering of labor standards. In this new model, "development" is privatized, with corporations—such as the moneylending banks—being imagined as the way forward. Microcredit assumes that poverty can be eradicated by the individualized hard work of the poor, not by larger social and structural measures, such as increasing wages. In much of the pro-microcredit literature, women are constantly referred to as "good credit risks," with this instrumental approach seeing women as more responsible for households, hence reinforcing existing patterns of oppressive sexual divisions of labor in all ways, despite the rhetoric of "empowerment."[29] The extension of microcredit into societies plagued by austerity has served to structurally weaken local communities, depleting crucial reserves of solidarity and mutuality as individuals are "poverty-pushed" into competition with one another. As it has expanded in the wake of austerity, microcredit is fundamentally fraught because it is founded on the dubious belief that the market and democracy are synonymous, and indeed an unquestionable orthodoxy.

Such practices of cybernetic rent farming are not exclusive to rich nations like the UK; indeed many poorer nations are now at the frontier of experiments in surveillance and debt extraction. Kenya, known as Africa's "Silicon Savannah" and center of technological innovation in the continent, is an illustrative example. As in much of the poorer world, in Kenya, many people live on a day-to-day basis, without the security of accumulated money to provide a buffer to unexpected expenses. People would get by often with the aid of loans embedded in reciprocal relations, or "peer-to-peer credit systems"—to use an economist term for the ancient practice—which have long bound communities together, allowing for complex arrangements of negotiation and mutual aid. As reciprocal relations have been stretched and subsumed through modernization, these practices become more difficult to sustain, thus providing an opportunity for fin-tech firms to swoop in and provide easy access to monetary credit—and hence easy access to profit through interest extracted on debt. Millions of Kenyans now borrow money at steep interest rates through many different mobile apps, with perhaps the most famous being one developed by Safaricom, Africa's biggest tech firm. In places such as Kenya, it is comparatively easy for fin-tech corporations to dodge the paltry protections and limited regulations offered by the state, making it a ripe frontier for experimentation.[30]

Globally, these developments are propelled by the dubious promise of "fortune at the bottom of the pyramid," a business pundit idea that encouraged global corporations to operate in the South, under the belief that through promoting consumerism and credit/debt in the poor world they could lift billions from poverty and simultaneously make lots of money.[31] Again, this runs on the sunny yet problematic assumption that profit maximization is always and automatically an unambiguous social good. Nevertheless, extending credit/debt to the poorest is an increasingly important development at the intersection of globalization and surveillance. Cybernetic technology has overcome many of the issues that hampered the early expansion of microcredit, including high transaction costs, a lack of automation, lack of commercial infrastructure, and a lack of surveillance to minimize the risk of the rent seekers. The global spread of smart-phones has lifted many of these impediments to extending debt relations to the "bottom of the pyramid," which along with structural global inequalities and the tendency toward intensifying financialization that set in after the Global

Financial Crisis, have converged to set the conditions for the current credit/debt boom. Promoted by the development industry, major financial firms, global bureaucracies like the World Bank, fin-tech start-ups and the tech-titans, as well as powerful states like China, cybernetic usury swims in rhetoric of empowerment, inclusion, and convenience that serves to actively conceal the raw profitability of perpetual debt.

AGAINST CASH

In China, rather than leave openings for foreign corporations, these credit-rating issues are being addressed by the state. To develop a credit-rating system fit for the twenty-first century's "Socialist market economy system," the State Council picked eight Chinese corporations and issued them with licenses to develop systems and algorithms for the Social Credit System. This outsourcing went to some of the biggest players in the Chinese tech-sector, who are also some of the world's biggest tech-titans. Many of these corporations had already been developing components that could be added to the system. In July 2017, this process stalled, with the People's Bank of China pulling back on plans to license the firms. Regulators expressed concerns over potential conflicts of interest, with most of the worry focusing on the fact that the big tech firms are reluctant to share their data with rival platforms, thus making it difficult to establish a comprehensive score for people. This shows the tension between the centralized state and the competition between the corporations to achieve monopoly. Despite this change of tack, the government is still determined to go ahead with the project, and much can be learned from developments thus far.

One of the most important of the eight original Chinese companies is Alibaba, a key collaborator in the creation of the Social Credit System. This sprawling conglomerate has a market capitalization of approximately US$481 billion—around the same as Poland's GDP. Alibaba introduced Alipay, a payment system that allows people to buy things offline and transfer money to other Alipay account holders. For example, if someone wanted to buy a bowl of rice porridge from a street vendor, they could use their mobile computing-machine to take a photo of a QR (quick response) code, type in the amount—say 3 yuan—and hit go. Then, the vendor checks their device, confirms that the money has been transferred, and the transaction is settled. These days, it applies to basically everything, all but replacing cash: even musicians busking on the street have QR codes for donations. Alibaba's system is vast, overtaking PayPal back in 2013 as the world's largest mobile payment platform. In 2018, Alipay has 54 percent of the market, followed by WeChat Pay, owned by the tech-titan Tencent, with 40 percent of what is functionally a duopoly dominating an enormous market. At the end of the first quarter of 2019, these two Chinese tech-titans have market capitalizations of US$472 billion and US$440 billion respectively, putting them in at the number six and seven highest slots of any publicly listed corporation globally. These giant numbers reflect the power of these tech-titans, as well as a notable shift of cybernetic power toward China.

The Chinese cashless sector has expanded dramatically, from 3.5 percent of all market transactions in 2011, to over 80 percent in 2017. In 2017, this means that around $8 trillion of transactions took place in China, which utterly dwarfs the $62 billion worth of mobile transactions in the United States. The one letter difference that separates "billions" and "trillions" in the previous sentence can flatten the orders of magnitude that separate these figures. Put differently, for every $1 Americans spend via mobile transaction, Chinese citizens spend around $1,300.[32] This can present difficulties for foreigners in China, for one needs a government ID number in order to access the cashless system and ensure government oversight of all spending patterns. These enormous numbers point toward transformations in social practice in China on a grand scale. The ways in which people are going about their everyday lives are being increasingly mediated by computing-machines, with this privatized arrangement giving more opportunities for techno-finance to extract profits and hence social power from the whole arrangement. In addition to collecting transaction fees, Alibaba and Tencent extract tremendous amounts of surveillance data, all of which is being mined for advertising purposes, as well as feeding into their respective credit scoring businesses, Tencent Credit and Sesame Credit, as well as into the State Council's overarching Social Credit System. Again, cybernetic surveillance plays a key role in facilitating the concentration and centralization of power at the apex of social hierarchies.

These kinds of practices are part of the uneven global drive for a "cashless society." Around the world, at least outside of financial hubs, many banks are shutting down cash machines and closing branches in an attempt to push people to use cybernetic banking systems. In a parallel way to how Google funnels people onto the Web through its privatized search-engine, the financial giants want to funnel people's spending habits through their privatized systems. In both cases, the control of surveillance data is a key motivation for it can lead to increased power and profit. Financial organizations have a motive to push for total digitization of payments because it allows them to scrape money off each transaction in the form of fees while leaving a valuable trail of surveillance data that can be groomed over by algorithms to monitor, predict, and manipulate people's behavior. A similar desire for such insights is also behind many retail surveillance schemes, such as customer loyalty programs and frequent flyer schemes that expanded in the 1980s. These data sets can be used by credit raters to determine someone's apparent debt worthiness and hence the ability for a creditor to profit from extracting interest. Banks are motivated to cut costs and hence boost profits; rather than paying humans to have jobs as bank tellers, or replenishing the cash in ATMs, many of these flesh-and-blood employees continue to be replaced by computing-machines.

Furthermore, full digitization means that that money never leaves the banking system, and hence it can be better exploited by the financiers. Contrast this to cash payments; money in its physically embodied form as a state-approved token is a kind of public utility designed to facilitate market transactions and circulation of commodities. Withdrawing cash removes the money from the banking system. Indeed every use of cash is, for techno-finance, a missed opportunity to profit from the increasingly fine-grained surveillance of consumer habits, fees, and other techniques of wealth extraction; hence there are strong motivations for finance's struggle against cash. Finance and the state are extremely intertwined, making it difficult to know where one begins and the other ends. These days, the "revolving door" between finance and the state provides a vivid indication of this, yet the process goes back centuries to when the world's first bankers in Genoa provided the funds for Spain's various wars of conquest in the long sixteenth century.[33] This process increased in fits and starts, up until it went exponential during the financialization of world capitalism in the 1970s. As a result, contemporary governments have largely gotten on board with the push against cash, as they are attracted to the ability it grants them to monitor and control people through surveillance. Other aspects of the state, such as central banks, are opposed to private payment systems that they cannot directly surveil, a problem China is seeking to avoid by having the authoritarian state take a central role in the process. A different story is projected by the finance industries' public relations campaigns. They claim to give consumers more flexible digitized options in response to consumer demand for more digitized "convenience," to use one of capitalism's most fetishized concepts. Likewise, arguments can be made that cashless societies have less possibilities for corruption owing to the increased powers of surveillance over the flow of money, at least for the majority of people. Having said this, some kinds of cryptocurrencies can be used anonymously and hence have potential for privacy and corruption despite being entirely cashless. Plainly, many people find the advent of digitized money advantageous; however, if the option of converting money-as-data into cash is removed—as is the end goal of the cashless society—then the ability to avoid surveillance of purchase becomes drastically reduced while the power of financial institutions is drastically increased.[34]

The removal of cash alters the materiality of how transactions take place. Classic capitalism imagined a buyer purchasing goods from a seller, with cash functioning as the medium to facilitate the circulation of commodities in the supposedly competitive marketplace. Yet, when cash is removed and the system is digitized, the process becomes more abstract: money-as-data does not move between the buyer and seller in a direct way but in a way mediated and controlled by distant and powerful financial bureaucracies. These monopolistic corporations are empowered by their gatekeeper position in the process, facilitating circulation while also projecting control over it. In analog technology, cash is resilient, requiring little energy-intensive infrastructure. Crucially, it does not leave data traces that the surveillance engines of technocrats and advertisers can scrape up and process as they attempt to project their various aspirations and neuroses into everyday life (other than perhaps, traces of cocaine left on notes).[35]

Likewise, the shift to cashless transactions has consequences in people's everyday practices. One report for the American Psychological Association found that people are much more inclined to spend freely when using a credit card as opposed to cash. This comes in part from the different practices of physically handing over hard-earned tokens in the form of cash, as opposed to initiating transactions between distant financial computing-machines. With cash there is a moment in which one may pause and reconsider the purchase, with this moment and its thought being a barrier for profit.[36] Following this, it is easy to see how spending becomes even easier when one moves from using a credit card—which is kept in a wallet and is associated with money-as-cash—to a smart-phone payment. This would simply be yet another usage for the "universal machine," and hence a structural incentive to spend. Such systems actively encourage consumerism, and increasingly gambling, as well as a tendency toward increasing social indebtedness, both of which benefit the processes of capital accumulation. Indeed, encouraging consumerism is essential to dealing with the ongoing crises of overproduction that plague capitalism. The differences in the technologies of payments is a factor in the explosion of consumer debt over the last four decades, a situation that has increased finance's ability to extract money from other people's productive labor.

Another step in this direction began in China in 2017 with the first usage of facial recognition technology to pay for a commodity, thus further reducing the barriers to consumption and thereby facilitating capital accumulation. Alibaba unveiled the world's first "smile and pay" system at a Kentucky Fried Chicken franchise in Hangzhou, where a consumer "simply" had to smile at a camera to automatically pay.[37] Of course, there is nothing remotely "simple" about this process, which requires multiple layers of extremely complex and energy intensive infrastructure upon which biometric data is extracted, algorithmically processed, financial accounts accessed, money-as-data transacted (with possible repercussions to one's Social Credit/Debt Score), with the entire thing being overseen and mediated by powerful and distant forces. These technologies are spreading. At the time of writing in 2019, a test is under way at Shenzen's central station whereby subway tickets are being issued via facial-recognition payment systems.[38] There is a curious echo of the nineteenth-century information revolution here. As noted in chapter 1, in the Gilded Age, tickets were issued with biometric data punched into it in order to minimize fraud, with this practice inspiring the creation of electric tabulating machines, an important step in the history of computing. Then, a century-and-a-half later, biometric data on trains is again at the cutting edge of the automation of social control.

There are clear incentives from the perspective of cybernetic capital to increase these movements away from analog cashless. Globally, the push for a cashless society is very uneven, with Scandinavian countries and China at the vanguard. It is also thriving in the poorer world, particularly in places where the financial elites have great power. One famous example was seen in the botched experiment in India pushed by the ruling Bharatiya Janata Party, a Hindu nationalist organization with historic links to authoritarianism and ethno/religio racism. In a surprise announcement on television at 8 p.m. on November 8, 2016, Prime Minister Narendra Modi rendered 86 percent of the country's currency worthless outside of banks overnight. He was ostensibly framing the move as a way to fight a series of frightening problems—the informal economy, corruption, illegal activity, and terrorism. The move disproportionally hurt India's poor, with it being felt very acutely in cash-reliant rural communities and by those in positions of precarious labor. The experiment was broadly considered a disaster. It failed to achieve its stated goal of formalizing the informal economy and caused much suffering. It was a classic example of a technological solution— through banks and digital payments—and the flawed belief that whizzy technology could solve a deep-set social "problem."[39]

Elsewhere in the world, imposed cashlessness has been used as an explicit control strategy. For example, in 2007 the Australian government ordered a sweeping "intervention" into the lives of Aboriginal people of the remote Northern Territory. The intervention was led by the national military in response to a supposed emergency following allegations of rampant child sexual abuse in remote Aboriginal communities. While these allegations were challenged at the time, it should be noted that in the ensuing years there has not been a single prosecution for such abuse, thus casting additional doubt on the original justification. Nevertheless, having successfully depicted Aboriginal communities as violent, depraved, and dangerous places, the state sent soldiers marching in to impose new rules. The intervention serves as a reminder that "invasion is a structure, not an event," with the persistent and ongoing effects of settler-colonialism bleeding across Australian history.

The intervention saw the structures of invasion pushed onto indigenous people through, among other things, increased surveillance, control, extraordinarily harsh penalties—such as six months potential jail time for a single can of beer—and "income management" welfare strategies. Following the recommendations of Andrew "Twiggy" Forrest— a white billionaire, who it should be noted extracted his fortune while acting as the CEO of a mining corporation digging up Aboriginal lands—

the Australian government proceeded to introduce cashless welfare.[40] This means that 80 percent of the sub-poverty line welfare money given to the unemployed must pass through a state-issued cashless payment card that only works in certain shops for certain goods, not unlike a high-tech surveilling version of the United States Federal "food stamp" program. Only 20 percent is deposited into their normal bank account, to be spent however the recipient chooses. This system means that the majority of purchases become an object for surveillance and control, with the card structurally restricting the everyday dignity and choices of those forced into accepting its automated discipline.

This introduction resulted in many regressive developments, such as Aboriginal-only supermarket ques. Furthermore, there is no evidence that cashless welfare reduces drug and alcohol abuse, not does it heighten the possibility of employment. Owing to decades of automation, outsourcing, privatization, and deregulation, Australia suffers from structural unemployment. In 2019, there are record high numbers of job seekers versus job opportunities, with an average of sixteen people applying for each job. Despite the manifest lack of jobs, the blame is placed on the unemployed themselves: "welfare dependency" is framed as the problem, not, for example, expanding inequality, financial globalization, or colonialism. From its inception under military imposition in indigenous communities, the practice has expanded to other sites across the country. The trial version of this scheme has cost the government $18.9 million, which breaks down to over $10,000 per person. Meanwhile, unemployed benefits are only about $14,448, which is 30 percent below the poverty line, a dismal figure that translates into debt, shame, and degradation. About half of the government's spending on this scheme went to Indue, a financial services corporation that was subcontracted to operate the system. This is an example of how one group's poverty can be another's business opportunity. Systems like this are a cybernetic twist in the long history of "overseeing the poor."[41]

Techno-market fixes for structural and social problems are pushed by development industry organizations such as the so-called Better Than Cash Alliance, which runs through the United Nations Capital Development Fund, an institution that seeks to financialize the poor. The Alliance notes with alarm, "More than 2 billion people in the world are still unable to participate in the formal financial system. The majority are women." As is common in these realms, the Alliance evokes the global category of the "unbanked," a collection of 1.7 billion people largely in the poor world who do not have a bank account. This quarter of humanity, in all their diversity, are grouped together and defined in the negative through their lack of integration into the systems of global financial extraction. And yet, the "unbanked" is not "just a self-evident category or a label for some already existing problem or pathology, the unbanked is a method of social sorting key to the ways in which the economic lives of precarious populations are 'made up' and rendered governable."[42] Nevertheless, after having noted this problem/opportunity, the Alliance devotes its sizable resources to accelerating "the transition from cash to digital payments in order to reduce poverty and drive inclusive growth" by working with thirty countries, as different as Colombia, Ethiopia, Pakistan, the Philippines, and the Solomon Islands. Their rosy world-saving rhetoric gains a different inflection when one notes that decidedly self-interested financial corporations like Citigroup, Mastercard, and Visa fund them. It is worth pausing and considering critically how the different politics are inherent in the respective technologies of cash and digital money.[43]

The idea that all economic transactions should go through formalized, centrally managed, systems of surveillance is very new—and very problematic. Across human history, the majority of people lived, either largely or entirely, outside the reach of money systems, with anthropology providing many examples of the various practices used in place of money.[44] People got the goods they needed to survive by a great diversity of means, often characterized by informal arrangements made through specific place-based relations that were mediated by face-to-face interactions. Reciprocal relations were used within local communities bound together by kinship structures, and the exchange of precious goods and barter objects were only used for economic exchange with outsiders. Money, as broadly understood, came along with the first states and with it being imposed by conquering armies. Throughout human history, the practices of using money have become increasingly abstract. Across thousands of years and various cultures, currency objects have moved from coinage forged of precious metals, to coins forged of common metals that could not be debased, to credit notes, and then to paper money that was pegged onto a systematized gold standard. This process of abstraction massively intensified in the 1970s when money went cybernetic, where it exists as numbers in the databases of networked computing-machines. This abstraction has allowed for an enormous increase in the power of money to make money without a foundation in productive activity, which is to say it has increased the power of finance.[45]

CARROTS AND STICKS

Meanwhile back to China, where under the tech-titan Alibaba's umbrella lies Ant Financial Services Group, and beneath that Sesame Credit, one of the State Council's former prospective license holders for the Social Credit System. This corporation's initiative has provided the state with some of the infrastructure for the public system. Firstly, Alibaba has not revealed the "complex algorithm" used to reduce people to a single number. It has, however, revealed a number of factors that are taken into consideration in this black box process. Credit history and fulfilment capacity are central, with the algorithms going over people's payment histories and their ability to service debts. Behavior and preferences are implicated in this, with the algorithms drawing conclusions about people according to their actions as gathered by cybernetic surveillance. Algorithms might note a person's shopping habits and see them as a measure of their character, with higher scores going to those with higher levels of consumption, with this dubious measure being seen as an unquestioned good. For example, someone seen spending money on luxuries—imported whisky, perfumes, designer brands—could see their score go up; whereas someone who spends their money on things frowned upon by moralistic elites—violent computer games, cheap alcohol, anything vaguely considered subversive—could see their score fall.[46]

The credit score can also be affected by many other social practices. If someone jaywalks and a CCTV camera with facial recognition systems pins it on them (correctly or otherwise), the score may drop. If one makes a reservation at a restaurant and fails to show up without cancelling, the score may drop. If someone is found cheating in an online game, their score may drop. Conversely, if one has the luxury of spending an hour in the gym each day, exercising in an effort to have their body conform to some fetishized ideal, then their score may rise. The Social Credit System gets literally vampiric, for if one donates a liter of blood they can gain six points. Social relations between friends online is also a factor in determining one's Social Credit score. Sesame Credit gives points for sharing what they call "positive energy" online. Announcing publicly on social media how great China is or how well the economy is going can lift one's score. Social relations are also significant, as a person's score is connected to their friends' scores. So, if one is friendly with someone with a high score, who is always posting wonderful things about the status quo, that will likely reflect well. Conversely, one does not want to associate with a dissident, lest their score be negatively impacted. Alibaba maintains that there are no penalties for friends making negative comments, but it is not hard to imagine this trajectory. Indeed, this possibility played out in science fiction in the episode "Nosedive" for the popular British series *Black Mirror* and was taken even further by the Japanese anime series *Psycho-Pass*, a gruesome saga that draws much from the sci-fi writings of Philip K. Dick.[47] When any such bureaucratic system is introduced, it is always flanked by ways in which it can be gamed, along with the possibilities of subverting and resisting it.

The Social Credit System is designed to punish people if the computing-machines determine that they have broken "trust." The State Council's planning document summarizes its intention thus stating it will allow "the trustworthy to roam everywhere under heaven while making it hard for the discredited to take a single step." This translates to an elaborate system of automated carrots and sticks. On the carrot side of the equation, Alibaba gives instant loans to anyone whose points get to a certain level (as long as the credit is spent on their products). Achieve a slightly higher score and you can get a loan to spend anywhere. Get a higher score again, and you will be fast-tracked for a visa to visit Europe. Having a higher Social Credit score leads to cheaper public transport and shorter wait times in hospitals. These examples have parallels around the world whereby governments and corporations attempt to use "nudge" tactics to push people into being better consumers, workers, or citizens from the perspective of power. On the stick side of the equation, in 2016, the State Council's General Office released a policy document elaborating the effects of having a low Social Credit Score. The document is quite detailed, with wide-reaching proposals on how to punish those deemed untrustworthy by the algorithm. For example, it suggests that a person with a low score be restricted on their ability to receive government subsidies or support. A low score would also make renting a property or finding a job more difficult. As of early 2018, 11 million flights and 4 million train trips have been blocked by the system owing to people's low scores. At the end of 2017, a list of 8.8 million people has been put online to publicly shame them as debtors. Indeed, assembling debtor lists as part of a name-and-shame campaign was one of the first steps taken toward the Social Credit System. Low-scoring people will be the focus of more intensive police surveillance and frisking. The document recommends restricting a low scorer's ability to catch trains and aircraft, visit hotels and restaurants, send their children to high-fee schools, or to build or renovate a house. According to the system, failing to pay an interest-bearing loan to an unproductive rentier class of financiers is seen as socially reprehensible and worthy of automated punishment.[48] There is a long global history of "debtors' prisons," carceral institutions designed for the destitute to work off their debts. While most of these prisons were shut down across the nineteenth century as humanitarian reforms, there has been an uneven backslide into similar practices, particularly in the United States since the crisis in global capitalism set in during the 1970s. There many poor people are arrested and imprisoned—often in privatized, profit-seeking prisons—for failing to pay a debt, often in the form of a fine. This is particularly concerning with fines increasingly being used as a means to extract much needed revenue for municipal governments from the poorest of people. That this avenue is taken over, say, taxing the rich, only serves to intensify spiraling inequalities.[49]

The State Council's policy document specifically forbids a person with a low score from being employed in high management, finance, the legal sector, the military, or as a civil servant, and would disallow membership of the Communist Party. There are a few ways that the system could function against the powerful, thus tapping into a popular anti-corruption sentiment. As of 2017, 1,100 government officials have been blacklisted, and the names of 33,000 companies that have violated laws and regulations have also been published. This kind of do-it-yourself retribution system comes as an attempt to patch up a historically weak legal and judicial system in China, where such concerns for justice have been sidelined by the quest for massive growth. While there is potential for the system to exert some control over the powerful, it is decidedly made to serve the interests of the elite, to project a normative vision on society, and to exert control from above. This is not only a Chinese phenomenon, for the inherent biases in data and algorithms serve to reproduce and intensify existing social inequalities, with problematic feedback loops.[50] As an inequality magnifier, the Social Credit System's automated carrots-and-sticks approach even extends to one's love life. One of the eight companies selected to develop the system's infrastructure is Baihe, China's biggest online dating company. The dating app teamed up with Alibaba to allow its members to show off their good credit ratings. Baihe promotes people with good credit scores, giving them a better standing on their website, thus increasing their chance of getting a date. Showcasing some of the norms embedded in the system, Zhuan Yirong, Baihe's vice president explains: "A person's appearance is very important. But it's most important to be able to make a living. Your partner's fortune guarantees a comfortable life."[51]

As the credit/debt relations spread across the social body, it is abundantly clear on which side of the divide lies the real power. In 2017, a joint notice issued by the Publicity Department of the Central Committee of the Communist Party of China, the Supreme People's Court, and the China Banking Regulatory Commission advised authorities across the country that they must establish a debtors list. Debtors are to be listed on online platforms as a public-shaming punishment for their dishonesty. Some of China's provinces have taken this to another level and use enormous screens in public spaces to shame debtors by displaying people's names and mugshots. The photographic practice of the mugshot evolved in parallel with the institution of modern police and soon become organized in vast archives of images composed of data extracted from those subjected to the disciplinary apparatus. "The bodies—workers, vagrants, criminals, patients, the insane, the poor, the colonized races—are taken one by one: isolated in a shallow, contained space; turned full face and subjected to an unreturnable gaze; illuminated, focused, measured, numbered and named; forced to yield to the minutest scrutiny of gesture and features. Each device is the trace of a wordless power, replicated in countless images, wherever the photographer prepares an exposure in police cell, prison, mission house, hospital, asylum, or school."[52] These dynamics qualitatively intensify as such portraits of criminality are digitized in a searchable, centralized cybernetic system. Then, when played in public on giant LED screens, they are a performance of discipline, part of an increasingly tightly woven structure of social control.

About 200 million surveillance cameras are scattered unevenly across China, with this coming to around one camera per seven citizens. At present, plans are emerging to weave this swarm of cameras into a single network. In Chongqing, a pilot program called "Sharp Eyes" has been implemented whereby all security cameras are networked into a centralized, data-sharing system that will merge to create a comprehensive surveillance dossier on every person, combining medical records, online purchases, social media engagements, and so on, all linked to the national ID card system and a picture of their face—a compulsory practice at birth in many, many countries. The program takes its name from a Mao era slogan: "the masses have sharp eyes." In a cybernetically enhanced echo of China's history of state repression, the system encourages citizens to report any suspicious activity and thereby participate in their own surveillance.[53]

Furthermore, the data accumulated in this surveillance bank can be sold to any interested party, with an array of data brokers springing up to capitalize on this, ranging from the thorough to the fraudulent. Two Chinese reporters working for the *Southern Metropolis Daily* discovered that for 700 yuan (around US$100) and with the national ID number of a targeted person, they could easily buy enormous amounts of data about a consenting fellow journalist. They could see a detailed and fully accurate five-year history of the target's places of residence, their bank account numbers and deposit records, car registration, all plane and train journeys, every hotel room they had stayed in, and so on. Pay a little more and they could get access to live locational data from the target's smartphone. The journalist's story ran under a headline that began with the word "Terrifying!," with this scandal serving as a reminder that the public is not necessarily thrilled about the rise of this surveillance apparatus. Significantly, information purchased from the data brokers was not intended for public distribution, and yet for a fee it was all available. This implies that the data is being leaked or hacked from insecure databases, pointing to possible corruption and/or inadequate security. It shows how a centralized authoritarian state surveillance project can be crosscut into a decentralized, chaotic free-for-all/war-of-all-against-all where anyone with $100 can be a Little Big Brother. This situation has grim social ramifications that greatly amplify the potential for revenge, rivalries, jealousy, stalking, harassment, and abuse.[54]

Despite all this, one research project found that the Social Credit/ Debt System enjoys a high degree of approval from the very people rated by the system. It found that 80 percent of respondents either somewhat or strongly approved of the system, 19 percent staying neutral, and only 1 percent either somewhat or strongly disapproving. While these results surely reflect the nature of conducting surveys in an authoritarian surveillance state, this alone does not account for the results. Many people, particularly the wealthy and the elderly, interpreted the system through an individualized framework that focuses on the perceived benefits and convenience. Furthermore, there is an implicit assumption that the surveillance and calculations of Social Credit are conducted impartially and objectively; indeed, this seems to be a condition for people's approval. It should come as no surprise that frames of interpretation—which smile, nod, and totally neglect questions of social power—are championed by the state-controlled media system.

While much of this is distinct to the dynamics of China, the Social Credit/Debt System is providing a model of control that other states are learning from. For example, the Australian city of Darwin is drawing on elements of China's system as part of its "smart-city" reorganization, with these deeply problematic developments being reconfigured in a nominally free and democratic country.[55] Indeed, such practices are rapidly globalizing.

GLOBALIZING CONTROL

Like many of the examples across this chapter, China is hardly unique. Indeed, data brokering has become a massive surveillance industry. Some of today's top data brokers are old, such as Equifax, which was founded in the United States in 1899 as a credit rating company that specialized in working for insurance companies wanting to conduct risk assessments and set premiums. Equifax now frames itself as a "data analytics" firm—a euphemism for surveillance—and has a revenue of US$3.1 billion. Other big players in these types of surveillance industries include the American company Acxiom, which provides three thousand attributes and scores on 700 million people in the United States, Europe, and elsewhere. Likewise, Oracle categorizes people into thousands of categories providing thirty thousand attributes on over 2 billion consumer profiles. Each of these multi-billion-dollar companies profit tremendously from selling surveillance. For decades, this largely invisible industry has expanded alongside the intensification of cybernetic capitalism, driven by the enormous power that fin-tech capital has over the public life. There are strong links between the consumer data broker industry and consumer debt. The extracted data traces encoded in these for-profit databases encapsulate a great asymmetrical power relation, topped by almost unilateral knowledge: data brokers know tremendous amounts about people, yet the people surveyed know almost nothing about the data brokers. This is the one-way mirror of surveillance.[56]

A sliver of light was shone on this dark sector after a 2019 law was passed in the state of Vermont in the United States that required that companies who buy and sell third-party personal data register—with 121 companies coming out of the woodwork, to use a far too analog expression. The law requires that the companies only have to register; they don't have to disclose who they have in their databases, what data they collect, or who buys it, nor does it allow people to access their own data. It does try to push these firms to provide an opt-out. If one wants to opt out, they have to go through all 121 companies individually, enacting tedious and bureaucratic processes themselves.[57] These companies make up an important part of the overarching surveillance apparatus that has come into being, a vast and multi-faceted cybernetic formation.[58] It sprawls across many fields—such as advertising, business IT, risk data, marketing data, and management—with associated practices, including identity verification, fraud detection, background checks, tenant screening, loyalty programs, predictive marketing, "internet of things," welfare provisions, and so on. Many different industries are now integrated into the sprawling surveillance industries that characterize early twenty-first-century cybernetic capitalism. Of course this includes the tech-titans (Alibaba, Amazon, Apple, etc.); financial services (Blackrock, Deutsche Bank, Goldman Sachs, etc.); the telecom and service providers (AT&T, China Mobile, Samsung, Telefónica, etc.); media publishing (Asahi Shimbun, Disney, News Corp, etc.); retail (pharmacies, hospitality, automotive, etc.); and the public sector, with its interests in welfare, healthcare, education, utilities, policing, and so on.[59] Beyond all of that lurks the military agencies, the NSA, CIA, NRO, and so on, and their mercenary collaborators. Collectively, this apparatus of cybernetic capitalism extracts tremendous amounts of data from people's activities, data that is processed by surveillance engines in order to project power: to intensify capital accumulation and exert social control.

One slice of this project for social control specifically takes aim at the body, especially the human face, through facial recognition technology. Behind the buzz of this booming industry lurk many assumptions and devices with built-in bias that sits atop layers of unresolved questions, such as whether emotions can be reliably measured from a face, whether they are universal, and how they can be classified. Crucial politico-ethical questions are again, largely absent from the narrow calculus of power. Amazon announced in mid-2019 that their facial recognition software can now recognize human fear. In parallel to this ominous announcement, Amazon was meeting with the United States' Immigration and Customs Enforcement and its Customs and Border Patrol, seeking to sell its surveillance ware to the state. A tech-titan like Amazon will be in a powerful position to profit from the increasing fixation on the U.S.-Mexico border as zone of control, with up to US$950 million up for grabs at the beginning of 2020.[60] In such contexts these biometric systems are more than systems for recognizing and representing faces; rather they can be interpreted as a portrait of social control. These systems represent bodies made object, coded, divided, individuated, and subjected to neural network technology, the functioning of which is not understood by their operators nor their subjects. The social image that results is an interrogation room where the iconic one-way mirror is replaced by a black box, a networked computing-machine that both detects and projects fear.[61]

Soon after the invention of photography in the nineteenth century, some criminologists began to paw through mug shots of law breakers and draw strange conclusions. Some believed criminals were "throwbacks," less evolved than law-abiding humans and identifiable because of particular facial features. These arguments were bound up with the rise of eugenics, as well as ideas of racial purity, ideas that have been shown to be outright racist and classic weapons of social control. This debate is resurfacing today with two scientists working at Shanghai Jiao Tong University claiming that their facial recognition technology can predict criminality. They have machine vision algorithms that measure data points on people's faces in order to compare photos of criminals and non-criminals. Through the AI neural network, the researchers claim that they could correctly distinguish criminals from non-criminals through photos with an accuracy of 89.5 percent. For example they claim that the curvature of the upper lip is 23 percent larger for criminals than for non-criminals. Through such measurements, the authors claim to have built a machine that can automatically make a reliable inference on criminality. This is problematic for many reasons, not least because crime has never been a neutral category. What is crime, what actions count as criminal, and who has the power to decide this are the result of historical processes and social power. After an outcry, the authors stated that they were totally surprised by the reaction, and they defended their work claiming that it "is only intended for pure academic discussions." While on the personal level of the researchers, this may be so, but when put into the larger frame of how integral the techno-sciences are to the contemporary power systems under conditions of cybernetic capitalism, these defenses ring hollow.[62]

The Chinese government is at the forefront of developing and implementing surveillance and artificial intelligence to project social control. A whitepaper published by a government think tank, the China Academy of Information and Communication Technology, describes how the state intends to use surveillance systems to automate censorship and control public opinion. They claim that artificial intelligence "can predict the development trajectory for Internet incidents, strengthen early-warning capabilities as events evolve, pre-emptively intervene in and guide public sentiment to avoid mass online public opinion outbreaks, and improve social governance capabilities."[63] At the time of writing in 2019, such systems of control are currently being tested to try and crush the uprising in Hong Kong, with the protestors being labeled "terrorists" and "hooligans" and so forth, while the city functions as a colonial crucible for refining techniques and technologies of control.

This is an example of cybernetic surveillance systems being used to preemptively police a populace and defend an unequal social order. While China provides an explicitly authoritarian manifestation of this development, "predictive policing," a much-hyped "revolution" in policing, is currently active and increasing in many states around the world. Often discussed through references to science fiction—in particular Philip K. Dick's short story *The Minority Report* (1956), later made into a film (2002)—the reality is a more drab convergence of standard criminology, rational choice theory, and crime-mapping techniques drawn together into software that allows data mining and predictive analytics to process cybernetic surveillance.[64] Perhaps the most famous corporation engaging in these practices is U.S. based PredPol, a company that sports the commercial slogan "What. Where. When. Predict critical events and gain actionable insight with PredPol®, The Predictive Policing Company™." This corporation has held contracts with numerous U.S. and UK cities, with millions of people having unevenly fallen under its secretive scope. PredPol's software functions by plotting the history of crime data onto a map of the city, with this data set being processed by secret algorithms so as to make predictions about where crime may occur in the future, and thus where police should focus their gaze. Police can search a map of the city—with PredPol's data being projected onto Google Maps—and use it to decide where to patrol. In this case, once again, surveying preempts surveillance. Drawing from cop-show fantasies and science fiction, it is often imagined as being able to prevent big ticket crime, like murder, yet again, the reality is less sensational. Algorithmic policing is far more effective at predicting misdemeanor crime—vagrancy, loitering, vandalism, disorderly conduct, minor drug offenses, and so on—for these are strongly correlated to the geography of the city and the socio-economic profile of a suburb. Then, considering the segregated nature of U.S. cities, it is also a strong proxy for race; thus, while the algorithms might be "colorblind," its very functioning draws on and reinforces structural racism. In practice, predictive policing software creates strong cybernetic feedback loops: the software focuses police activity in an area with more historical crime data; additional police presence sees that more crime data is gathered; the software sends more police to the area—as well as justifying its own existence. Meanwhile, increasing numbers of poor people have to pay fines to underfunded municipalities—with fine farming attempting to plug the revenue gap lost by failing to tax the wealthy—while prisons fill with people accused of essentially victimless crimes. Furthermore, in a U.S. context—where people die at the hands of the police every day—this is a matter of much controversy, particularly given the racialized nature. Nevertheless, systems of surveillance and policing using secret corporate algorithms continue to expand beyond any kind of public oversight.[65]

One of the pathbreaking ways that China is employing AI and surveillance to project control is by becoming the first known state to use artificial intelligence to explicitly racially profile its citizens. Through the vast, centralized system of cameras peppered across the country, the government employs facial recognition software that can apparently identify Uyghurs, a persecuted indigenous, ethnic minority of eleven million people largely in Xinjiang, a region four times the size of Germany in the west of China. Several billion-dollar startups have developed this software, which is designed to allow the state to spy on Uyghurs as they go about their lives, both in Xinjiang, and across many other parts of the country. This comes together with other practices of intensive and authoritarian surveillance of Uyghurs, including DNA testing, as part of a new generation of automated racism. There is a long pedigree of automated racism in other parts of the world; for example, American facial recognition technology is infamously white-centric, a fact that fits with the structural racism.[66] There is a key distinction between an implicitly racist technology and an outright and purposefully racist technology. In China this is particularly problematic as an entire people have been collectively categorized as "terrorist" owing to a scattering of sporadic, autonomous, and short-lived bouts of violence initiated by groups like the Eastern Turkestan Islamic Movement. Furthermore, Xinjiang is a strategically important location of the Chinese elite, being the site of much oil extraction, coal mining, and natural gas production, among other resources. Additionally, as it borders eight other countries— Mongolia, Russia, Kazakhstan, Kyrgyzstan, Tajikistan, Afghanistan, Pakistan, and India—Xinjiang is also central to the massive infrastructure project, the ambitious Belt and Road initiative, a gamble whereby China seeks to become a continental superpower on a global scale. This project seeks to bind Eurasia together via networks of high-speed trains, oil and gas pipelines, and 5G telecommunications webs, all under the watchful eye of China's centralized state and outside of the control of the sea-faring rival power of the United States. All up, the Belt and Road initiative is one of the most powerful and important projects of globalization in the early twenty-first century, and one that unavoidably pivots on Xinjiang.

After the "global war on terror" shuddered into being in 2001, the Bush administration bullied the UN General Assembly to adopt a resolution requiring all member states to adopt anti-terror laws, which was in part an open invitation for regimes around the world to smuggle in oppressive laws that suited their local context.[67] China uses the geo-political climate of global "terror" to inspire the justification for the development of vast prison camps—called "concentration camps" by the World Uyghur Congress and "vocational training centers" by the Chinese State—that currently hold around two million Uyghurs prisoner behind razor-wire fences and watchtowers. President Xi laid the ground for this immense repression back in 2014 when he called for an all-out "struggle against terrorism, infiltration and separatism" using the "organs of dictatorship," and showing "absolutely no mercy."[68] This secret speech was among a large stash of Communist Party documents leaked to the New York Times in 2019. The leaks also revealed the scripts that government officials are to follow when they face queries from relatives asking why their loved ones have been imprisoned. According to the leaked script, if an official is directly asked by a relative of the disappeared: "Did they commit a crime?" then they are instructed to respond by acknowledging that they did not, before stating: "It is just that their thinking has been infected by unhealthy thoughts." All up, this leak gives an unprecedented insight into the inner workings of the thought policing and repression at play in China, showing it to be extremely coercive, threatening, bureaucratically Kafkaesque, and intimately interwoven with surveillance as it engages.[69] As an entire people have been criminalized, there are many things that could result in an Uyghur being sent to a camp, including having the wrong style of beard, wearing a headscarf, praying, attending mosque, practicing funeral rituals, having friends or family abroad, traveling alone, refusing alcohol or tobacco, or even owning camping equipment. Combined with the mass bulldozing of ancient mosques, the ban on giving Uyghur names to their children or teaching them Muslim texts, it has rapidly become a large-scale program of cultural genocide.[70]

Outside the network of prison camps, much of Xinjiang populated regions have been transformed in an extension of the prison. It is now one of the most surveilled regions in the world. Comparing it to other places of extreme large-scale surveillance does not bode well for China's Uyghur. Israel has created a high-tech surveillance state that keeps an extremely close watch on Palestinians, including 1.8 million who possess a second-class Israeli citizenship (or 20 percent of Israel's total population), 1.8 million people living on the Gaza Strip—arguably the world's largest prison—a further 3.3 million in the West Bank, as well as a further 3 million Palestinian refugees living in Jordan, Lebanon, and Syria. Surveillance is key to projecting control over a targeted people in order to maintain the social inequalities and injustices of the overarching system. As with China, Israel exhibits a combination of settler colonialism, "war on terror" justifications, geopolitical power struggles, control of resources, apartheid style structural racism, and rising ethno-nationalist authoritarianism. All are enabled by the powerful military-industrial complexes and high-tech control systems.[71] One point of this comparison is to note that if one wishes to criticize China over the brutality imposed on Xinjiang, it would be hypocritical not to turn the same critical gaze upon other instances of massive, race-based control systems, of which Israel provides a shining example. In light of this comparison, perhaps the point of the "re-education camps" may not be about the re-education of those imprisoned, but rather the "educational" component may be aimed outward as a deterrent to the rest of China and to those beyond the Middle Kingdom. Parallels can be seen between this and the need to maintain a permanent threat to silence those seeking some negotiated alternative to mandated and illegal boundaries, harassment, and confinement in Israel-Palestine. The lesson that the prison camps emit is that the project of control will go forward and those who oppose its progress shall be crushed. The camps allow for the exception to become the norm.[72]

In Xinjiang, the surveillance systems discussed across this chapter come together to project intense social control. Many, many people have been arrested, imprisoned, beaten, and tortured as a result of these technologies. Many more live precarious, debt-riddled lives as a result of them. Conversely, others may get some sense of convenience, security, and parasitic wealth from these very same technologies. The social relations that these technologies embody are woven with domination and exploitation, both the high-tech pattern recognition, and the low-tech beatings in cold rooms.

CONCLUSION

With thousands upon thousands of data points on each person in the rich and richer world, the tremendous techno-social concentration of surveillance power makes the medieval *Domesday Book* seem crude.

Yet, like its ancient precursor, there are inevitably countless errors in this data, with it being plagued by omissions, ambiguities, and conflicting systems. Despite these very real and consequential errors, these systems show how societies are being remade by centralized power as part of a project of social control that is worthy of an apocalyptic title.

This chapter has used China's Social Credit/Debt System as a way of demonstrating the complex dynamics of globalization and surveillance in its latest high-tech version. It shows a compelling case of how financial mechanisms interlock with other systems of social control, by combining mass surveillance, gamified corporate loyalty programs, and debt peonage. As many of the examples cited above suggest, it is easy to see the system as a thoroughly dystopian prospect. However, this is not to encourage a "naughty China" perspective, as is common amongst foreign reporting on the project. For instance, in 2016, *The Economist* ran an article titled "China Invents the Digital Totalitarian State," which unproblematically claimed, "Big-data systems in democracies are not designed for social control. China's explicitly would be." Expressing such a view requires one to take a seriously blinkered view of history and social power. Plainly, similar technocratic systems of social control exist under the U.S. model, albeit with different patterns. Google, Facebook, Amazon, and the other Silicon Valley tech-titans have a similar girth of surveillance, as too do the NSA, NRO, NGV, CIA, DIA, and other such military-intelligence Three Letter Acronyms (TLA), while Wall Street's financial predations are infamous and unparalleled. *The Economist* can only make this claim through unproblematically assuming that democracy and the so-called free market are synonymous terms, hence blinding themselves to the very real exercise of power in the corporate sphere and its deep and enduring connections to the state.[73]

By putting the developments in China in parallel with those of the hegemonic U.S. model, and its various implications in the Global South, it is revealing to illustrate their similarities and differences. The market has been described as "Leviathan in sheep's clothing." Playing with that evocative metaphor, the U.S. tech-titans like Google seek to project themselves as benevolent and neutral: they wear electric sheep costumes, all cuddly and trustworthy. If one looks closely it is possible to glimpse that terrible cyborg eye of power gazing out of all that fluffy, synthetic wool. In China it's a different model, with the party-state taking up its "leading role" in driving and constructing a technocratic control apparatus. Here the Leviathan does not need an electric sheep costume, although it adorns its muscular, cybernetic flesh with woolly hide armor. In both cases, the behemoths function to extract wealth, concentrate power, and project control, with surveillance being a key to its concentration and centralization. Either way, the message from the beast is the same: you will pay your debt, and you will conform.[74]

Conclusion

The Limits of Control

ACCUMULATION, SOLIDARITY, AND POSSIBILITIES

Fifty years ago, an insightful philosopher of technology noted that cybernetic systems of computing-machines were becoming almost god-like in their ability to survey and control everyday life, with increasing omniscience and omnipotence: "In the end, no action, no conversation, and possibly in time no dream or thought would escape the wakeful and relentless eye of this deity: every manifestation of life would be processed into the computer and brought under its all-pervading system of control. This would mean, not just the invasion of privacy, but the total destruction of autonomy: indeed the dissolution of the human soul."[1] This unheeded warning successfully sets the stakes of the globalization and automation of surveillance. Not only the structures of power, but also what it means to be human is transformed by the extension of systems of surveillance. To unravel these transformations in social practice, we need to grapple with both politico-ethical questions as well as complex philosophic dilemmas. Through creating dense material webs of dependence—all based on complex infrastructure, huge amounts of energy extraction, and so much waste—cybernetic systems curtail, enable, and altogether reconstitute the possibilities of being able to creatively participate in society, within open-ended nature.[2]

As this book has so far argued, surveillance has long historical roots, being thoroughly entangled with power under capitalist modernity and the militaristic and scientific powers that it musters. Surveillance is a social practice that involves watching over something in order to project control over it. It involves extracting data from a limited slice of reality—thereby reducing the infinite complexity of nature to something that can be represented—which can grant an organization power that can then be projected over unruly subjects. Frequently, this power is used to defend and extend unequal power relations, serving to concentrate and centralize power. In chapter 1, I looked at some deep origins of this way of seeing, noting how surveillance was preceded by surveying, thus giving it strong connections to the enclosure movements that created private property and facilitated imperialism. Focusing on the crucible of colonialism, the chapter showed how—via panopticons and the nineteenth century's information revolution—surveillance became increasingly entangled with technology and empire. Chapter 2 continued this narrative into the twentieth century, focusing on the United States in the Cold War and how the conjoined twins of control—the nuclear bomb and the computing-machine—where born of the military-industrial complex and proceeded to reorganize the world order. It noted that the rise of cybernetics has enabled surveillance's control project to be thoroughly integrated with networked computing-machines and their increasing ability to mediate and reconstitute social processes, often according to the interests of powerful and distance forces.

Building on this understanding of cybernetic capitalism, chapter 3 used Google as an exemplar of twenty-first-century surveillance and as a way to discuss how computers are used to surveil the world and reshape social practice. Likewise, chapter 4 used China's Social Credit System as a way into discussions of financialization, debt, and the Global South, noting how these processes are being globalized. These two case studies showed how surveillance is used to intensify control while promoting consumerism and debt, with monopolistic corporations, the state, and financial sectors working to reorganize the world according to the demands of infinite accumulation. This material impossibility at the heart of capitalism—the desperate need for infinite and exponential expansion within finite nature, including finite human nature—is central to understanding the strange and increasingly unstable world we inhabit. As this book's narrative shows, under conditions of cybernetic capitalism, surveillance has frequently been used as a way to sell people things they do not need, rack up debt they cannot repay, compel them to work harder for systematically exploitative companies, and conform to government policy that works primarily in the monopolistic interests of the powerful. It is crucial to understand this dominant and dominating tendency while also recalling that "all modern control systems are riddled with contradictions."[3] By putting these contradictions at the forefront, it is possible to see how surveillance can both protect and persecute, simplify and complicate, personalize and dehumanize, and so on, and then how these contradictions are all entangled with the uneven power structures of capitalist modernity. Through focusing in on these contradictions, it is possible to gain insights into the current world order, as well as possible windows beyond it. In this spirit, this concluding chapter reviews and reflects on a few of the themes discussed previously in order to draw them into larger arguments, as well as to imagine possible pathways that these dynamics could take in the future—a grim, totalitarian vision or perhaps touching on the enduring possibility of alternatives.

SURVEILLANCE AS A SURROGATE FOR SOLIDARITY

Having looked at Google's cyber-empire and China's Social Credit System in the last two chapters, it may be helpful to draw some parallels between those two institutions. They are plainly very different—one is controlled by the State Council, the highest organ of the Chinese state; the other by an American corporation. They also have similarities: they are both very powerful in a hierarchical and centralized way, operate on vast scales, and use computing-machines and surveillance in order to project control. To begin drawing parallels between these two institutions, I will explore the rhetoric of "trust." In its clunky bureaucratic language, a policy document published by China's State Council states,

> All levels' Party and units are encouraged to use name list information concerning persons subject to enforcement for trust-breaking, integrate it into their own areas, professional scope and business activities, and implement credit supervision, warning and punishment over persons subject to enforcement for trust-breaking.[4]

Here and elsewhere, the State Council's vision for the Social Credit/ Debt System is filled with the rhetoric of trust, with the system being sold as an apparatus to automatically enhance trust and sincerity across society at large. This can be seen in the slogan coined for the release of AliPay—Alibaba's key Social Credit/Debt instrument—in 2004: "Trust makes it simple." Half a world away, Google is also fondly framing their dys/utopian vision with rhetoric of trust. An example of this can be seen in the corporation's self-styled philosophy that—under the heading "You can make money without doing evil"—states, "Our users trust our objectivity and no short-term gain could ever justify breaching that trust."[5] Another concise expression of their attitude toward trust comes via a top company spokesperson who repeats variations on a theme of "Trust is the most important currency online."[6] In different ways, both Google and China's State Council imagine trust through the lens of technology and the market. In a time when cybernetic capitalism reigns supreme, these kinds of ideological framing are unsurprising.

And yet, the social concept of trust goes deeper than this. Trust evokes a combination of confidence, reliance, dependence, and hope, thus making it a thoroughly subjective and cultural phenomenon. Trust is a form of human social relation that is extremely complex, dense with meaning and layers of particular histories—from personal to world-historic—which make the concept resistant to quantification. For example, consider all the density of meaning that constitutes deep social relations, be it between lovers, rivals, parents, or such, or the complexity of social practices, from a Balinese cockfight to a Korean shamanic wedding procession. Upon close anthropological inspection, these social practices are infinitely rich and open-ended, with innumerable lines tying each element to a larger social symbolic field, where the power structures of hierarchy, the organization of nature, the conceptualization of the human condition—with all of its desires and dilemmas—come into a dense ensemble of social meaning. This meaning-making is often composed of layers of ambiguity and ambivalence, complication, and contradiction, all woven into contextual and particular histories.[7] For all the material complexity involved in how computing-machines draw in surveillance data and process it, in some important respects it pales in comparison to the actual complexity of embodied social relationships. A system that tracks credit card purchases, or other such easily extractable data sets, is comparatively simplistic.

Complexity like this is a problem for power. Recall that Norbert Wiener's cybernetic system sought to reduce complexity in order to make predictions and project control (chapter 2). In that case, the complexity of artillery calculations was a problem for the Pentagon who used computing-machines to automate control of weaponry. This is significant, as all cybernetic surveillance since then has followed this broad trajectory: "watch over" to reduce complexity in order to make predictions and project control. Hence, the vast complexity of the natural world, which includes the social world, and the unpredictability of history is a problem for those who profit most from the unequal status quo. With roots stretching back to Francis Bacon in the long sixteenth century, the possibility of using scientific knowledge and technology to make predictions and to gain control has a deep history across capitalist modernity. Cybernetic surveillance participates in these developments by attempting to automate the oracle; to have machines reduce unpredictable people to credit scores, profiles for advertisers, persuadable numbers for electoral engineers, and so on, all to project control over their future, in order to secure the ongoing power.

Processes of surveillance and automated control are necessary at the gigantic scale at which China's State Council and Google operate. For the great majority of human history, trust has been made—and broken—largely on the personal level, with interactions being mediated by face-to-face communication. Consider Lewis Tappan, the original nineteenth-century American credit rater, and his need to personally meet those he extended credit to and make notes in his dossier recording his personal assessment of the debtor's character (chapter 4). Trust on a personal level requires interpretation to sense another's character and intentions, with much of it happening intuitively, through reading subtle signs in the form of embodied expression. This is not to suggest that this is necessarily ideal, for prejudice can easily flourish in face-to-face relations. Rather it is to argue that extending trust requires *interpretive labor*, effort to understand the other, to imagine things from their perspective, and to relate this to oneself in a particular social context. Calling this interpretive labor is significant in that it emphasizes the importance of interpretation for all social practices, acknowledging that the process requires work, and recognizing that it is bound up with uneven power relations. This is to say, the higher in a hierarchy one is, the less interpretive labor one needs to employ vis-à-vis subordinates; one can simply give orders. Those lower in the hierarchies need to pay closer attention to the actions of their supervisors—in various contexts a manager, police officer, prison guard, welfare officer, or a husband—in an attempt to avoid the punishments of power.[8]

Using interpretive labor to build trust is problematic for institutions like Google or China's State Council. Their titanic scales, greatly extended relations, and sharply unequal power arrangements make trust in the social sense of the term impossible; the interpretive labor would be too great. In order to maintain their own asymmetrical power, each turns to networked computing-machines and they see surveillance as a solution. They have computing-machines programmed in an attempt to automate and quantify trust in order to make it legible for distant government and corporate bureaucrats. To do this, they have surveillance-engines extract data from everyday life—using browser history, biometric data, social media communications, space-time coordinates, and so forth—from which they attempt to dramatically simplify trust, boiling it down to extremely reductive numbers—be it a Citizen Score, a threat rating, or the likelihood that one could be manipulated to engage as a gullible consumer. In these cases, and many, many more, interpretive labor is automated by surveillance-engines.

This is problematic because computing-machines cannot perform interpretive labor in the way that humans can, for the way that they "think" is radically different. Drawing from theorizing on hermeneutics and embodied cognition, interpretation is a fundamentally social practice and it occurs within and between creative, embodied beings. The thinking of computing-machines plays out with a totally different materiality whereby they *compute*, which is to say, determine by mathematical means. This is significant, for the word "computer" originated in English along with capitalist modernity in the long sixteenth century, when it referred to a person employed to perform calculative labor for surveying—thus again showing how surveying preceded surveillance (chapter 1). Then, the term passed to machines during the nineteenth-century "information revolution," before becoming completely mechanized after the rise of cybernetics. Now, of course, the computer is a machine and the earlier human profession is obsolete. Thus, in the term "computer" itself, we can see a history of how human intellectual practices have been automated, outsourced, and encoded into machines. So, calculative labor was thoroughly automated; then, as computing-machines have become more and more sophisticated, they have started to be able to approximate interpretive labor and other intellectual practices.

As a type of computing-machine, surveillance-engines are made to extract data traces from the world via sensors, which they encode into numbers for computation that can be used to simplify nature, make predictions, and project control. This process can be enacted at tremendous scales, with vast databases of centralized and searchable information available to be processed with algorithms and neural networking. This process can potentially reveal surprising patterns that are totally invisible to human interpreters, a process that can give people real insights into the world. Needless to say, these can be extremely powerful tools in the hands of the technocrats who wield them. While lacking the ability to interpret in the social sense of the term, surveillance-engines can powerfully automate aspects of interpretive labor and other intellectual practices, operating at scales, depths, and breadths that are totally beyond human capacities. Likewise, people act in the world in ways that are fundamentally creative and are totally beyond the ability of a computer-machine—or even the actors themselves—to fully grasp. This is the open-ended nature of the complexity of the material universe, with this very complexity being a problem for the narrow calculus of power and their attempts to simplify it in order to project control.[9] While the distinctions between the strong subjectivity that humans possess and the information processing systems of computing-machines are profound and enduring, it is plain that they are drawn together in our historic moment into the overarching power system of cybernetic capitalism. This was part of Wiener's original understanding of cybernetics: control and communication between the humans and the machine.[10]

Surveillance has not always been central to how social relations have been organized: the "global village" is a very different beast from traditional villages. Firstly, traditional villages, and other small-scale human social formations, do not necessarily engage in surveillance in the sense of "watching over," as one is not necessarily "above" one's neighbor in the sense that the state or the capitalist wields structural power over their citizens/employees. This is not to idealize such traditional arrangements; oppression can flourish there as well, albeit on a much smaller and less systematic scale. It is true that secrets are often scarce in village life, with others often knowing who is sleeping with who, or other such gossip gleaned from eavesdropping, spotting, and rumors. Crucially, this knowledge of others' actions came as a result of the inhabitants' lives being intimately bound to one another. For most of history, people have been embedded members of place-based communities, where their relationships with the people around them were primarily mediated by face-to-face relations. This is qualitatively different from the abstract technological surveillance-engines prying into personal details, scraping data traces from algorithmic processing to serve powerful and distant interests.[11] Abstract surveillance deals with categories, not characters. This problem has long roots, being one of the key reasons why the *Domesday Book* from almost a thousand years ago was given its apocalyptic name (chapter 4).

These qualitative differences are worth emphasizing, for centuries of enclosure movements and forcible displacements have seen waves of uprooting circle the globe, resulting in the traditional folkways being smashed and reorganized by the forces of capitalist modernity, with all of its technological and colonial formations. This has been particularly evident as agricultural regions have been devastated by war, debt, industrialization, and the pressures of the global market; enormous numbers of people have been forced to move to cities, driving a historically unparalleled urbanization process. Physically moving from the land to cities often severs the more intimate social connections of place-based communities, ripping apart the complex social fabric that has made up the bulk of the historical human experience. The cities and slums that the former rural dwellers now inhabit are vibrant places, where the old ways are remixed in creative ways. They do not simply disappear in a linear way; they are overlaid, hybridized, and reconstituted on different levels. Nevertheless, the scale and speed of the process of urbanization and globalization under capitalism, particularly since its cybernetic reconstitution, has undermined the older social orders.[12] China is a compelling case of this phenomenon, with the large-scale destruction of the old ways by breakneck processes of modernization. In China, the hugely intensifying levels of inequality released by this process have, among other things, contributed to a crisis in social trust. Deep distrust is common in everyday life, with much of it focused on local governments, although paradoxically, it appears to go along simultaneously with increased trust in the distant central government.[13]

Thus, in such an unrooted world, surveillance acts as something like a surrogacy for trust, albeit a problematic one that enables the concentration and centralization of power. As trust is abstracted from its embodied roots in everyday life where it is created through interpretive labor, it comes back into social organization as a techno-scientific process that radically enhances forms of social control. The abstract processes overlay more concrete ways of being, with for example a Citizen Score overlaying reciprocal relations. Framing this as "overlaying" is helpful, for it suggests that the less abstract ways of being don't simply disappear into a one-dimensional flattening, rather they persist in a layered and complex, contradictory way. The combination of scientific observation, technical invention, centralized political power, and elite economic extraction come together in a system that is enormously powerful but also deeply unstable. Compelled toward impossible dreams of infinite growth within finite nature, the cybernetic capitalist system is decidedly expansionist and colonial as it pushes into more and more parts of the world and life. As it goes, it can either replace or remake other ways of being and doing, other ways that are, on careful consideration, perhaps well worth preserving.[14]

Nevertheless, in these cases, surveillance becomes a substitute for solidarity, one that is necessary to the very functioning of global capitalism. This dominant and dominating social formation simply could not function without surveillance; the system of minority ownership and rule over a starkly unequal society, where exploitation is constitutional, social life is alienated, communication increasingly disembodied, and communities fragmented could not be reproduced without the overseers and their computing-machines and surveillance-engines. The organizing power of cybernetics is needed to exert control, for without the view from above, the abstracted elite could not try and mold the world according to their interests. This is to say that without cybernetic surveillance, capitalism as we know it would collapse.

CAPITALISM AS A SURVEILLANCE SYSTEM

With these observations in mind, it may be helpful to apply the concept of surveillance to capitalism itself, beginning with one of its seminal organizational forms: the corporation. Originally emerging in the long sixteenth century, the corporation has played a key role in global capitalism. This is not the place to explore the details of this long and complex saga, which has moved through early joint-stock companies, like the Dutch East India Company established in 1602, to the granting of legal personhood and limited liability in the nineteenth century; and the partial fall and rise of monopoly power in the twentieth century through to the unlimited political influence via advertising granted in the twenty-first century. From the onset, corporations were created as non-human entities, working with particular sets of powers. Curiously, the word "corporation" is derived from *corpus*, the Latin word for "body." They were created under the laws of states to have a continuous existence independent of the actual bodies of the people who make it up, thus capturing how across history, the corporation has become increasingly disembodied as it has been made more abstract. The last half millennium has borne witness to a notable intensification of corporations, with great increases in their size and scope, and their ability to organize the world. The contradictory forces of competition and monopoly, private wealth and state power, and the constant need for infinite accumulation within finite nature all serve to chase corporations around the world, undoubtedly making them major players in the uneven processes of globalization. In the following, I shall look at an aspect of the saga of corporations through the lens of surveillance in order to tease out some systemic patterns.[15]

Corporations are social formations that organize productive activity in the interests of their owners, the shareholders. Within a corporation, the highest decision-making authority is granted to the board of directors, who are chosen by the major shareholders. The board in turn appoints a chief executive officer (CEO) to manage the firm's daily affairs. The board determines the strategic direction for the company, deciding what, where, and how to produce goods or deliver services. The board of directors is sometimes called a board of *supervisors*. This is significant, for "supervise" and "supervision" tightly parallel with "surveillance," meaning the "view from above," with both words being drawn from Latin and their usage emerging in the long sixteenth century. A board of supervisors is a manifestation of a hierarchical and centralized structure that *watches over* human organization in order to exert control over it and to defend and extend its own social power. This is to say that, on the broadest level, corporations are internally organized as surveillance apparatuses.[16]

One part of corporate surveillance exists on the highest levels, with the super-visionary board—and the shareholders they serve—sitting above and outside the company. From this commanding position, the board of supervisors can influence all the major decisions a company makes, yet crucially they do not actually do the work: it is the workers who harvest the grain, sew the garment, assemble the car, and code the algorithm. Yet under the laws, traditions, ideologies, and violence of capitalism, whatever products are produced by workers immediately and automatically become the private property of the employer, and ultimately, the unworking external shareholders. Crucially, while shareholders do not produce the goods, they determine the entire production process. They employ a hierarchy of managers to surveil the organization and prepare reports to provide the hierarchy with an overview of the operations. From this vantage point, they seek to invest $X worth of capital and expect $X + $Y of capital in return. The bigger the +$Y the better, at least for the shareholders and their ability to structurally extract wealth from the labor of others and from natural processes. Indeed, this is part of the core secret of capitalism: money begets money, and the more money one has the more one can make with it, and the more social power one can wield over society.[17]

As they exist above and outside of the company, it is easy to see how they can have a very a different set of interests to their workers or the wider communities that may be affected by their practices. Should a company close a factory, fire all the workers, and reopen offshore where they can pay poorer people a fraction of the wages? This idea may be cooked up by the board of supervisors on behalf of their major shareholders with their structural interest in profit maximization and quick returns, yet it is less likely to be championed by the workers whose livelihoods are to be sacrificed and communities ruined. Should a company invest in having managers oversee the workers to make sure they are constantly working at or above maximum capacity? Should they try the same thing via technologies of remote control? Again, this may well make sense to the external, non-working elite, but is less likely to be supported by those coming under the painful pressures of increasing micro-management.

Milton Friedman's highly influential book *Capitalism and Freedom*, published in 1962, unambiguously declared that "there is only one social responsibility of business—to use its resources and engage in activities designed to increase its profits."[18] If one follows this and concentrates only on profit maximization, then all the infinite complexity and ambiguity of social nature vanishes, replaced by a clear and simple logic of accumulation *über alles*—profit above everything else. From this shockingly narrow gaze, there is no need to negotiate the different needs of various groups of consumers, workers, citizens, minorities, and so on; no need to engage with messy, contested concepts like security, capabilities, fairness, or social good; no need to have to reckon with the complications of history, uneven power, or ecological entanglement. Rather, Friedman recommends the single-minded pursuit of profit. He thereby embraces the view from above, to surveil and simplify the world in order to make it legible for power and thus to be able to reorganize the world according to the power of capital accumulation. Friedman justified this stark clarity with a direct reference to Adam Smith's mythological "Invisible Hand," interpreting it to assume that naked avarice would somehow be transmuted into gold by the glorious "free market." Following the economist's lead, many others cheered and jumped aboard this violently simple abstraction, offering economic rationale for "maximizing shareholder value."[19] This has had the effect of supercharging the inhuman logic of the corporation—organizations that are composed of people, but are actually non-human entities; they are legal constructs made from people machines and natural processes, sewn together with networks of communication and control.[20]

The ideas of profit maximization above all streamed from the high temples of economics and into corporate practice in the 1980s, being intimately associated with the solidification of "neoliberalism."[21] Many companies turned toward this mode of operation, with General Electric often being held up as an early leader of this transformation. Founded by Thomas Edison in 1889, almost a century later in 1981, the board of supervisors appointed Jack Welch to be CEO. Welch held this position for twenty years, overseeing the company's market value increase by 4,000 percent. This tremendous growth was achieved at a tremendous cost that neatly fell outside of the investors' narrow purview of profit maximization. A pincer action occurred, with all decisions being made to drive up profits at one end and to drive down expenses at the other. Costs were driven down by a brutal internal austerity project whereby the company slashed its internal spending, mercilessly firing hundreds of thousands of employees, including an annual purge of the bottom

10 percent of managers each year. Meanwhile, top managers were given stocks, thus shifting their relations from employee to owner, integrating them further into the logic of wealth extraction. This was accompanied by a pathological obsession with "cost efficiency," leading to an enormous outsourcing drive accompanied by a hostile push into the poorer world where they could pay poor people less to do the same work, thus profiting through exploiting and exacerbating global inequality.[22] Simultaneously, the firm shifted much of their focus from manufacturing to financial services, mimicking the financial markets they sought to impress. They were rewarded lavishly with tremendous stock prices, record-breaking payouts, and *Fortune* magazine dubbing Welch the "Manager of the Century."

So, if the board of supervisors watches over a corporation, projecting control to maximize the extraction of wealth, we may well ask the ancient question initially asked by Juvenal, a poet in Imperial Rome, "Who watches the watchmen?" As already noted, a company's super-visionary board is chosen by the major shareholders to represent their interests in capital accumulation. At this point it is worth considering who the "shareholders" actually are. In theory, anyone with surplus money can invest in the stock market, with some members of the middle classes around the world—historically known as the *petite bourgeoisie*—seeking to emulate the capitalists on a comparatively tiny scale by following this path. Also, some countries force workers to become investors through rules that require money to be paid into pension funds that invest in the market on their behalf in order to fund their own retirement, rather than rely on a public solution. These schemes serve to weld the fate of ordinary people more directly to the global market and its cyclically spasmodic fluctuations. These cases aside, in the context of the historic unprecedented inequality we now face, it is fair to state that the rich and mega-rich, who own the vast majority of the world's money, also own the vast majority of the world's shares.

In the United States in 2016 the top 10 percent of households owned 92 percent of all stocks, with the top 1 percent owning 50 percent of all the total stock.[23] Within the "1%," the concentration of ownership becomes more and more intense as one steps up to the 0.1%, the 0.01%, the 0.001%, and so on. Put inversely, the bottom 90 percent of Americans own only 8 percent of stock. While nationally based, on a global level such statistics would likely show even greater concentrations of wealth in the hands of a few. This enormously unequal ownership structure correlates to an enormously unequal decision-making structure, with power being strongly tied to private wealth, and the action of the corporations reflecting the interest of their rich owners, first and foremost. An insight into how this functions as a system can be gained by looking to the structures of investment and the systematic super-visionary power they wield over the corporate sphere.

Much of this takes place under the title "asset management." This refers to a commercial financial service whereby a company oversees pools of investment funds from which—for a fee—it promises to offer more returns than individual investors could get on their own or through a traditional bank. Asset management functions as a kind of "shadow bank," offering many of the same services as commercial banks but outside the regulations that govern that sector. It should also be noted that these firms invest heavily in each other, making them simultaneous rivals and allies, bound together in monopolistic competition.[24] As of 2017 there were seventeen transnational investment companies managing over one trillion U.S. dollars' worth of investment assets each (table C.1). Some of the names are well known, after their instrumental role in triggering the Global Financial Crisis that began in 2007, and some are not well known at all. Collectively, these firms oversee a massive $41.1 trillion worth of investments.[25]

It is worth pausing to reflect on this to ask this deceptively simple question: what is a trillion? The easy answer is 1,000,000,000,000; yet that torrent of zeros doesn't necessarily do justice to its scale. At a spending rate of $1 per second, it would take about twelve days to burn through a million, thirty-two years to burn through a billion, and 31,546 years to get through a trillion. The order of magnitude between these numbers is easy to overlook. The main point is to emphasize the obvious: a trillion dollars is an enormous sum of money. If we were to use extreme inequality as a starting place, a trillion dollars could, for example, be used to provide universal clean water and sanitation for every human on earth for about seven years. Globally, around one in four people have no choice but to regularly ingest contaminated drinking water, through which many diseases—such as diarrhea, cholera, dysentery, typhoid, and polio—can spread, to say nothing of the toxins that come from producing consumer goods and industrial agriculture.[26] According to the World Health Organization, diarrhea alone kills over two

Table C.1.　Top Asset Management Firms in Early 2017

Rank	Name	Country of Headquarters	Assets under Management (US$)
1	BlackRock	US	$5.4 trillion
2	Vanguard Group	US	$4.4 trillion
3	JP Morgan Chase	US	$3.8 trillion
4	Allianz SE (PIMCO)	Germany/US	$3.3 trillion
5	UBS	Switzerland	$2.8 trillion
6	Bank of America, Merrill Lynch	US	$2.5 trillion
7	Barclays plc	Great Britain	$2.5 trillion
8	State Street Global Advisors	US	$2.4 trillion
9	Fidelity Investments (FMR)	US	$2.1 trillion
10	Bank of New York Mellon	US	$1.7 trillion
11	AXA Group	France	$1.5 trillion
12	Capital Group	US	$1.4 trillion
13	Goldman Sachs Group	US	$1.4 trillion
14	Credit Suisse	Switzerland	$1.3 trillion
15	Prudential Finance	US	$1.3 trillion
16	Morgan Stanley & Co	US	$1.3 trillion
17	Amundi/Credit Agricole	France	$1.1 trillion
Total	**17 firms, 199 directors**		**$41.1 trillion**

Note: In 2017, BlackRock increased the amount of assets under its management by 22 percent, raising it to $6.29 trillion. It also happily reported a $1.2 billion tax benefit in the fourth quarter of 2017 as a direct result of Trump's tax cut package.

Source: Peter Phillips, Giants: The Global Power Elite (New York: Seven Stories Press, 2018).

million people each year, largely children, making it the world's biggest killer. If done in a thoughtful and public manner, a trillion-dollar investment could potentially make an enormous and concrete difference to the lives of the world's poorest people, for nobody in a world as rich as ours should have to shit themselves to death.[27]

Alternatively, a trillion dollars could also be invested to make the rich richer, and this is where the asset managing companies come in. Like all corporations, each of these investment firms has a board of supervisors. One study of seventeen of the biggest asset management firms found that there were 199 directors supervising the investment of $40 trillion.[28] So, the amount of people that could fit into a standard university lecture theatre oversee how this gargantuan concentration of money is invested. This does not imply that these directors are necessarily extremely rich—although many of them really are—for their personal wealth is secondary to the position they hold in supervising global capitalism in order to maximize the extraction of wealth for unproductive investors. This is not just an argument about them as particular people, for if they were to be replaced the structures within which they operate would exert the same pressures on their replacements. The structure of capitalisms compels them to invest the money they oversee into the most profitable ventures, which do not usually include providing basic services to poor people. Rather, they tend to invest in corporations that make enormous revenue—an area dominated by the big fossil fuel companies—or ones that are perceived as having a powerful ability to extract wealth and consolidate power that will pay off in the future, such as the surveillance-fueled tech-titans.[29] The asset management firms have such an enormous amount of money to invest, this translated into them taking significant control over the companies they invest in.

Take Amazon as an example. The top five institutional shareholders are Vanguard (11.06 percent), BlackRock (9.35 percent), FMR (6.45 percent), T. Rowe Price (5.76 percent), and State Street (5.71 percent), with four of these familiar from table C.1, and one, T. Rowe Price, narrowly falling shy of breaking the one-trillion-dollar mark with a mere $991 billion in 2017. Collectively, these five asset management firms control 38.33 percent of institutional shares, thus putting them in a powerful position to influence Amazon's practices.[30] Should Amazon do everything in its power to avoid paying tax? Should they develop a system to automatically surveil their employees and automatically fire them if they fall below standard, and all without supervisor intervention?[31] Should they fire as many workers as possible and replace them with robots? The handful of supervisors at the asset management firm play a key role in selecting Amazon's board of supervisors, and hence the answers to these questions.

While the top twenty asset management firms show a strong Atlantic orientation, all being headquartered in the United States and Europe, elsewhere there is another model of surveillance that successfully oversees huge large-scale capital accumulation. In China there are the "Big Four" commercial banks that supervise titanic amounts of investments (table C.2). Take the Industrial and Commercial Bank as an example. This organization is, by many measures, the largest bank in the world, with over US$4 trillion in assets. While semi-privatized, the Chinese Central Government holds around 70 percent of voting rights, which makes it a different kind of beast from shareholder dominated Blackrock or Vanguard. The state apparatus oversees the Big Four

Table C.2. China's "Big Four" State-Owned Commercial Banks, 2018

Rank	Name	CN¥ (trillions)	US$ (trillions)
1	Industrial and Commercial Bank	27,699,540	4.113
2	Agricultural Bank of China	22,609,471	3.357
3	China Construction Bank (2017 data)	22,124,383	3.285
4	Bank of China	21,267,275	3.157
Total		**93,700,669**	**13.912**

Sources: Industrial and Commercial Bank of China, "2017 Annual Report," http://v.icbc.com.cn/user files/Resources/ICBCLTD/download/2018/720180423.pdf; Bank of China, "2018 Annual Report," http://pic.bankofchina.com/bocappd/report/201903/P020190329601110675116.pdf; China Construction Bank, "Exploring the Blue Ocean: 2017 Annual Report," http://en.ccb.com/en/newinvestor/upload/20180817_1534487897/20180817143224827527.pdf; Agricultural Bank of China, "Joint Dedication to Build a Beautiful China: 2018 Annual Report," http://www.abchina.com/en/investor-relations/performance-reports/annual-reports/201903/P020190329665642073693.pdf.

Chinese banks, monopolizing and projecting power through their control over their investments. While this is a different model of extreme hierarchy—a publicly controlled way to increase private wealth—the explicit goal of the structure is capital accumulation.

While this book is not the place to analyze this in detail, there are some important parallels and distinctions to make between the two models of asset management. Despite their different modes of operating, the Chinese investment banks and the Atlantic asset management firms have strong parallels with respect to the extreme centralization and concentration of power that exists within their hierarchies. One draws directly on the power of an authoritarian state, and the other draws on the tyranny of elite shareholders, with the American state apparatus and its world-spanning military sitting behind it, with around eight hundred garrisons outside its territory (China, by contrast, has zero bases outside itself, although it is attempting to build some on fabricated islands in the contested South China Sea). Through providing profitable returns to unproductive external investors, they both oversee and exacerbate great inequality, and the decision-making power over investment falls to either state bureaucrats or financial mercenaries.

Surveillance is not only integral to the internal functioning of corporations—from managers overseeing workers, machines automating this, to the controlling board of supervisors—but moreover, surveillance is central to capitalism itself. Shareholders, particularly the institutional shareholders, supervise the corporations to extract the maximum amount of wealth possible. This wealth is then invested into more layers of surveillance to intensify the quest for further capital accumulation and the centralization of power that comes from "watching over" from above and outside in order to project control. Beyond any one shareholder or supervisor, the capitalist class as a whole "watches over" the system that bears their name. Capitalism is thus organized as a vast surveillance apparatus that enables the 1%—and their decimal-fraction superiors—to organize the world in ways that enable them to extract and concentrate as much wealth and power as possible. Building on long-term processes beginning in the long sixteenth century, this parasitic arrangement has deeply contradictory effects, with major material improvements in the lives of many around the world, incredible leaps in areas of knowledge, and the development of a multitude of new cultural forms.[32] And yet, all this was intimately bound up with war, genocide, slavery, and ecological catastrophes. To dismiss the darker side of this—as many celebrated mainstream analyses tend to do—is to neglect the complex and contradictory reality in which "progress" under capitalist modernity has been simultaneously liberating and destructive.[33] These constitutive dynamics have been visible for centuries, and yet in the early twenty-first century, they have become increasingly thunderous, with cascading, collapsing ecological systems, turbulent financial markets, decomposing political legitimacy, spreading civil wars, resurgent fascism, and totalitarian control projects all converging.[34]

Indeed, this points to a major contradiction in capitalism: those that sit at the apex of the system—such as the above-mentioned 199 directors of the biggest asset management firms or the big-shot CEOs of the tech-titans and other firms—have immense power and control over global capital; and yet should they deviate from the path of maximum extraction, they will be replaced by others willing to do the job: the inhuman logic of the structures they supposedly rule over overrules them. This results in an ethic of "If I don't do it, someone else will, probably a competitor," which provides additional justification for profit maximization, whatever the consequences. Paradoxically, this situation means that those atop capitalism simultaneously have great power and are totally powerless before the inhuman logic of infinite accumulation. Furthermore, this is connected to another even bigger contradiction: the vast system of control that has been developed over the centuries of capitalist modernity is increasingly out of control and is rapidly undermining the conditions for life to flourish on planet Earth.

"APRÈS MOI, LE DÉLUGE"

Of course, many of the supervisors are resisting and will continue to actively resist having their power curtailed by democratic organizations, because if worker-control became the dominant model, capitalism would be over. This curious phrase—"Après moi, le déluge" [After me, the flood]—is attributed to either Louis XV of France, or his lover, back in 1757. It is interpreted as meaning, after the fall of my reign, chaos, terror, and destruction will prevail—therefore you had better support me. The combination of ignorant arrogance and imaginative poverty in this phrase has long been seen as a poignant encapsulation of the attitude of capitalism.[35] It is highly relevant again as climate change, ecosystem collapse, mass migration, mass unemployment, civil war, and resource depletion continue to intensify and converge. Indeed, rapidly rising sea levels and melting polar ice caps give the phrase a darkly literal twist.

The convergence of the twenty-first-century remixes of fascism with cybernetic capitalism is not a hopeful combination; indeed, it is almost too easy to envision a potential dark future extending from many of the dynamics discussed throughout this book. Kernels of a cybernetic totalitarianism already exist in the present, lurking in the processes of dehumanization, in the imperial war machines, and the tremendous centralization and concentration of power that is facilitated by deep surveillance technologies, automated social control, and so much violence. These kinds of politics can thrive where stunted solidarity, indebtedness, ecological corrosion, and meaninglessness come together to shred social relations. Should the convergence of fascism and cybernetic capitalism continue to gather strength, then it has the potential to make the twentieth-century versions of totalitarianism seem crude.

At present, tens of millions of people from Xinjiang and Palestine are already various shades of imprisoned in what could be provocatively, but accurately, called cybernetic concentration camps (chapter 4). In these places, the logic of the camp spills out through the razor wire, and is projected outward by camera networks, watchtowers, and checkpoints to degrade the lives of entire sectors of society. Colonies have long acted as crucibles of social control, so it is fair to assume that the extreme surveillance of these colonies may continue their uneven creep toward the centers of power. As chapter 2 argued, whenever a society embraces a technology of domination, like the atomic bomb, it also embraces an inherent political structure of domination. The same goes for the automation of social control through surveillance. From this position, we can see that while the victims of surveillance suffer under technologies of domination, the perpetrators are not immune, they too are deformed and degraded: the dominator is dominated by domination.

In the rich world, cybernetic capitalists, militaries, and mercenaries already have extensive digital dossiers on billions of people, updated in real time with data traces drawn from many various aspects of everyday life being extracted and filed away. Most people in the rich world carry surveillance devices on their person virtually all of the time, recording almost every intimate movement of their lives. Imagine this: the little camera mounted on your smartphone records your face as you, say, skim over the daily news. It is not at all far-fetched to imagine that this video data ends up on a mercenary corporation's database as they subcontract data from an increasingly authoritarian (and worse) regime. The footage of your face is then fed through facial recognition algorithms, plus sentiment analysis software and an expression decoder, in order to automatically monitor your emotional reactions to the news in real time. Then, if the surveillance-engine captures patterns of the "wrong" kind of emotional responses—say a barely perceivable wince of disgust every time the government announces another step toward their glorious future—then you could end up on a Thoughtcrime watchlist, or worse. All the pieces of this already exist, developed by advertisers in their desperate need to produce consumers to keep the ruinous wheels of overproduction and capital accumulation spinning. How far this trajectory continues is yet to be determined by social struggles and the unpredictable nature of history's unfolding. Nevertheless, it is sobering to recall that we *already* live in a world that has totalizing surveillance, unprecedented inequality, predictive policing, collapsing ecosystems, and the possibility of extrajudicial summary executions by flying robots.

As the situations worsen, some sections of the elite may compromise and allow their power and resources to be redistributed for broader social good. Other sections already are and will continue to actively resist moving toward a more democratic and sustainable social system, preferring the totalitarian solution that profits them. These grim developments are well noted by sections of the cybernetic capitalist elite, who are actively working on contingency plans. These take the form of colonial fantasies about space, bioengineering away death, uploading minds, and other deranged ways to immortalize their power.[36]

One arc of this involves buying up large tracts of land in supposedly safe territories, like New Zealand, in order to move there when an acute global crisis unfolds; such as a large-scale war, an intense financial collapse, or a revolutionary uprising against the 1%. Many Silicon Valley tech-billionaires have put such plans in action, with for example, fueled-up private jets waiting in Nevada for the sole purpose of escaping the United States. These members of the super-rich imagine living in luxury bunker fortresses, waited on by robots, and defended by drones; tiny islands of immense wealth and security in a burning, miserable world. In this grim colonial vision, the vast majority of the world's people are rendered "surplus humanity."[37]

Whether these dreadful possibilities come into being or not depends in very significant ways upon ordinary people and whether they continue to acquiesce. Outside the elite, and the power structures that support them, many ordinary people are already resisting and will continue to resist moving to more democratic and sustainable systems of organization. Around the world, significant numbers of people seem to be giving up on the concept of democracy, degraded as it is by the logic of capital (chapter 3), preferring rather to choose domination, to submit before a control structure.[38] This is partly explainable because many cultures and identities are thoroughly integrated into the power systems of surveillance and control.

Surveillance is not just about external powers, but also about how these views have been internalized into subjectivities of consumption and cultures of surveillance. For surveillance "is no longer merely something external that impinges on our lives," with it going from "being an institutional aspect of modernity or a technologically enhanced mode of social discipline or control" to become thoroughly internalized, forming "part of everyday reflections on how things are and of the repertoire of everyday practices."[39] The eager uptake of so-called smart devices with their fetishization of narrowly understood convenience and efficiency is one of the best examples of this phenomenon. There is a rise of a kind of Taylorism of the self via fitness trackers and other self-surveillance devices that promise the possibility of optimization and maximizing efficiency, all while selling intimate data extracted to dubious third parties with unknown and ill-thought through consequences. These devices allow the "auto-exploiting subject" to carry around its "own labor camp; here, it is perpetrator and victim at one and the same time."[40] Likewise, the pervasiveness of social media creates a kind of marketplace of selves whereby people "share" curated exposures of themselves on vast corporate networks that allow for the mutual surveillance of participants, with this level of surveillance playing out as the iceberg tip of the unilateral surveillance of the cybernetic capitalism that underpins it. This is significant, for consumerism is structurally essential to contemporary capitalism and needed to absorb the overproduction of goods. New "needs need new commodities; new commodities need new needs and desires; the advent of consumerism augurs the era of 'inbuilt obsolescence' of goods offered on the market and signals a spectacular rise in the waste-disposal industry."[41] This breeds strong contradictions, for a society of consumers must appear to gratify their needs and produce happiness, while simultaneously working to promote insatiability. In this context, the surveillance-commodification complex of cybernetic advertising also functions as "a way of breaking down the solidarity of cultural collectives by instructing individuals in what they are supposed to desire."[42] All of this shows how the dynamics of cybernetic surveillance have been woven into the subjectivities and cultures of consumption in ways that require a struggle against these kinds of subjectivities and cultures, as well as against external structural power.

The future world that surveillance-engines of cybernetic capitalism are aiding to bring about is a world of spiraling inequality, where those at the systems techno-finance apex reach dizzying levels of riches at the direct expense of the majority of the world. This is paralleled by a grotesque concentration and centralization of social power in the hands of a tiny global elite. It is an enormously bureaucratic world, with an unreadable mass of deeply boring privacy statements, terms, and conditions, and an array of global administrators pushing standardization and upholding intellectual property rights in order to ensure the effective extraction of profits. It is a world where these bureaucracies are defended, extended, and enforced by spies, police, military, and mercenary powers. It is an unstable world, driven by the ruinous capitalist doctrine of infinite growth within finite nature, including finite human nature, a world where short attention spans and fractured consciousness is paralleled by processes of toxification and collapsing ecosystems. Pincered between the blades of extermination and extinction, this is a world of abstract information in your pocket, disembodied communication, and endless consumption—a world that is just so damned "convenient."

"ANOTHER WORLD IS POSSIBLE"

Famously encoded into the World Social Forum's Charter of Principles in São Paulo, Brazil, back in 2001, the phrase "another world is possible" carries in it a succinct and enduringly important message.[43] It suggests that the current dominant and dominating world order is the long-term result of a particular arrangement of power—political, economic, cultural, and ecological—which is the result of particular historic and social processes: this is to say that things could be otherwise. The surveilled world described herein unfolded largely due to the long-term dynamics that extend from the desperate need for capital accumulation, and the concentration and centralization of social power thanks to control of bureaucratic, scientific, and militaristic forces. The world in which capitalist modernity has developed is, of course, far more complex than these organizing principles, thus making the social formations on which they are based ripe with contradiction. For instance, over the same five-hundred-year period, aspects of democracy have developed as well, with society controlled from above and outside being challenged by society organized from below and within.[44] It is within such contradictions that the possibilities of alternatives to the ruinous trajectory described above can spring forth. These possibilities exist beyond the limits of control, outside of the narrow calculus of power and the violent simplifications of its surveillance. For the actual existing complexity of social ecology—with all its unpredictability, staggering diversity, living labor, and collective creativity—is far beyond understanding from above, let alone controllable.

One way an aspect of these contradictions could be resolved is in the sphere of production, an enormous area of life that is currently dominated by the surveilling power of capitalism. Instead of workplaces being controlled from above and outside, such as by shareholder surveillance, they can be organized from within and below. The concept of a "worker-controlled co-operative" is helpful here in illustrating how productive work can be organized democratically while avoiding systematic surveillance. Worker-controlled co-ops are based on the simple principle that those who do the work should be the ones to make decisions over the production process. Under this model, there are no external shareholders unproductively profiting on the labor of others, and no managers projecting downward control. Likewise, distant state bureaucrats are not directly controlling the organization. Rather the workers themselves should be the ones to make the decisions in the contexts of the local communities they serve. This fundamental difference leads to a very distinct power structure to what is found under the shareholder or traditional state ownership systems. Any profit generated by the productive activity of a worker co-op is either reinvested in the organization itself or is returned to its members, with this decision falling on the workers themselves in a democratic manner.

When workforces and communities organize themselves and decide how economic activity should be shaped, they are likely to make sharply different decisions in comparison to those that make sense only from capitalism's surveilling gaze. Under capitalism, capital must accumulate, a process that involves surveilling control, systematic wealth extraction, and power concentration as organizing principles. By contrast, worker-control has completely different organizing principles, allowing workers to think through decisions from within and below, rather than above and outside. For example, workers are unlikely to agree to move production to poorer countries to increase profits, for this would mean the end of their own jobs. Likewise, it would be tough to get workers to agree to pay top managers exorbitant salaries while allowing their own wages to stagnate. It would also be more difficult to convince them to spill toxins into their own environments or to work with dangerous machinery. On the contrary, they would be much more likely to provide safe workplaces and benefits to workers, such as daycare for children. The long-term direct interest in their local community and bottom-up organization of a worker-control structure would result in entirely different possibilities and organizing principles— wealth extraction versus co-operation; power attached to wealth versus power attached to work; distant versus local; above and outside versus below and within. Worker-controlled co-operatives can exert structural pressures that can help to resolve some of the most pressing problems in global capitalism, not as a cure-all, but by going to the heart of the surveilling logics of domination. [45]

As the increasingly converging crises—driven in a large part by the forces of war and finance—continue to rip through the social fabric of our communities, this will very likely be accompanied by increasing public anger at the ruinous status quo and add urgency to the need to seek alternatives. While some anger could well turn to various shades of fascism as a solution, much of it could turn in the opposite direction. It is not far-fetched to imagine a wave of worker-controlled take-overs following in the wake of an intensifying crisis, for this has happened many times before. Curiously, this kind of social organization of production often appears spontaneously and flourishes in the cracks of capitalism, with examples over the last century blossoming in places as diverse as Algeria and Argentina, Spain and Syria, Ukraine and the United States. Flourishing co-operative production could be part of a broader democratic movement that could demand that governments force major corporations to undergo processes of democratic reconstitution, forcing them to answer to social demands rather than surveilling extraction and control from above.[46]

While this is not the place to explore the various ways in which processes of democratization could lead to very different kinds of world, the imaginative exercise is crucial. Picture a different global organization, one founded on small, locally run communities with large degrees of participation on decision-making processes, worker-control over co-operative production, and frugal, low-consumption lifestyles. Such highly self-sufficient communities could be organized primarily on the face-to-face level, and from that basis extend beyond their locality into larger confederations, each run on democratic principles. Such nested confederations could scale up all the way to global levels, which is highly necessary to confront the planetary scale of problems that plague our world. Such a model would result in a totally different form of globalization than what we find today: one grounded in democracy from below, rather than projected down via surveillance from above. In addition to being potentially ecologically sustainable, deeply democratic, and allowing social justice and equality to be meaningful lived concepts, such communities would require little internal surveillance to function. Their members would be able to conduct the necessary interpretive labor to build the social trust, reciprocity, co-operation, and solidarity that is necessary to support such society. This is not a utopian proposal, for such a situation would necessarily be riddled with conflict and disagreement, negotiation and compromise—in short, politics. Rather, the claim is that while such an organization would undoubtedly create problems, they would be more manageable than the existential crises that have been brought about by five centuries of global capitalism.

Should society move in this direction, such a form of democracy could drastically curtail the need for surveillance, in its militarized, commodified form as a technology of domination. It is important to note that other aspects of surveillance, such as its reducing complexity in order to make predictions and gain power, would not have to be discarded. Rather, this kind of abstract thinking, monitoring, and calculations can give crucially important insights into the world, insights that could be put to the service of democratically determined goals, in contrast to the centralization of power and wealth. Indeed, it may well be that much could be redeemed from cybernetic technologies if they were thoroughly reworked from a human scale according to bottom-up logics of democracy and if ecological principles were seriously reckoned with. This is indeed an urgent area for theoretical and practical investigation.

Plainly, such a world would require radical structural change from the dominant and dominating way in which the world is currently organized, with its obsession with endless growth, production, and consumerism; colonization and patriarchy; accumulation and control. It would require significant cultural transformations to detangle subjectivities from desiring surveillance and endless consumption in order to build social solidarity. Large political, economic, cultural, and ecological transformations are desperately necessary in order to keep our ecosystems alive and our common humanity intact. Some parts of this struggle are very new—such as the power of the techno-science brought forth by militaries, intellectuals, and capital—and other parts are very old. Indeed, for millennia revolutionary movements have often been brought together around the core demands: "Cancel the debts and redistribute the land"—demands that are as apt as ever in today's world.[47] Such a framing helps to conceive this as a global and intergenerational project, a kind of "long revolution" of democracy, a world-wide struggle for the commons. Such processes are necessary to bring about the conditions for collective well-being, which is to say the conditions for human flourishing within nature, in order to create the conditions where meaningful lives can be lived. These dilemmas are deeply political and ethical, bearing on what kind of world we create, what kind of lives we would live, and what kind of creatures we could become. It remains a critically important task to imagine such possibilities, and furthermore to concretely act to create kernels of them in the cracks and contradictions of the current order that could take root, grow, and blossom forth as the crisis in the ruinous status quo continues to deepen.[48]

Back during the global protests that erupted around the world in 1968, the Parisian manifestation of this Great Refusal saw radicals graffiti the city's walls with the evocative slogan: "*soyez réalistes, demandez l'impossible*" (be realistic, demand the impossible). Cut to half a century later and inequality and toxification are reaching world-ruining levels while, paradoxically, many seem to find it easier to imagine the end of the world rather than the end of capitalism. In this context, it is plain that a strong argument can be made that the world still needs to be turned upside down, hence the spirit of the '68 slogan still holds. Nevertheless, to play with the phrase, capitalism is somehow seen by many as "realistic" even though it demands the impossible: infinite, exponential expansion within finite nature. Indeed, much of the calamitous trajectory of the present is driven by this impossible, insatiable, and dominating desire: the project of control that is out of control. Thus, to flip the slogan on its head: *be impossible, demand the realistic*. There is a provocative and radical case to be made for being impossible to the disastrous status quo—refuse, resist, rebel, and revolt while fostering creativity, curiosity, courage, and compassion—and demand the realistic: a democratic and sustainable world held in common.

Notes

PRELUDE

1. Giovanni Arrighi, *Adam Smith in Beijing: Lineages of the Twenty-First Century* (London: Verso, 2007); Sean Cubitt, *Finite Media: Environmental Implications of Digital Technologies* (Durham, NC: Duke University Press, 2017).

2. Adam Greenfield, *Radical Technologies: The Design of Everyday Life* (London: Verso, 2017), 31–62.

3. Emily West, "Amazon: Surveillance as a Service," *Surveillance & Society* 17, no. 1/2 (2019).

4. WikiLeaks, "Amazon Atlas," https://wikileaks.org/amazon-atlas/releases.

5. Hillary Hoffower, "We Did the Maths to Calculate How Much Money Jeff Bezos Makes in a Year, Month, Week, Day, Hour, Minute, and Second," *Business Insider (Australia)*, January 10, 2019, https://www.businessinsider.com.au/what-amazon-ceo-jeff-bezos-makes-every-day-hour-minute-2018-10.

6. Thomas Piketty, *Capital in the Twenty-First Century*, trans. Arthur Goldhammer (Cambridge, MA: The Belknap Press, 2014).

7. David Lyon, "Surveillance, Snowden, and Big Data: Capacities, Consequences, Critique," *Big Data & Society* (2014); *Surveillance after Snowden* (London: Polity, 2015).

8. Aaron Gregg, "Amazon Launches New Cloud Storage Service for U.S. Spy Agencies," *Washington Post*, November 20, 2017, https://www.washingtonpost.com/news/business/wp/2017/11/20/amazon-launches-new-cloud-storage-service-for-u-s-spy-agencies.

9. Florian Henckel von Donnersmarck, *The Lives of Others* (Buena Vista International, 2006); Anna Funding, *Stasiland: Stories from Behind the Berlin Wall* (New York: HarperCollins, 2003).

CHAPTER 1: SURVEYING SURVEILLANCE

1. Mark Juergensmeyer et al., eds., *The Oxford Handbook of Global Studies* (Oxford: Oxford University Press, 2018); Manfred Steger and Paul James, eds., *Globalization: The Career of a Concept* (London: Routledge, 2015).

2. David Lyon, *Surveillance Studies: An Overview* (Cambridge: Polity Press, 2007).

3. Manfred B. Steger, *Globalization: A Very Short Introduction*, 3rd ed. (Oxford: Oxford University Press, 2013); *The Global Studies Reader*, 2nd ed. (Oxford: Oxford University Press, 2014); Manfred B. Steger and Paul James, *Globalization Matters: Engaging the Global in Unsettled Times* (Cambridge: Cambridge University Press, 2019).

4. Andy Flemming and Aureliein Mondon, "The Radical Right in Australia," Oxford Handbooks Online, https://www.oxfordhandbooks.com/view/10.1093/oxfordhb/9780190274559.001.0001/oxfordhb-9780190274559-e-32; John Hinkson, "Trump and the Fascist Prospect," *Arena Journal* 47/48 (2017).

5. Franco "Bifo" Berardi, *Heroes: Mass Murder and Suicide* (London: Verso, 2015), 93–118.

6. APA, "Victorian Extremist Phillip Galea Planned to Bomb Leftwing Premises, Police Say," *The Guardian*, October 31, 2016, https://www.theguardian.com/australia-news/2016/oct/31/victorian-extremist-phillip-galea-planned-to-bomb-leftwing-premises-police-say; Martin McKenzie-Murry, "How Reclaim Australia Hid a 'Terrorist,'" *The Saturday Paper*, August 13, 2016, https://www.thesaturdaypaper.com.au/news/law-crime/2016/08/13/how-reclaim-australia-hid-terrorist/14710104003610.

7. John Gilliom, *Overseers of the Poor: Surveillance, Resistance, and the Limits of Privacy* (Chicago: University of Chicago Press, 2001); Ken Loach, *I, Daniel Blake* (eOne Films, 2016).

8. Lyon, *Surveillance Studies*, 134–35.

9. Behrouz Boochani, *No Friend but the Mountains* (Sydney: Picador, 2018).

10. Philip Dorling, "Asio Eyes Green Groups," *Sydney Morning Herald*, April 12, 2012, https://www.smh.com.au/politics/federal/asio-eyes-green-groups-20120411-1wsba.html.

11. Anonymous, "Security Culture: A Comprehensive Guide for Activists in Australia," (Inventati.org, 2013); Aziz Choudry, ed., *Activists and the Surveillance State: Learning from Repression* (London: Pluto Press, 2019).

12. Jack Warshaw and Friends, "If They Come in the Morning," *Misfits Migrants and Murders*, https://jackwarshaw.bandcamp.com/track/if-they-come-in-the-morning-2; Angela Y. Davis, ed., *If They Come in the Morning: Voices of Resistance* (London: Verso, 2016).

13. David A. Bell, *The First Total War: Napoleon's Europe and the Birth of Warfare as We Know It* (Boston: Mariner Books, 2008, reprint).

14. Robin Blackburn, *The American Crucible: Slavery, Emancipation and Human Rights* (London: Verso, 2013).

15. Giovanni Arrighi, *The Long Twentieth Century: Money, Power and the Origin of Our Times* (London: Verso, 2010); Fernand Braudel, *Civilization and Capitalism, 15th–18th Century: The Perspective of the World* (Oakland: University of California Press, 1992); Silvia Federici, *Caliban and the Witch: Women, the Body and Primitive Accumulation* (New York: Autonomedia, 2014); Jason W. Moore, *Capitalism in the Web of Life: Ecology and the Accumulation of Capital* (London: Verso, 2015); Lewis Mumford, *Technics and Civilization* (New York: Harbinger Books, Harcourt, Brace & World, 1963); Immanuel Wallerstein, *World-Systems Analysis: An Introduction* (Durham: Duke University Press, 2004).

16. Alfred W. Crosby Jr., ed., *The Columbian Exchange: Biological and Cultural Consequences of 1492*, 30th anniversary ed. (Santa Barbara: Praeger, 2003); Karl Marx, *Capital: A Critique of Political Economy*, trans. Ben Fowkes, 3 vols., vol. 1 (Westminster: Penguin Classics, 1976), 247.

17. Chandra Mukerji, *From Graven Images: Patterns of Modern Materialism* (New York: Columbia University Press, 1983), 79–130.

18. Mark Monmonier, *How to Lie with Maps*, 2nd ed. (Chicago: University of Chicago Press, 1996); Timothy Erik Ström, "Mapping Google Maps: Critiquing an Ideological Vision of the World," https://researchdirect.westernsydney.edu.au/islandora/object/uws%3A47394 (thesis, Western Sydney University, 2018); Denis Wood, *The Power of Maps*, ed. John Fels (New York: Guilford, 1992).

19. Clifford Geertz, "Form and Variation in Balinese Village Structure," *American Anthropologist* 61, no. 6 (1959); Geertz, *The Interpretation of Cultures: Selected Essays* (New York: Basic Books, 1973).

20. Torin Monahan, *Surveillance in the Time of Insecurity* (New Brunswick: Rutgers University Press, 2010), 116.

21. Paul James, *Globalism, Nationalism, Tribalism: Bringing Theory Back In* (London: Sage, 2006), 198.

22. Alfred W. McCoy, *Policing America's Empire: The United States, the Philippines, and the Rise of the Surveillance State* (Madison: University of Wisconsin Press, 2009), 37.

23. Rob Kitchin and Martin Dodge, *Code/Space: Software and Everyday Life* (Cambridge: MIT Press, 2011), 137–57.

24. Marx, *Capital*, 1.

25. Federici, *Caliban and the Witch*; *Re-Enchanting the World: Feminism and the Politics of the Commons* (Oakland: PM Press, 2019); David Harvey, *The New Imperialism* (Oxford: Oxford University Press, 2005).

26. Timothy D. Searchinger et al., "Assessing the Efficiency of Changes in Land Use for Mitigating Climate Change," *Nature* 564 (2018); Greg Wilpert and Alexander Zaitchik, "Amazon in Danger of Total Destruction under Brazil's Right-Wing President Bolsonaro," The Real News Network, July 12, 2019,

https://therealnews.com/stories/amazon-in-danger-of-total-destruction-under
-brazils-right-wing-president-bolsonaro.

27. Roger J. P. Kain and Elizabeth Baigent, *The Cadastral Map in the Service
of the State: A History of Property Mapping* (Chicago: University of Chicago Press,
1992), 130.

28. Ibid., 130–32.

29. Carolyn Merchant, *Autonomous Nature: Problems of Prediction and Control
from Ancient Times to the Scientific Revolution* (New York: Routledge, 2016); Moore,
Capitalism in the Web of Life; James C. Scott, *Seeing Like a State: How Certain Schemes
to Improve the Human Condition Have Failed* (New Haven, CT: Yale University Press,
1998), 11–22; Vandana Shiva, *Monoculture of the Mind: Biodiversity, Biotechnology
and the Third World* (Penang, Malaysia: Third World Network, 1993).

30. Eduardo Galeano, *Hunter of Stories*, trans. Mark Fried (London: Constable,
2019), 14.

31. John Patrick Montaño, *The Roots of English Colonialism in Ireland* (Cambridge: Cambridge University Press, 2011), 155–56.

32. Karl Marx and Friedrich Engels, *The Communist Manifesto* (New York:
Signet Classic, 2011).

33. E. P. Thompson, *Customs in Common* (London: Penguin Books, 1991),
164.

34. David Harvey, "Cosmopolitanism and the Banality of Geographical Evils,"
Public Culture 12, no. 2 (2000): 549; David N. Livingstone, *The Geographical Tradition: Episodes in the History of a Contested Enterprise* (Oxford: Blackwell, 1992),
216–59.

35. Adam Smith, *An Inquiry into the Nature and Causes of the Wealth of Nations*
(Chicago: University of Chicago Press, 1977), 947.

36. Matthew H. Edney, *Mapping an Empire: The Geographical Construction of
British India 1765–1843* (Chicago: Chicago University Press, 1997).

37. Jerry Brotton, *A History of the World in Twelve Maps* (London: Penguin
Group, 2012); David S. Landes, *Revolutions in Time: Clocks and the Making of
the Modern World* (Cambridge: Harvard University Press, 1983); Dava Sobel and
William J. H. Andrewes, *The Illustrated Longitude* (New York: Walker Publishing
Company, 1998); Ström, "Mapping Google Maps."

38. Edney, *Mapping an Empire*, 293.

39. Matthew S. Anderson, "Samuel Bentham in Russia," *The American Slavic
and East European Review* 15 (1956).

40. Jeremy Bentham, *Panopticon, Constitution, Colonies, Codification*, 11 vols.,
vol. 4, The Works of Jeremy Bentham (Edinburgh: William Tait, 1838–1843).

41. Michel Foucault, *Discipline and Punish: The Birth of the Prison* (New York:
Vintage Books, 1995). See also the 2003 special issue of *Surveillance & Society*
called "Foucault and Panopticism Revisited" (vol. 1, no. 3).

42. John Bowring, "Report on Egypt and Candia" (Great Britain: House of Commons, Sessional Papers, 1840).

43. Timothy Mitchell, *Colonising Egypt* (Cambridge: Cambridge University Press, 1988).

44. Antonio Gramsci, *Selections from the Prison Notebooks of Antonio Gramsci* (New York: International Publishers, 1971); Raymond Williams, *Marxism and Literature* (Oxford: Oxford University Press, 1977).

45. Karl Polanyi, *The Great Transformation: The Political and Economic Origins of Our Time* (Boston: Beacon Press, 2001), 14, 190.

46. Blackburn, *The American Crucible*; Polanyi, *The Great Transformation*, 14, 190.

47. Eduardo Galeano, *Open Veins of Latin America: Five Centuries of the Pillage of a Continent*, trans. Cedric Belfrage (New York: Monthly Review Press, 1997), 199; Eric Hobsbawm, *The Age of Empire: 1875–1914* (London: Abacus, 2013), 72, 362; Eric R. Wolf, *Europe and the People without History* (Los Angeles: University of California Press, 2010), 290–94.

48. James Gleick, *The Information: A History, a Theory, a Flood* (London: Fourth Estate, 2012), 147–48; Armand Mattelart, *The Invention of Communication*, trans. Susan Emanuel (Minneapolis: University of Minnesota Press, 1996).

49. Gleick, *The Information*, 148.

50. David Harvey, *The Condition of Postmodernity: An Enquiry into the Origins of Cultural Change* (Oxford: Basil Blackwell 1989), 240–59; Hobsbawm, *The Age of Empire*, 76.

51. Gleick, *The Information*; Armand Mattelart, *Networking the World: 1794–2000*, trans. Liz Carey-Libbrecht and James A. Cohen (Minneapolis: University of Minnesota Press, 2000); John Tagg, *The Burden of Representation: Essays on Photographies and Histories* (Basingstoke: Macmillan Education, 1988).

52. Karl Marx, "Letter from Karl Marx to Nikolai Danielson in St. Petersburg, 10 April 1879," https://www.marxists.org/archive/marx/works/1879/letters/79_04_10.htm.

53. Arrighi, *The Long Twentieth Century*, 249; Jeffry A. Frieden, *Global Capitalism: Its Fall and Rise in the Twentieth Century* (New York: W. W. Norton, 2006), 19–20.

54. Hobsbawm, *The Age of Capital*, 77–78.

55. Benedict Anderson, *Imagined Communities: Reflections on the Origin and Spread of Nationalism*, revised ed. (London: Verso Books, 2006), 184.

56. Sidney Mintz, "Plantations and the Rise of a World Food Economy: Some Preliminary Ideas," *Review (Fernand Braudel Center)* 34, no. 1/2 (2011).

57. Fredrick Wilslow Taylor, *The Principles of Scientific Management* (Champaign: Book Jungle, 2009), 27.

58. Harry Braverman, *Labor and Monopoly Capital: The Degradation of Work in the Twentieth Century*, 25th anniversary ed. (New York: Monthly Review Press, 1998), 73–74, emphasis in original.

59. John Hinkson et al., eds., *Cold War to Hot Planet: Fifty Years of Arena* (Melbourne: Arena Publications, 2016), 12–27; Hobsbawm, *The Age of Empire*, 45.

60. Frieden, *Global Capitalism*, 159–64.

61. Vladimir Illich Lenin, "The Taylor System—Man's Enslavement by the Machine," March 13, 1914, https://www.marxists.org/archive/lenin/works/1914/mar/13.htm; "The Immediate Tasks of the Soviet Government," https://www.marxists.org/archive/lenin/works/1918/mar/x03.htm.

62. Hannah Arendt, *The Origins of Totalitarianism* (New York: Harcourt, Brace, Jovanovich, 1973), 137.

63. McCoy, *Policing America's Empire*.

CHAPTER 2: THE ATOM AND THE WATCHTOWER

1. Jozef Rotblat, "The Hydrogen-Uranium Bomb," *Bulletin of the Atomic Scientists* XI, no. 5 (1955): 177.

2. John Hinkson, "New World or Worlds Unravelling?," *Arena Magazine*, June 19, 2018, https://arena.org.au/new-world-or-worlds-unraHvelling-by-john-hinkson; Manfred B. Steger, *The Rise of the Global Imaginary: Political Ideologies from the French Revolution to the Global War on Terror* (Oxford: Oxford University Press, 2008), 133–34.

3. Jason W. Moore, "The Capitalocene, Part I: On the Nature and Origins of Our Ecological Crisis," *Journal of Peasant Studies* 44, no. 3 (2017); Colin N. Waters et al., "Can Nuclear Weapons Fallout Mark the Beginning of the Anthropocene Epoch?," *Bulletin of the Atomic Scientists* 71, no. 3 (2015); James Westcott, "Written in Stone: In the Race for Geology's Highest Accolade—a 'Golden Spike'—Do Advocates of the Anthropocene Sell Their Ideas Short?," https://aeon.co/essays/is-rushing-to-declare-the-anthropocene-also-human-error.

4. Langdon Winner, *The Whale and the Reactor: A Search for Limits in an Age of High Technology* (Chicago: University of Chicago Press, 1986), 34.

5. Tilman Ruff, "Nuclear Promises," *Arena Magazine*, no. 162 (2019): 19–22.

6. David F. Noble, *Forces of Production: A Social History of Industrial Automation* (New York: Alfred A. Knopf, 1984), xi.

7. Daniel Guerin, *Fascism and Big Business* (New York: Pathfinder, 1973); John Hinkson, "Globalization and New World Order," in *Cold War to Hot Planet: Fifty Years of Arena*, ed. John Hinkson et al. (Melbourne: Arena Publications, 2016); C. Wright Mills, *The Power Elite* (Oxford: Oxford University Press, 2000); Lewis Mumford, *The Myth of the Machine: The Pentagon of Power* (New York: Harcourt Brace Jovanovich, 1970), 181.

8. Vannevar Bush, "Science the Endless Frontier" (Office of Scientific Research and Development, 1945).

9. John Hinkson et al., eds., *Cold War to Hot Planet: Fifty Years of Arena* (Melbourne: Arena Publications, 2016); Mumford, *The Myth of the Machine*; Fred Turner, *From Counterculture to Cyberculture: Stewart Brand, the Whole Earth Network, and the Rise of Digital Utopianism* (Chicago: University of Chicago Press, 2006).

10. Francis Bacon, "The New Atlantis," Project Gutenberg, https://www.gutenberg.org/files/2434/2434-h/2434-h.htm.

11. Mumford, *The Myth of the Machine*, 118–19.

12. Edward W. Said, *Culture and Imperialism* (New York: Vintage Books, 1994), xix.

13. Vannevar Bush, "Report of the National Defense Research Committee for the First Year of Operation, June 27, 1940, to June 28, 1941," http://docs.fdrlibrary.marist.edu/psf/box2/a13f19.html.

14. Lewis Mumford, *Technics and Civilization* (New York: Harbinger Books, 1963), 91.

15. David A. Bell, *The First Total War: Napoleon's Europe and the Birth of Warfare as We Know It* (Boston: Mariner Books, 2008; reprint ed.); Joel Kovel, *Against the State of Nuclear Terror* (Boston: South End Press, 1983), 49; Kevin Robins and Frank Webster, "Cybernetic Capitalism: Information, Technology, Everyday Life," in *The Political Economy of Information*, ed. Vincent Masco and Janet Wasko (Madison: University of Wisconsin Press, 1988).

16. Flo Conway and Jim Siegelman, *Dark Hero of the Information Age: In Search of Norbert Wiener the Father of Cybernetics* (New York: Basic Books, 2006); Norbert Wiener, "A Scientist Rebels," *The Atlantic* (January 1947).

17. Theodor Adorno and Max Horkheimer, *Dialectic of Enlightenment* (London: Verso, 1979); Carol Cohn, "Sex and Death in the Rational World of Defense Intellectuals," *Signs* 12, no. 4 (1987); Daniel Ellsberg, *The Doomsday Machine: Confessions of a Nuclear War Planner* (New York: Bloomsbury, 2017).

18. S. M. Amadae, *Rationalizing Capitalist Democracy: The Cold War Origins of Rational Choice Theory* (Chicago: University of Chicago Press, 2003); Sankaran Krishna, *Globalization & Postcolonialism: Hegemony and Resistance in the Twenty-First Century*, ed. Terrel Carver and Manfred Steger, Globalization (Lanham, MD: Rowman & Littlefield).

19. Jeffry A. Frieden, *Global Capitalism: Its Fall and Rise in the Twentieth Century* (New York: W. W. Norton, 2006), 262.

20. Nick Turse, "Donald Trump's First Year Sets Record for U.S. Special Ops: Elite Commandos Deployed to 149 Countries in 2017," *The Nation*, December 14, 2017, https://www.thenation.com/article/donald-trumps-first-year-set-a-record-for-use-of-special-operations-forces.

21. Giovanni Arrighi, *The Long Twentieth Century: Money, Power and the Origin of Our Times* (London: Verso, 2010), 306–7; Frieden, *Global Capitalism*.

22. F. A. Hayek, *The Road to Surfdom* (London: Routledge, 2001); Karl Popper, *The Open Society and Its Enemies* (London: Routledge, 2011); Joseph Schumpeter, *Capitalism, Socialism and Democracy* (London: Routledge, 2006). A summary of their fears can be found in Amadae, *Rationalizing Capitalist Democracy*, 15–23.

23. Michael Pembroke, *Korea: Where the American Century Began* (Melbourne: Hardie Grant, 2018).

24. Eric Hobsbawm, *The Age of Extremes: 1914–1991* (London: Abacus, 2013), 229.

25. David Holloway, "Innovation in Science: The Case of Cybernetics in the Soviet Union," *Science Studies* 4, no. 4 (1974); Slava Gerovitch, "The Cybernetics Scare and the Origins of the Internet," *Baltic Worlds*, February 11, 2010, http://balticworlds.com/the-cybernetics-scare-and-the-origins-of-the-internet.

26. Eden Medina, *Cybernetic Revolutionaries: Technology and Politics in Allende's Chile* (Cambridge: MIT Press, 2011); Peter Kornbluh, *The Pinochet File: A Declassified Dossier on Atrocity and Accountability* (New York: The New Press, 2003).

27. Noble, *Forces of Production*.

28. Joshua Oppenheimer, "The Act of Killing" (Det Danske Filminstitut, 2012); "The Look of Silence" (Why Not Productions, 2014); Geoffrey B. Robinson, *The Killing Season: A History of the Indonesian Massacres, 1965–66* (Princeton: Princeton University Press, 2018).

29. Robins and Webster, "Cybernetic Capitalism," 99–100.

30. Mumford, *The Myth of the Machine*, 130–96.

31. Noble, *Forces of Production*, 57.

32. Ibid.

33. David Harvey, *A Brief History of Neoliberalism* (Oxford: Oxford University Press, 2005); Naomi Klein, *The Shock Doctrine: The Rise of Disaster Capitalism* (London: Penguin Group, 2007); Vijay Prashad, *The Darker Nations: A People's History of the Third World*, ed. Howard Zinn (New York: The New Press, 2007); Vijay Prashad, *The Poorer Nations: A Possible History of the Global South* (London: Verso, 2014); Manfred B. Steger and Ravi K. Roy, *Neoliberalism: A Very Short Introduction* (Oxford: Oxford University Press, 2010); *Globalisms: The Great Ideological Struggle of the Twenty-First Century* (Lanham, MD: Rowman & Littlefield, 2009); Immanuel Wallerstein, *World-Systems Analysis: An Introduction* (Durham, NC: Duke University Press, 2004).

34. Gilles Deleuze, "Postscript on the Societies of Control," *October* 59 (Winter 1992).

35. Cynthia Enloe, *Globlization and Militarism: Feminists Make the Link*, 2nd ed. (Lanham, MD: Rowman & Littlefield, 2016); Yasha Levine, "Google and Encryption: Why True User Privacy Is Google's Biggest Enemy," *Pando*, https://archive.today/bDecl; William J. Mitchell, *City of Bits: Space, Place, and the Infobahn* (Cambridge: MIT Press, 2000), 107–8; Tiqqun, *The Cybernetic Hypothesis* (thean archistlibrary.org, 2010), 9, emphasis in original.

36. Nick Turse, *Kill Anything That Moves: The Real American War in Vietnam* (New York: Metropolitan Books, 2013).

37. Philip Jones Griffiths, *Agent Orange: "Collateral Damage" in Viet Nam* (London: Trolley Books, 2004).

38. Paul N. Edwards, *The Closed World: Computers and the Politics of Discourse in Cold War America* (Cambridge, MA: MIT Press, 1996).

39. John Williamson, "What Washington Means by Policy Reform," Peterson Institute for International Economics, http://www.iie.com/publications/papers/paper.cfm?researchid=486.

40. Kate Bedford, *Developing Partnerships: Gender, Sexuality and the Reformed World Bank* (Minneapolis: University of Minnesota Press, 2009); Ha-Joon Chang, *Bad Samaritans: The Guilty Secrets of Rich Nations and the Threat to Global Prosperity* (London: Random House Business Books, 2007); Sean Cubitt, *Finite Media: Environmental Implications of Digital Technologies* (Durham, NC: Duke University Press, 2017), 86–95; Heung-soon Im, *Factory Complex: The Exploitation of Female Laborers in the South Korean Workplace* (video, 2015); Naomi Katz and David Kemnitzner, "Fast Forward: The Internationalization of the Silicon Valley," in *Women, Men, and the International Division of Labor*, ed. June C. Nash and Maria P. Fernandez-Kelly (Albany: SUNY Press, 1984); Kenneth Surin, "Hostage to an Unaccountable Planetary Executive: The Flawed 'Washington Consensus' and Two World Bank Reports," in *World Bank Literature*, ed. Amitava Kumar (Minneapolis: University of Minnesota Press, 2003); World Bank, *The East Asian Miracle: Economic Growth and Public Policy* (Oxford: Oxford University Press, 1993).

41. Marc Levinson, *The Box: How the Shipping Container Made the World Smaller and the World Economy Bigger* (Princeton, NJ: Princeton University Press, 2006), 6.

42. Levinson, *The Box*, 6; Ned Rossiter, *Software, Infrastructure, Labor: A Media Theory of Logistical Nightmares* (New York: Routledge, 2017); Anna Tsing, "Supply Chains and the Human Condition," *Rethinking Marxism* 21, no. 2 (2009).

43. BBC, "The Box," BBC, http://news.bbc.co.uk/2/hi/in_depth/business/2008/the_box/default.stm.

44. Lester Donald Earnest, "How the Biggest Military-Industrial-Congressional Fraud of the 20th Century Launched More Frauds and the Internet," https://web.stanford.edu/~learnest/nets; Paul Jay and Lester Donald Earnest, "Cold War Radar System a Trillion Dollar Fraud—Lester Earnest on Rai," https://therealnews.com/stories/cold-war-radar-system-a-trillion-dollar-fraud-lester-ernest-on-rai-1-4.

45. James Bridle, *New Dark Age: Technology and the End of the Future* (London: Verso, 2018), 35; SABRE, "The Sabre Story," https://www.sabre.com/files/Sabre-History.pdf.

46. "Bush Rejects Taliban Offer to Hand Bin Laden Over," *The Guardian*, https://www.theguardian.com/world/2001/oct/14/afghanistan.terrorism5.

47. Arthur Holland Michel, "How Rogue Techies Armed the Predator, Almost Stopped 9/11, and Accidentally Invented Remote War," https://www .wired.com/2015/12/how-rogue-techies-armed-the-predator-almost-stopped -911-and-accidentally-invented-remote-war.

48. BBC, "Trump Revokes Obama Rule on Reporting Drone Strike Deaths," *BBC News*, https://www.bbc.com/news/world-us-canada-47480207.

49. Aiden Warren, "Globalization, Security and Drones," ed. Ali Farazmand, *Global Encyclopedia of Public Administration, Public Policy, and Governance* (Berlin: Springer, 2017), https://link.springer.com/referenceworkentry/ 10.1007%2F978-3-319-31816-5_3195-1.

50. Dan Gettinger, "Drones Operating in Syria and Iraq," *Center for the Study of the Drone* (Bard College, 2016), https://dronecenter.bard.edu/files/2016/12/ Drones-in-Iraq-and-Syria-CSD.pdf.

51. Tom Engelhardt and Nick Turse, *Terminator Planet: The First History of Drone Warfare, 2001–2050* (Lexington, KY: Dispatch Books, 2012); Warren, "Globlization, Security and Drones."

52. Giorgio Agamben, *Stasus: Civil War as a Political Paradigm* (Stanford, CA: Stanford University Press, 2015); Franco "Bifo" Berardi, "The Coming Global Civil War: Is There Any Way Out?," *e-flux* 69 (2016); Grégoire Chamayou, *A Theory of the Drone*, trans. Janet Lloyd (New York: The New Press, 2015).

53. Aiden Warren and Aleksei Hillas, "Lethal Autonomous Robotics: Rethinking the Dehumanization of Warfare," *UCLA Journal of International Law and Foreign Affairs* 22, no. 2 (2018).

CHAPTER 3: WELCOME TO THE MACHINE

1. That's Google's 2013 revenue divided by the number of minutes in a year: $59,830,000,000 ÷ 525,600 = $113,832. This calculation flattens the fluctuations that characterize the flux of their actual revenue generation but can serve as an indication.

2. Danny Sullivan, "Google Still World's Most Popular Search Engine by Far," http://searchengineland.com/google-worlds-most-popular-search-engine-148089; Danny Sullivan, "Google Still Doing at Least 1 Trillion Searches per Year," January 16, 2015, http://searchengineland.com/google-1-trillion-searches-per-year-212940.

3. Sergey Brin et al., "What Can You Do with a Web in Your Pocket?," *Bulletin of the IEEE Computer Society Technical Committee on Data Engineering* (1998); Sergey Brin and Lawrence Page, "The Anatomy of a Large-Scale Hypertextual Web Search Engine," Stanford University, http://infolab.stanford.edu/~backrub/google.html.

4. Nafeez Ahmed, "How the CIA Made Google: Inside the Secret Network behind Mass Surveillance, Endless War, and Skynet—Part 1," https://medium .com/insurge-intelligence/how-the-cia-made-google-e836451a959e; "Why Google Made the NSA: Inside the Secret Network behind Mass Surveillance, Endless War,

and Skynet—Part 2," https://medium.com/insurge-intelligence/how-the-cia-made
-google-e836451a959e.

5. Nick Turse, *The Complex: How the Military Invades Our Everyday Lives*
(London: Faber and Faber, 2008), 16.

6. Brin and Page, "The Anatomy of a Large-Scale Hypertextual Web Search
Engine," 21.

7. Matteo Pasquinelli, "Google's Pagerank Algorithm: A Diagram of Cognitive Capitalism and the Rentier of the Common Intellect," in *Deep Search*, ed.
Konrad Becker and Felix Stalder (Piscataway, NJ: Transaction Publishers, 2009);
Timothy Erik Ström, "Mapping Google Maps: Critiquing an Ideological Vision of
the World" (Western Sydney University, 2018).

8. Vincent Mosco, *To the Cloud: Big Data in a Turbulent World* (Boulder, CO:
Paradigm, 2014).

9. Google, "How Search Works," https://www.google.com/insidesearch/how
searchworks/thestory.

10. Sean Cubitt, *Finite Media: Environmental Implications of Digital Technologies* (Durham, NC: Duke University Press, 2017); Timothy Erik Ström, "Abstraction and Production in Google Maps: The Reorganisation of Subjectivity, Materiality and Labour," *Arena Journal* 47/48 (2017).

11. Anders S. G. Andrae and Thomas Edler, "On Global Electricity Usage of
Communication Technology: Trends to 2030," *Challenges* 6, no. 1 (2015).

12. Sean Cubitt, *Finite Media*; James Bridle, *New Dark Age: Technology and the
End of the Future* (London: Verso, 2018); Vincent Mosco, *To the Cloud*; Timothy
Erik Ström, "The Road Map to Brave New World: Cartography and Capitalism
from Gulf Oil to Google," *Culture Unbound* 9, no. 3 (2018).

13. Anthony L Kimery, "While Fending Off DOJ Subpoena, Google Continues Longstanding Relationship with US Intelligence," *Homeland Security Today*,
January 25, 2006, https://archive.is/skEkN; Tory Newmyer, "Can a Silicon Valley
Insider Save Ohio's Economy?," *Fortune*, http://fortune.com/2012/06/03/can-a
-silicon-valley-insider-save-ohios-economy.

14. Steven Levy, *In the Plex: How Google Thinks, Works, and Shapes Our Lives*
(New York: Simon & Schuster, 2011), 83.

15. Shoshana Zuboff, *The Age of Surveillance Capitalism: The Fight for a Human
Future at the New Frontier of Power* (London: Profile Books, 2019).

16. Graham Charlton, "Do 50% of Adults Really Not Recognise Ads in Search
Results?," April 27, 2016, https://searchenginewatch.com/2016/04/27/do-50-of
-adults-really-not-recognise-ads-in-search-results; Larry Kim, "The War on 'Free'
Clicks: Think Nobody Clicks on Google Ads? Think Again!," *WordStream*, August
19, 2019, http://www.wordstream.com/blog/ws/2012/07/17/google-advertising.

17. Christian Fuchs, *Digital Labour and Karl Marx* (New York: Routledge,
2014); Jakob Rigi and Robert Prey, "Value, Rent, and the Political Economy of
Social Media," *Information Society* 31, no. 5 (2015); Dallas W. Smythe, *Dependency*

Road: Communications, Capitalism, Consciousness, and Canada, ed. Melvin J. Voiget, *Communication and Information Science* (Norwood, NJ: Ablex, 1981), 22–51.

18. Siva Vaidhyanathan, *The Googlization of Everything (And Why We Should Worry)* (Berkeley: University of California Press, 2011), 3.

19. William Burroughs, *Naked Lunch* (London: Flamingo, 1993); Levy, *In the Plex*, 229.

20. Paul Baran and Paul Sweezy, *Monopoly Capital: An Essay on the American Economic and Social Order* (Monthly Review Press, 1966); David Harvey, *Seventeen Contradictions and the End of Capitalism* (London: Profile Books, 2014), 131–45; Robert W. McChesney, *Digital Disconnect: How Capitalism Is Turning the Internet against Democracy* (New York: The New Press, 2013), 36–41.

21. Zuboff, *The Age of Surveillance Capitalism*, 212.

22. Zygmunt Bauman, *Consuming Life* (Cambridge: Polity Press, 2007), 57, empahsis in original.

23. Mosco, *To the Cloud*, 42–43.

24. Sean Cubitt, *Finite Media*, 108; William Davies, *The Happiness Industry: How the Government and Big Business Sold Us Well-Being* (London: Verso, 2015); Raymond Williams, *Culture and Materialism: Selected Essays* (London: Verso, 2005), 170–95.

25. Adam Greenfield, *Radical Technologies: The Design of Everyday Life* (London: Verso, 2017).

26. Nick Couldry and Andreas Hepp, *The Mediated Construction of Reality* (Cambridge: Polity, 2016).

27. Hackernoon, "How Much Time Do People Spend on Their Mobile Phones in 2017?," https://hackernoon.com/how-much-time-do-people-spend-on-their-mobile-phones-in-2017-e5f90a0b10a6; iPass, "Two Thirds of Mobile Professionals Feel Anxious without Wi-Fi, Says Ipass Report," https://www.ipass.com/press-releases/two-thirds-mobile-professionals-feel-anxious-without-wi-fi-says-ipass-report.

28. Ström, "Mapping Google Maps."

29. Ibid.

30. Natasha Dow Schüll, *Addiction by Design: Machine Gambling in Las Vegas* (Princeton, NJ: Princeton University Press, 2014); Zuboff, *The Age of Surveillance Capitalism*, 449–53.

31. Jeffrey H. Kuzenkoff and Scott Titsworth, "The Impact of Mobile Phone Usage on Student Learning," *Communication Education* 62, no. 3 (2013).

32. Adrian F. Ward et al., "Brain Drain: The Mere Presence of One's Own Smartphone Reduces Available Cognitive Capacity," *Journal of the Association for Consumer Research* 2, no. 2 (2017).

33. Nicholas Carr, *The Shallows: How the Internet Is Changing the Way We Think, Read and Remember* (London: Atlantic Books, 2010); Paul Lewis, "'Our Minds Can Be Hijacked': The Tech Insiders Who Fear a Smartphone Dystopia," https://www.theguardian.com/technology/2017/oct/05/smartphone-addiction-silicon

-valley-dystopia; Lynne Malcolm and Muditha Dias, *The Myth of Multitasking* (Podcast: All in the Mind, 2015), https://www.abc.net.au/radionational/programs/allinthemind/the-myth-of-multitasking/6743356; Thomas Metzinger, *The Ego Tunnel: The Science of the Mind and the Myth of the Self* (New York: Basic Books, 2009).

34. Joshua Brustein, "Your Boss Would Like You to Wear a Jawbone Fitness Tracker," https://www.bloomberg.com/news/articles/2014-12-10/jawbone-up-for-groups-a-plan-to-get-employers-to-buy-fitness-bands; Fitbit, "Fitbit for Corporate Wellness," https://www.fitbit.com/content/assets/group-health/FitbitWellness_Info Sheet.pdf.

35. Mac McClelland, "I Was a Warehouse Wage Slave," https://www.mother jones.com/politics/2012/02/mac-mcclelland-free-online-shipping-warehouses -labor; Richard Salame, "The New Taylorism," https://www.jacobinmag.com/2018/ 02/amazon-wristband-surveillance-scientific-management.

36. Liz Sly, "U.S. Soldiers Are Revealing Sensitive and Dangerous Information by Jogging," https://www.washingtonpost.com/world/a-map-showing-the-users -of-fitness-devices-lets-the-world-see-where-us-soldiers-are-and-what-they-are -doing/2018/01/28/86915662-0441-11e8-aa61-f3391373867e_story.html.

37. Raymond Williams, *Communications* (Ringwood, Victoria: Penguin Books, 1966), 17.

38. Astra Taylor, *Democracy May Not Exist, But We'll Miss It When It's Gone* (London: Verso, 2019).

39. Gabrielle Lynch, Justin Willis, and Nic Cheeseman, "Claims about Cambridge Analytica's Role in Africa Should Be Taken with a Pinch of Salt," *The Conversation*, https://theconversation.com/claims-about-cambridge-analyticas-role-in -africa-should-be-taken-with-a-pinch-of-salt-93864; Jane Mayer, "New Evidence Emerges of Steve Bannon and Cambridge Analytica's Role in Brexit," *New Yorker*, https://www.newyorker.com/news/news-desk/new-evidence-emerges-of-steve-ban non-and-cambridge-analyticas-role-in-brexit.

40. Catalist, "About Catalist," https://www.catalist.us/about.

41. Michael Scherer, "Inside the Secret World of the Data Crunchers Who Helped Obama Win," *Time*, November 7, 2012, http://swampland.time .com/2012/11/07/inside-the-secret-world-of-quants-and-data-crunchers-who -helped-obama-win.

42. Garrett M. Graff, "The Polls Are All Wrong. A Startup Called Vivis Is Our Best Hope to Fix Them," https://www.wired.com/2016/06/civis-election-polling -clinton-sanders-trump.

43. Michael Scherer, "Friended: How the Obama Campaign Connected with Young Voters," *Time*, November 20, 2012, http://swampland.time.com/2012/11/20/ friended-how-the-obama-campaign-connected-with-young-voters.

44. Jane Mayer, "The Reclusive Hedge-Fund Tycoon behind the Trump Presidency," *New Yorker*, https://www.newyorker.com/magazine/2017/03/27/the -reclusive-hedge-fund-tycoon-behind-the-trump-presidency; TRNN, "The Bizarre

Billionaire That Backed Bannon and Made Trump President," *The Real News Network*, November 2, 2017, https://therealnews.com/stories/the-bizarre-billionaire-that-backed-bannon-and-made-trump-president.

45. Amina Elahi, "Civis Analytics Lands $22 Million to Expand Data-Powered Problem Solving," *Chicago Tribune*, November 30, 2016, https://www.chicagotribune.com/business/blue-sky/ct-civis-analytics-funding-22-million-bsi-20161130-story.html.

46. Civis, "Our Mission," https://www.civisanalytics.com/mission.

47. FEC, "Civis Analytics, 2015–2016," Federal Election Comission, https://www.fec.gov/data/disbursements/?data_type=processed&recipient_name=civis+analytics&two_year_transaction_period=2016&min_date=01%2F01%2F2015&max_date=12%2F31%2F2016; "Cambridge Analytica, 2015–2016," https://www.fec.gov/data/disbursements/?data_type=processed&committee_id=C00580100&recipient_name=cambridge+analytica&two_year_transaction_period=2016&min_date=01%2F01%2F2015&max_date=12%2F31%2F2016.

48. Google, "Ten Things We Know to Be True," https://www.google.com/about/philosophy.html.

49. Schmidt's quotes were taken from *HuffPostTech*, "Google CEO on Privacy (Video): 'If You Have Something You Don't Want Anyone to Know, Maybe You Shouldn't Be Doing It,'" http://www.huffingtonpost.com/2009/12/07/google-ceo-on-privacy-if_n_383105.html; Holman Jenkins, "Google and the Search for the Future," *Wall Street Journal*, http://online.wsj.com/news/articles/SB10001424052748704901104575423294099527212; Derek Thompson, "Google's CEO: 'The Laws Are Written by Lobbyists,'" http://www.theatlantic.com/technology/archive/2010/10/googles-ceo-the-laws-are-written-by-lobbyists/63908.

50. Perhaps the best guide to the Snowden leaks and their implications is David Lyon, *Surveillance after Snowden* (London: Polity, 2015). For a "firsthand" account, see Glen Greenwald, *No Place to Hide: Edward Snowden, the NSA and the Surveillance State* (London: Hamish Hamilton, 2014) and Laura Poitras's Academy Award–winning documentary, *Citizenfour* (2015).

51. James Bridle, *New Dark Age*, 161–86; Lyon, *Surveillance after Snowden*.

52. Stephanie DeVos, "The Google-NSA Alliance: Developing Cybersecurity Policy at Internet Speed," *Fordham Intellectual Property, Media and Entertainment Law Journal* 21, no. 1 (2011).

53. Jeff Bercovici, "At Ted, Google's Larry Page Says NSA Spying Threatens Democracy," https://www.forbes.com/sites/jeffbercovici/2014/03/19/at-ted-googles-larry-page-says-nsa-spying-threatens-democracy; David Dayen, "The Android Administration," https://theintercept.com/2016/04/22/googles-remarkably-close-relationship-with-the-obama-white-house-in-two-charts.

54. Jason Leopold, "Exclusive: Emails Reveal Close Google Relationship with NSA," http://america.aljazeera.com/articles/2014/5/6/nsa-chief-google.html; Robert Scheer, *They Know Everything about You: How Data-Collecting Corpora-*

tions and Snooping Government Agencies Are Destroying Democracy (New York: Nation Books, 2015).

55. Benjamin H. Bratton, "The Black Stack," *e-flux* 53 (2014).

56. Vint Cerf, "Sop Workshop 160: Global Trends to Watch: The Erosion of Privacy and Anonymity and the Need of Transparency of Government Access Requests," http://paranoia.dubfire.net/2011/11/two-honest-google-employees -our.html; Christopher Soghoian, "Two Honest Google Employees: Our Products Don't Protect Your Privacy," http://paranoia.dubfire.net/2011/11/two-honest -google-employees-our.html.

57. Jessica E. Vascellaro, "Google Agonizes on Privacy as Ad World Vaults Ahead," *Wall Street Journal*, http://online.wsj.com/articles/SB10001424052748703 309704575413553851854026.

58. Levy, *In the Plex*, 45.

59. Brin and Page, "The Anatomy of a Large-Scale Hypertextual Web Search Engine."

60. Levy, *In the Plex*, 94; Eric Schmidt and Jonathan Rosenberg, *How Google Works* (London: John Murry, 2014), 80–81.

61. Lewis, "'Our Minds Can Be Hijacked.'"

CHAPTER 4: THE OVERLORDS OF AUTOMATED DEBT

1. Henry C. Darby, *Domesday England* (Cambridge: Cambridge University Press, 1977); OpenDomesDay.org, https://opendomesday.org/place/TL4933/ wicken-bonhunt.

2. China State Council, "State Council General Office Some Opinions Concerning the Construction of a Social Credit System," China Copyright and Media, https://chinacopyrightandmedia.wordpress.com/2007/03/23/state-council-general -office-some-opinions-concerning-the-construction-of-a-social-credit-system.

3. "Planning Outline for the Construction for a Social Credit System (2014– 2020)," China Copyright and Media, https://chinacopyrightandmedia.wordpress .com/2014/06/14/planning-outline-for-the-construction-of-a-social-credit-sys tem-2014-2020.

4. Ibid.

5. David Harvey, *Abstract from the Concrete* (Cambridge, MA: Sternberg Press, 2017).

6. David Barboza, "In Chinese Factories, Lost Fingers and Low Pay," *New York Times*, https://www.nytimes.com/2008/01/05/business/worldbusiness/05sweatshop .html.

7. Lixin Fan, "Last Train Home" (Canada: Zeitgeist Films, 2009); Jia Zhangke, "24 City" (China: MK2 Diffusion, 2008).

8. Min Jiang and King-Wa Fu, "Chinese Social Media and Big Data: Big Data, Big Brother, Big Profit?," *Policy & Internet* 10, no. 4 (2018); Aofei Lv and Ting Lou,

"Authoritarian Practices in the Digital Age Asymmetrical Power between Internet Giants and Users in China," *International Journal of Communication* 12 (2018): 3877–3895; Samantha Hoffman, "Programming China: The Communist Party's Autonomic Approach to Managing State Security," *Merics China Monitor* 44 (2017).

9. David Graeber, *Debt: The First 5,000 Years* (New York: Melville House, 2012); Maurizio Lazzarato, *The Making of the Indebted Man* (Cambridge: Semiotext(e), 2012).

10. Max Weber, "Politics as Vocation," in *From Max Weber: Essays in Sociology*, ed. H. H. Gerth and C. Wright Mills (New York: Oxford University Press, 1946); original italics.

11. Graeber, *Debt*, 391.

12. Matthew Desmond, *Evicted: Poverty and Profit in the American City* (New York: Crown, 2016); David Graeber, *The Utopia of Rules: On Technology, Stupidity, and the Secret Joys of Bureaucracy* (Brooklyn: Melville House, 2015).

13. Aristotle, "Politics," MIT, http://classics.mit.edu/Aristotle/politics.1.one.html; *Ezekiel*, 18:10–13; Joshua Vincent, "Historical, Religious and Scholastic Prohibition of Usury: The Common Origins of Western and Islamic Financial Practices," Seton Hall University, https://scholarship.shu.edu/cgi/viewcontent.cgi?referer=https://www.google.com/&httpsredir=1&article=1600&context=student_scholarship.

14. Graeber, *Debt*.

15. Giovanni Arrighi, *Adam Smith in Beijing: Lineages of the Twenty-First Century* (London: Verso, 2007); Cheng Hao, "The Death and Revival of Usury in China: An Institutional Analysis," *Journal of Economic Issues* 52, no. 2 (2018).

16. Federal Reserve, "Consumer Credit," https://www.federalreserve.gov/releases/g19/HIST/cc_hist_mt_levels.html.

17. Federal Reserve, "Mortgage Debt Outstanding," https://www.federalreserve.gov/data/mortoutstand/current.htm.

18. Robert Armstrong, "US Credit Card Interest Rates Hit 25-Year High," *Financial Times*, https://www.ft.com/content/47fa19fe-b56e-11e9-bec9-fdcab53d6959.

19. Cédric Durand, *Fictitious Capital: How Finance Is Appropriating Our Future*, trans. David Broder (London: Verso, 2017); Lorie Kornish, "Consumer Debt Is Set to Reach $4 Trillion by the End of 2018," CNBC, https://www.cnbc.com/2018/05/21/consumer-debt-is-set-to-reach-4-trillion-by-the-end-of-2018.html; Richard Wilkinson and Kate Pickett, *The Spirit Level: Why More Equal Societies Almost Always Do Better* (London: Allen Lane, 2009); Jackie Wang, *Carceral Capitalism* (South Pasadena, CA: Semiotext(e), 2018).

20. Rob Aitken, "'All Data Is Credit Data': Constituting the Unbanked," *Competition & Change* 21, no. 4 (2017); James C. Scott, *Seeing Like a State: How Certain Schemes to Improve the Human Condition Have Failed* (New Haven, CT: Yale University Press, 1998).

21. Christian Parenti, *The Soft Cage: Surveillance in America from Slavery to the War on Terror* (New York: Basic Books, 2003), 91–99.

22. U.S. Securities and Exchange Commission, 2018, https://www.sec.gov/Article/whatwedo.html.

23. LenddoEFL, "Unleashing Global Economic Potential with Alternative Data," https://include1billion.com; Bailey Klinger, "The Test of Entrepreneurship: Revolutionizing SME Finance," The Organization of American States, https://www.oas.org/en/sedi/desd/IIDialogo/presentations/Bailey_Klinger.pdf.

24. "Psychometrics: Tests of Character," *Economist*, https://www.economist.com/finance-and-economics/2016/09/29/tests-of-character.

25. Privacy International, "Fintech's Dirty Little Secret? Lenddo, Facebook and the Challenge of Identity," October 23, 2018, https://privacyinternational.org/long-read/2323/fintechs-dirty-little-secret-lenddo-facebook-and-challenge-identity.

26. Patrick Collinson and Rupert Jones, "Wonga Collapses into Administration," *The Guardian*, https://www.theguardian.com/business/2018/aug/30/wonga-collapses-into-administration; Tim Lewis, "With Wonga, Your Prosperity Could Count on an Algorithm," *The Guardian*, https://www.theguardian.com/money/2011/oct/16/wonga-algorithm-lending-debt-data.

27. Milford Bateman, *Why Doesn't Microfinance Work? The Destructive Rise of Local Neoliberalism* (London: Zed Books, 2010); Naomi Klein, *The Shock Doctrine: The Rise of Disaster Capitalism* (London: Penguin, 2007).

28. Susan George, *A Fate Worse Than Debt: A Radical New Analysis of the Third World Debt Crisis* (London: Penguin, 1990); IMF, "Annual Report: Economic Surveillance," https://www.imf.org/external/pubs/ft/ar/2017/eng/economic-surveillance.htm.

29. Kate Bedford, *Developing Partnerships: Gender, Sexuality and the Reformed World Bank* (Minneapolis: University of Minnesota Press, 2009); Robin G. Isserles, "Microcredit: The Rhetoric of Empowerment, the Reality of 'Development as Usual,'" *Women's Studies Quarterly* 31, no. 3/4 (2003); Supriya Singh, *Globalization and Money: A Global South Perspective* (Lanham, MD: Rowman & Littlefield, 2013).

30. Kevin P. Donovan and Emma Park, "Perpetual Debt in the Silicon Savannah," *Boston Review*, https://bostonreview.net/class-inequality-global-justice/kevin-p-donovan-emma-park-perpetual-debt-silicon-savannah.

31. C. K. Prahalad and Stuart L. Hart, "The Fortune at the Bottom of the Pyramid," *Strategy + Business* 26 (2002).

32. iResearch, "China's Third-Party Mobile Payment Report" (Beijing: iResearch, 2017).

33. Giovanni Arrighi, *The Long Twentieth Century: Money, Power and the Origin of Our Times* (London: Verso, 2010); Fernand Braudel, *Civilization and Capitalism, 15th–18th Century: The Perspective of the World* (Oakland: University of California Press, 1992).

34. Zygmunt Bauman, *Consuming Life* (Cambridge: Polity Press, 2007).

35. Brett Scott, "In Praise of Cash," *Aeon*, https://aeon.co/essays/if-plastic-replaces-cash-much-that-is-good-will-be-lost.

36. Priya Raghubir and Joydeep Srivastava, "Monopoly Money: The Effect of Payment Coupling and Form on Spending Behavior," *Journal of Experimental Psychology* 14, no. 3 (2008), https://www.apa.org/pubs/journals/releases/xap143213.pdf.

37. Amanda Lee, "Alipay Rolls Out World's First 'Smile to Pay' Facial Recognition System at KFC Outlet in Hangzhou," *South China Morning Post*, September 1, 2017, https://www.scmp.com/tech/start-ups/article/2109321/alipay-rolls-out-worlds-first-smile-pay-facial-recognition-system-kfc.

38. Li Tao, "You Will Soon Be Able to Pay Your Subway Fare with Your Face in China," *South China Morning Post*, March 13, 2019, https://www.scmp.com/tech/innovation/article/3001306/you-can-soon-pay-your-subway-ride-scanning-your-face-china.

39. Christophe Jalil Nordman and Isabelle Guérin, "The Shock of Indian Demonetisation: A Failed Attempt to Formalise the Economy," *The Conversation*, April 3, 2018, https://theconversation.com/the-shock-of-indian-demonetisation-a-failed-attempt-to-formalise-the-economy-93328.

40. Rachel Siewert, "Ten Years of Intervention," *Arena Magazine*, no. 148 (June 2017); Nicolas Rothwell, "Colonial Turbulence in the North," *Arena Magazine*, no. 148 (June 2017), 11–17. Issue 148 of *Arena Magazine* was dedicated to exploring the intervention and is full of important articles on the topic.

41. AUWU, "It's Time! Raise Newstart!," Australian Unemployed Workers' Union, https://unemployedworkersunion.com/raise-newstart-now; DSS, "Cashless Debit Card," Department of Social Services, Australian Government, https://www.dss.gov.au/families-and-children/programmes-services/welfare-conditionality/cashless-debit-card-overview; John Gilliom, *Overseers of the Poor: Surveillance, Resistance, and the Limits of Privacy* (Chicago: The University of Chicago Press, 2001); Vinnies.org.au, "What's Wrong with the Cashless Debit Card?," St Vincent de Paul Society, https://www.vinnies.org.au/page/Publications/National/Factsheets_and_policy_briefings/What_s_wrong_with_the_cashless_welfare_card.

42. Aitken, "'All Data Is Credit Data.'"

43. BTCA, "Better Than Cash Alliance," https://www.betterthancash.org.

44. Singh, *Globalization and Money*.

45. Paul James, *Globalism, Nationalism, Tribalism: Bringing Theory Back In* (London: Sage, 2006), 133–57.

46. Rachel Botsman, "Big Data Meets Big Brother as China Moves to Rate Its Citizens," https://www.wired.co.uk/article/chinese-government-social-credit-score-privacy-invasion; Matthew Carney, "Leave No Dark Corner," Australian Broadcasting Corporation, New York: Infobase, 2018.

47. Naoyoshi Shiotani, "Psycho-Pass" (Fuji TV [Noitamina], 2012); Joe Wright, "Nosedive," in *Black Mirror* (Endemol Shine, UK, 2016).

48. Tara Francis Chan, "China's Social Credit System Has Blocked People from Taking 11 Million Flights and 4 Million Train Trips," *Business Insider*, https://www.businessinsider.com.au/china-social-credit-system-blocked-people-taking-flights-train-trips-2018-5; Liu Xuanzun, "Social Credit System Must Bankrupt Discredited People," *Global Times*, http://www.globaltimes.cn/content/1103262.shtml.

49. Wang, *Carceral Capitalism*.

50. Cathy O'Neil, *Weapons of Math Destruction: How Big Data Increases Inequality and Threatens Democracy* (New York: Crown, 2016).

51. Celia Hatton, "China 'Social Credit': Beijing Sets up Huge System," *BBC News*, https://www.bbc.com/news/world-asia-china-34592186.

52. John Tagg, *The Burden of Representation: Essays on Photographies and Histories* (Basingstoke, UK: Macmillan Education, 1988), 64.

53. Simon Denyer, "China's Watchful Eye," *Washington Post*, January 7, 2018, https://www.washingtonpost.com/news/world/wp/2018/01/07/feature/in-china-facial-recognition-is-sharp-end-of-a-drive-for-total-surveillance.

54. David Bandurski, "Cashing in on Dystopia," SupChina, January 3, 2017, https://supchina.com/2017/01/03/cashing-in-on-dystopia.

55. Peter Rogers, "Is China's Social Credit System Coming to Australia?," *The Conversation*, May 28, 2019, https://theconversation.com/is-chinas-social-credit-system-coming-to-australia-117095; Manfred B. Steger and Paul James, *Globalization Matters: Engaging the Global in Unsettled Times* (Cambridge: Cambridge University Press, 2019), 209–29.

56. Leanne Roderick, "Discipline and Power in the Digital Age: The Case of the US Consumer Data Broker Industry," *Critical Sociology* 40, no. 5 (2014).

57. Steven Melendez, "A Landmark Vermont Law Nudges over 120 Data Brokers Out of the Shadows," *Fast Company*, March 2, 2019, https://www.fastcompany.com/90302036/over-120-data-brokers-inch-out-of-the-shadows-under-landmark-vermont-law.

58. Christl Wolfie, "Corporate Surveillance in Everyday Life" (Vienna, Austria: Cracked Labs, 2017).

59. Ibid., 13.

60. Lucas D. Introna and David Wood, "Picturing Algorithmic Surveillance: The Politics of Facial Recognition Systems," *Surveillance & Society* 2, no. 2/3 (2004); Julie Bort, "Amazon Adds Fear Detection and Age Ranges to Its Facial-Recognition Tech as the Border Patrol Looks to Award a $950 Million Contract," *Business Insider*, August 14, 2019, https://www.businessinsider.com.au/amazon-fear-detection-age-ranges-added-facial-recognition-rekognition-tech-2019-8; Jeremy W. Crampton, "Platform Biometrics," *Surveillance & Society* 17, no. 1/2 (2019).

61. Tagg, *The Burden of Representation*, 76.

62. Stephen Jay Gould, *The Mismeasure of Man* (New York: W. W. Norton, 1996); Tagg, *The Burden of Representation*; Xiaolin Wu and Xi Zhang, "Automated Inference on Criminality Using Face Image + Responses to Critiques on Machine

Learning of Criminality Perceptions," arXiv.org, May 26, 2017, https://arxiv.org/pdf/1611.04135.pdf.

63. CDT, "White Paper Outlines Potential Uses of AI," *China Digital Times*, November 19, 2018, https://chinadigitaltimes.net/2018/11/white-paper-outlines -potential-uses-of-artificial-intelligence.

64. Philip K. Dick, "The Minority Report," in *Minority Report* (London: Gollancz, 2002); Steven Spielberg, *Minority Report* (DreamWorks Pictures, 2002).

65. Caroline Haskins, "Dozens of Cities Have Secretly Experimented with Predictive Policing Software," *Vice*; O'Neil, *Weapons of Math Destruction*, 84–104; Christian Parenti, *Lockdown America: Police and Prisons in the Age of Crisis* (London: Verso, 2008); Wang, *Carceral Capitalism*, 228–59; Aleš Završnik, ed. *Big Data, Crime and Social Control* (Abingdon, UK: Routledge, 2018).

66. Paul Mozur, "One Month, 500,000 Face Scans: How China Is Using A.I. to Profile a Minority," *New York Times*, April 14, 2019, https://www.nytimes .com/2019/04/14/technology/china-surveillance-artificial-intelligence-racial-pro filing.html; Wang, *Carceral Capitalism*.

67. Kim Lane Scheppele, "From a War on Terrorism to Global Security Law," 2013, https://www.ias.edu/ideas/2013/scheppele-terrorism.

68. Xi, cited in Austin Ramzy and Chris Buckley, "The Xinjiang Papers: 'Absolutely No Mercy': Leaked Files Expose How China Organized Mass Detentions of Muslims." *New York Times*, November, 16, 2019, https://www.nytimes.com/interactive/2019/11/16/world/asia/china-xinjiang-documents.html.

69. Ramzy and Buckley, "The Xinjiang Papers."

70. Chris Buckley, "China Is Detaining Muslims in Vast Numbers. The Goal: 'Transformation,'" *New York Times*, September 8, 2018, https://www.nytimes .com/2018/09/08/world/asia/china-uighur-muslim-detention-camp.html; David Palumbo-Liu, "The Ongoing Persecution of China's Uyghurs," *Jacobin*, June 1, 2019, https://jacobinmag.com/2019/06/china-uyghur-persecution-concentra tion-camps; Bernhard Zand, "A Surveillance State Unlike Any the World Has Ever Seen," *Der Spiegel*, July 26, 2018, https://www.spiegel.de/international/ world/china-s-xinjiang-province-a-surveillance-state-unlike-any-the-world-has -ever-seen-a-1220174.html.

71. William A. Cook, ed., *The Plight of the Palestinians: A Long History of Destruction* (New York: Palgrave Macmillan, 2010); Saree Makdisi, *Palestine Inside Out: An Everyday Occupation* (New York: W. W. Norton, 2008); Vijay Prashad, ed., *Letters to Palestine: Writers Respond to War and Occupation* (London: Verso, 2015); Edward W. Said, *The Question of Palestine* (New York: Vintage Books, 1992); Eyal Weizman, *Hollow Land: Israel's Architecture of Occupation* (London: Verso, 2017).

72. Giorgio Agamben, *Means without End*, trans. Cesare Casarino and Vincenzo Binetti (Minneapolis: University of Minnesota Press, 2000).

73. "Creating a Digital Totalitarian State: China's Social-Credit System," *Economist* 421, no. 9020 (2016).

74. Fredric Jamerson, "Postmodernism and the Market," *Socialist Register* (1990): 106; Karl Marx, *Capital: A Critique of Political Economy*, trans. Ben Fowkes, 3 vols., vol. 1 (Westminster, UK: Penguin Classics, 1976).

CONCLUSION

1. Lewis Mumford, *The Myth of the Machine: The Pentagon of Power* (New York: Harcourt Brace Jovanovich, 1970), 274–75.

2. Franco "Bifo" Berardi, *The Soul at Work: From Alienation to Autonomy*, trans. Francesca Cadel and Mecchia Giuseppina (New York: Semiotext(e), 2009); Shoshana Zuboff, *The Age of Surveillance Capitalism: The Fight for a Human Future at the New Frontier of Power* (London: Profile Books, 2019).

3. William Burroughs, "The Limits of Control," *Semiotext(e)* III, no. 1 (1978): 41.

4. China State Council, "Opinions Concerning Accelerating the Construction of Credit Supervision, Warning and Punishment Mechanisms for Persons Subject to Enforcement for Trust-Breaking," China Copyright and Media, September 25, 2016, https://chinacopyrightandmedia.wordpress.com/2016/09/25/opinions-con cerning-accelerating-the-construction-of-credit-supervision-warning-and-punish ment-mechanisms-for-persons-subject-to-enforcement-for-trust-breaking.

5. Google, "Ten Things We Know to Be True," https://www.google.com/about/ philosophy.html.

6. Jonathan Rosenberg, "The Meaning of Open," Google Official Blog, December 21, 2009, http://googleblog.blogspot.com.au/2009/12/meaning-of-open.html; Eric Schmidt and Jonathan Rosenberg, *How Google Works* (London: John Murry, 2014).

7. Clifford Geertz, *The Interpretation of Cultures: Selected Essays* (New York: Basic Books, 1973).

8. David Graeber, *The Utopia of Rules: On Technology, Stupidity, and the Secret Joys of Bureaucracy* (Brooklyn: Melville House, 2015).

9. Nick Couldry and Andreas Hepp, *The Mediated Construction of Reality* (Cambridge: Polity, 2016); Byung-Chul Han, *Psychopolitics: Neoliberalism and New Technologies of Power* (London: Verso, 2017); Vincent Mosco, *To the Cloud: Big Data in a Turbulent World* (Boulder, CO: Paradigm, 2014); Timothy Erik Ström, "Mapping Google Maps: Critiquing an Ideological Vision of the World" (thesis, Western Sydney University, 2018).

10. Norbert Wiener, *Cybernetics: Or Control and Communication in the Animal and the Machine* (New York: Technology Press, 1948).

11. John Hinkson, "Trump and the Fascist Prospect," *Arena Journal* 47/48 (2017); John Hinkson et al., eds., *Cold War to Hot Planet: Fifty Years of Arena* (Melbourne: Arena Publications, 2016); Paul James, *Globalism, Nationalism, Tribalism: Bringing Theory Back In* (London: Sage, 2006).

12. Mike Davis and Daniel Bertrand Monk, eds., *Evil Paradises: Dreamworlds of Neoliberalism* (New York: The New Press, 2007); David Harvey, *Seventeen Contradictions and the End of Capitalism* (London: Profile Books, 2014); Paul James, *Urban Sustainability in Theory and Practice: Circles of Sustainability* (London: Routledge, 2015); Jan Nederveen Pieterse, *Globalization and Culture: Global Mélange*, ed. Manfred Steger and Terrell Carver, Globalization (Lanham, MD: Rowman & Littlefield, 2009).

13. Yingnan Joseph Zhou and Shuai Jin, "Inequality and Political Trust in China: The Social Volcano Thesis Re-Examined," *China Quarterly* 236 (2018).

14. Simon Cooper, *Technoculture and Critical Theory: In the Service of the Machine?* (London: Routledge, 2002); James, *Globalism, Nationalism, Tribalism*; Langdon Winner, *The Whale and the Reactor: A Search for Limits in an Age of High Technology* (Chicago: University of Chicago Press, 1986).

15. Joel Bakan, *The Corporation: The Pathological Pursuit of Profit and Power* (New York: Free Press, 2005); Fernand Braudel, *Civilization and Capitalism, 15th–18th Century: The Perspective of the World* (Oakland: University of California Press, 1992); Karl Marx and Friedrich Engels, *The Communist Manifesto* (New York: Signet Classic, 2011).

16. Richard Wolff, "Democracy at Work: A Cure for Capitalism" (Chicago: Haymarket, 2012).

17. Karl Marx, *Capital: A Critique of Political Economy*, trans. Ben Fowkes, 3 vols., vol. 1 (Westminster, UK: Penguin Classics, 1976).

18. Milton Friedman, *Capitalism and Freedom* (Chicago: University of Chicago Press, 2002), 133.

19. Michael C. Jensen and William H. Meckling, "Theory of the Firm: Managerial Behavior, Agency Costs and Ownership Structure," *Journal of Financial Economics* 3, no. 4 (1976); Geoff Sharp, "Constitutive Abstraction and Social Practice," *Arena* 70 (1985); Alberto Toscano, "The Open Secret of Real Abstraction," *Rethinking Marxism* 20, no. 2 (2008).

20. Sean Cubitt, *Finite Media: Environmental Implications of Digital Technologies* (Durham, NC: Duke University Press, 2017), 34; Mumford, "The Myth of the Machine."

21. Berardi, *The Soul at Work*; Pierre Bourdieu, "The Essence of Neoliberalism" (December 1998), http://mondediplo.com/1998/12/08bourdieu; Noam Chomsky, *Profit over People: Neoliberalism and Global Order* (New York: Seven Stories Press, 1999); David Harvey, *A Brief History of Neoliberalism* (Oxford: Oxford University Press, 2005); Manfred B. Steger and Ravi K. Roy, *Neoliberalism: A Very Short Introduction* (Oxford: Oxford University Press, 2010).

22. J. P. Donlon, "GE CEO Jeff Immelt on the Future of GE and of American Manufacturing," *Chief Executive*, March 10, 2014, https://chiefexecutive.net/ge-ceo-jeff-immelt-on-the-future-of-ge-and-of-american-manufacturing.

23. Heidi Chung, "The Richest 1% Own 50% of Stocks Held by American Households," *Yahoo Finance*, January 17, 2019, https://au.finance.yahoo.com/news/the-richest-1-own-50-of-stocks-held-by-american-households-150758595.html.

24. Harvey, *Seventeen Contradictions and the End of Capitalism.*

25. Peter Phillips, *Giants: The Global Power Elite* (New York: Seven Stories Press, 2018); Stefania Vitali, James B. Glattfelder, and Stefano Battiston, "The Network of Global Corporate Control," *PLoS ONE* 6, no. 10 (2011).

26. Cubitt, *Finite Media.*

27. Sophie Hares, "The Cost of Clean Water: $150 Billion a Year, Says World Bank," Reuters, August 28, 2017, https://www.reuters.com/article/us-global-water-health/the-cost-of-clean-water-150-billion-a-year-says-world-bank-idUSKCN 1B812E; WHO, "Waterborne Disease Related to Unsafe Water and Sanitation" World Health Organization, https://www.who.int/sustainable-development/housing/health-risks/waterborne-disease/en.

28. Phillips, *Giants.*

29. Cédric Durand, *Fictitious Capital: How Finance Is Appropriating Our Future*, trans. David Broder (London: Verso, 2017).

30. Nasdaq, "Amazon.com, Inc. Ownership Summary," https://www.nasdaq .com/symbol/amzn/ownership-summary.

31. Julie Bort, "Amazon's Warehouse-Worker Tracking System Can Automatically Fire People without a Human Supervisor's Involvement," *Business Insider*, April 26, 2019, https://www.businessinsider.com.au/amazon-system-automatically-fires-warehouse-workers-time-off-task-2019-4.

32. Steven Pinker, *Enlightenment Now: The Case for Reason, Science, Humanism, and Progress* (New York: Viking, 2018).

33. Theodor Adorno and Max Horkheimer, *Dialectic of Enlightenment* (London: Verso, 1979); Zygmunt Bauman, *Liquid Modernity* (Cambridge: Polity Press, 2000); Jason Hinkel, "An Open Letter to Steven Pinker (and Bill Gates, for That Matter) about Global Poverty," *Climate & Capitalism*, February 4, 2019, https://climateandcapitalism.com/2019/02/04/letter-to-steven-pinker-about-global-poverty; Karl Polanyi, *The Great Transformation: The Political and Economic Origins of Our Time* (Boston: Beacon Press, 2001).

34. Franco "Bifo" Berardi, *And: Phenomenology of the End: Sensibility and Connective Mutation* (Los Angeles: Semiotext(e), 2015); Naomi Klein, *This Changes Everything: Capitalism vs. the Climate* (London: Allen Lane, 2014); Robert W. McChesney, *Digital Disconnect: How Capitalism Is Turning the Internet against Democracy* (New York: The New Press, 2013); Jason W. Moore, *Capitalism in the Web of Life: Ecology and the Accumulation of Capital* (London: Verso, 2015); Christian Parenti, *The Tropic of Chaos: Climate Change and New Geography of Violence* (New York: Nation Books, 2011); Richard Wolff, *Capitalism's Crisis Deepens: Essays on the Global Economic Meltdown* (Chicago: Haymarket, 2016).

35. Marx, *Capital*, 1, 381.

36. Timothy Erik Ström, "Twenty Years of Google: Abstract and Control," *Arena Magazine* (October-November 2018), no. 156.

37. Olivia Carville, "The Super Rich of Silicon Valley Have a Doomsday Escape Plan," *Bloomberg*, September 5, 2018, https://www.bloomberg.com/features/2018 -rich-new-zealand-doomsday-preppers; Melinda Hinkson, "In Humanity's Wake," *Arena Journal* 51/52 (2018); Evan Osnos, "Doomsday Prep for the Super-Rich," *New Yorker*, January 30, 2017, https://www.newyorker.com/magazine/2017/01/30/ doomsday-prep-for-the-super-rich; Douglas Rushkoff, "Survival of the Richest," OneZero, July 5, 2018, https://medium.com/s/futurehuman/survival-of-the-richest -9ef6cddd0cc1; Ström, "Twenty Years of Google."

38. Erich Fromm, *The Fear of Freedom* (London: Routledge & Kegan Paul, 1960).

39. David Lyon, "Surveillance Culture: Engagement, Exposure, and Ethics in Digital Modernity," *International Journal of Communication* 11 (2017).

40. Han, *Psychopolitics*, 61.

41. Zygmunt Bauman, *Consuming Life* (Cambridge: Polity Press, 2007), 31.

42. Cubitt, *Finite Media*, 108.

43. FSM, "About the World Social Forum," World Social Forum, https:// fsm2016.org/en/sinformer/a-propos-du-forum-social-mondial; Manfred B. Steger, James Goodman, and Erin K. Wilson, *Justice Globalism: Ideology, Crisis, Policy* (London: Sage, 2013).

44. Ellen Meiksins Wood, *Democracy against Capitalism: Renewing Historical Materialism* (Cambridge: Cambridge University Press, 1995).

45. Michael Albert, *Parecon: Life after Capitalism* (London: Verso, 2003); Robin Hahnel, *Of the People, by the People: The Case for a Participatory Economy* (London: Soap Box, 2012); Wolff, "Democracy at Work"; Wolff, *Capitalism's Crisis Deepens: Essays on the Global Economic Meltdown*.

46. Mark Boothroyd, "Self Organisation in the Syrian Revolution," *The Project: A Socialist Journal*, August 14, 2016, http://www.socialistproject.org/issues/ august-2016/self-organisation-syrian-revolution; Chomsky, *Profit over People*; John Curl, *For All the People: Uncovering the Hidden History of Cooperation, Cooperative Movements, and Communalism in America* (Oakland, CA: PM Press, 2009); Avi Lewis and Naomi Klein, "The Take" (Canada: First Run Features/Icarus Films, 2004); Arundhati Roy, *Capitalism: A Ghost Story* (London: Verso, 2015).

47. David Graeber, *Debt: The First 5,000 Years* (New York: Melville House, 2012), 8.

48. Berardi, *The Soul at Work*; Franco "Bifo" Berardi, *The Uprising: On Poetry and Finance* (New York: Semiotext(e) Intervention, 2012); Murray Bookchin, *The Ecology of Freedom: The Emergence and Dissolution of Hierarchy*, 4th ed. (AK Press, UK, 2004); Noam Chomksy, "Destroying the Commons: How the Magna Carta

Became a Minor Carta," TomDispatch.com, July 22, 2012, http://www.tomdispatch .com/post/175571/tomgram%3A_noam_chomsky%2C_the_great_charter%2C_its _fate%2C_and_ours/#more; Silvia Federici, *Re-Enchanting the World: Feminism and the Politics of the Commons* (Oakland, CA: PM Press, 2019); Vandana Shiva, *Earth Democracy: Justice, Sustainability, and Peace*, 2nd ed. (London: Zed Books, 2016); Bhaskar Sunkara, *The Socialist Manifesto: The Case for Radical Politics in an Era of Extreme Inequality* (London: Verso, 2019); Ted Trainer, "An Anarchism for Today: The Simpler Way," *Capitalism Nature Socialism* (2018); Raymond Williams, *The Long Revolution* (Ringwood, Victoria: Pelican Books, 1971).

BIBLIOGRAPHY

ABC. "Joint Dedication to Build a Beautiful China: 2018 Annual Report." Agricultural Bank of China. http://www.abchina.com/en/investor-relations/perfor mance-reports/annual-reports/201903/P020190329665642073693.pdf.

Adorno, Theodor, and Max Horkheimer. *Dialectic of Enlightenment*. London: Verso, 1979 [1944].

Agamben, Giorgio. *Means without End*. Translated by Cesare Casarino and Vincenzo Binetti. Minneapolis: University of Minnesota Press, 2000.

———. *Stasus: Civil War as a Political Paradigm*. Stanford, CA: Stanford University Press, 2015.

Ahmed, Nafeez. "How the CIA Made Google: Inside the Secret Network behind Mass Surveillance, Endless War, and Skynet—Part 1." https://medium.com/ insurge-intelligence/how-the-cia-made-google-e836451a959e.

———. "Why Google Made the NSA: Inside the Secret Network Behind Mass Surveillance, Endless War, and Skynet—Part 2." https://medium.com/insurge -intelligence/how-the-cia-made-google-e836451a959e.

Aitken, Rob. "'All Data Is Credit Data': Constituting the Unbanked." *Competition & Change* 21, no. 4 (2017): 274–300.

Albert, Michael. *Parecon: Life after Capitalism*. London: Verso, 2003.

Amadae, S. M. *Rationalizing Capitalist Democracy: The Cold War Origins of Rational Choice Theory*. Chicago: University of Chicago Press, 2003.

Anderson, Benedict. *Imagined Communities: Reflections on the Origin and Spread of Nationalism*. Revised ed. London: Verso Books, 2006.

Anderson, Matthew S. "Samuel Bentham in Russia." *American Slavic and East European Review* 15 (1956).

Andrae, Anders S. G., and Thomas Edler. "On Global Electricity Usage of Communication Technology: Trends to 2030," *Challengers* 6 (2015).

Anonymous. "Security Culture: A Comprehensive Guide for Activists in Australia." Inventati.org, 2013. https://www.inventati.org/securityau.

Arendt, Hannah. *The Origins of Totalitarianism.* New York: Harcourt, Brace, Jovanovich, 1973.

Aristotle. "Politics." MIT. http://classics.mit.edu/Aristotle/politics.1.one.html.

Armstrong, Robert. "US Credit Card Interest Rates Hit 25-Year High." *Financial Times,* August 6, 2019. https://www.ft.com/content/47fa19fe-b56e-11e9-bec9 -fdcab53d6959.

Arrighi, Giovanni. *Adam Smith in Beijing: Lineages of the Twenty-First Century.* London: Verso, 2007.

———. *The Long Twentieth Century: Money, Power and the Origin of Our Times.* London: Verso, 2010.

Australian Associated Press (APA). "Victorian Extremist Phillip Galea Planned to Bomb Leftwing Premises, Police Say." *The Guardian,* October 31, 2016. https:// www.theguardian.com/australia-news/2016/oct/31/victorian-extremist-phillip -galea-planned-to-bomb-leftwing-premises-police-say.

Australian Unemployed Workers' Union (AUWU). "It's Time! Raise Newstart!" Australian Unemployed Workers' Union. https://unemployedworkersunion .com/raise-newstart-now.

Bacon, Francis. "The New Atlantis." Project Gutenberg. https://www.gutenberg .org/files/2434/2434-h/2434-h.htm.

Bakan, Joel. *The Corporation: The Pathological Pursuit of Profit and Power.* New York: Free Press, 2005.

Bandurski, David. "Cashing in on Dystopia." SupChina, January 3, 2017. https:// supchina.com/2017/01/03/cashing-in-on-dystopia.

Bank of China (BoC). "2018 Annual Report." Bank of China. http://pic.bankof china.com/bocappd/report/201903/P020190329601110675116.pdf.

Baran, Paul, and Paul Sweezy. *Monopoly Capital: An Essay on the American Economic and Social Order.* New York: Monthly Review Press, 1966.

Barboza, David. "In Chinese Factories, Lost Fingers and Low Pay." *New York Times,* January 5, 2008. https://www.nytimes.com/2008/01/05/business/world business/05sweatshop.html.

Bateman, Milford. *Why Doesn't Microfinance Work? The Destructive Rise of Local Neoliberalism.* London: Zed Books, 2010.

Bauman, Zygmunt. *Consuming Life.* Cambridge: Polity Press, 2007.

———. *Liquid Modernity.* Cambridge: Polity Press, 2000.

BBC. "The Box." *BBC News,* http://news.bbc.co.uk/2/hi/in_depth/business/2008/ the_box/default.stm.

———. "Trump Revokes Obama Rule on Reporting Drone Strike Deaths." *BBC News,* March 7, 2019. https://www.bbc.com/news/world-us-canada-47480207.

Bedford, Kate. *Developing Partnerships: Gender, Sexuality and the Reformed World Bank.* Minneapolis: University of Minnesota Press, 2009.

Bell, David A. *The First Total War: Napoleon's Europe and the Birth of Warfare as We Know It*. Reprint ed. Boston: Mariner Books, 2008.

Bentham, Jeremy. *Panopticon, Constitution, Colonies, Codification*. The Works of Jeremy Bentham. 11 vols. Vol. 4, Edinburgh: William Tait, 1838–1843.

Berardi, Franco "Bifo." *And: Phenomenology of the End: Sensibility and Connective Mutation*. Los Angeles: Semiotext(e), 2015.

———. "The Coming Global Civil War: Is There Any Way Out?" *e-flux* 69 (2016).

———. *Heroes: Mass Murder and Suicide*. London: Verso, 2015.

———. *The Soul at Work: From Alienation to Autonomy*. Translated by Francesca Cadel and Mecchia Giuseppina. New York: Semiotext(e), 2009.

———. *The Uprising: On Poetry and Finance*. Semiotext(e) Intervention, 2012.

Bercovici, Jeff. "At TED, Google's Larry Page Says NSA Spying Threatens Democracy." *Forbes*, March 19, 2014. https://www.forbes.com/sites/jeffbercovici/2014/03/19/at-ted-googles-larry-page-says-nsa-spying-threatens-democracy.

Blackburn, Robin. *The American Crucible: Slavery, Emancipation and Human Rights*. London: Verso, 2013.

Boochani, Behrouz. *No Friend but the Mountains*. Sydney: Picador, 2018.

Bookchin, Murray. *The Ecology of Freedom: The Emergence and Dissolution of Hierarchy*. 4th ed. AK Press, UK, 2004.

Boothroyd, Mark. "Self Organisation in the Syrian Revolution." *The Project: A Socialist Journal*, August 14, 2016. http://www.socialistproject.org/issues/august-2016/self-organisation-syrian-revolution.

Bort, Julie. "Amazon's Warehouse-Worker Tracking System Can Automatically Fire People without a Human Supervisor's Involvement." *Business Insider*, April 26, 2019. https://www.businessinsider.com.au/amazon-system-automatically-fires-warehouse-workers-time-off-task-2019-4.

———. "Amazon Adds Fear Detection and Age Ranges to Its Facial-Recognition Tech as the Border Patrol Looks to Award a $950 Million Contract." *Business Insider*, August 14, 2019. https://www.businessinsider.com.au/amazon-fear-detection-age-ranges-added-facial-recognition-rekognition-tech-2019-8.

Botsman, Rachel. "Big Data Meets Big Brother as China Moves to Rate Its Citizens." *Wired*, October 21, 2017. https://www.wired.co.uk/article/chinese-government-social-credit-score-privacy-invasion.

Bourdieu, Pierre. "The Essence of Neoliberalism." *Le Monde diplomatique*, December 1998. http://mondediplo.com/1998/12/08bourdieu.

Bowring, John. "Report on Egypt and Candia." Great Britain: House of Commons, Sessional Papers, 1840.

Bratton, Benjamin H. "The Black Stack." *e-flux* 53 (2014).

Braudel, Fernand. *Civilization and Capitalism, 15th–18th Century: The Perspective of the World*. Oakland: University of California Press, 1992.

Braverman, Harry. *Labor and Monopoly Capital: The Degradation of Work in the Twentieth Century*. 25th Anniversary ed. New York: Monthly Review Press, 1998.

Bridle, James. *New Dark Age: Technology and the End of the Future.* London: Verso, 2018.

Brin, Sergey, Rajeev Motwani, Lawrence Page, and Terry Winograd. "What Can You Do with a Web in Your Pocket?" *Bulletin of the IEEE Computer Society Technical Committee on Data Engineering* (1998).

Brin, Sergey, and Lawrence Page. "The Anatomy of a Large-Scale Hypertextual Web Search Engine." Stanford University. http://infolab.stanford.edu/~backrub/google.html.

Brotton, Jerry. *A History of the World in Twelve Maps.* London: Penguin Group, 2012.

Brustein, Joshua. "Your Boss Would Like You to Wear a Jawbone Fitness Tracker." *Bloomberg*, December 10, 2014. https://www.bloomberg.com/news/articles/2014-12-10/jawbone-up-for-groups-a-plan-to-get-employers-to-buy-fitness-bands.

BTCA. "Better Than Cash Alliance." https://www.betterthancash.org.

Buckley, Chris. "China Is Detaining Muslims in Vast Numbers. The Goal: 'Transformation.'" *New York Times*, September 8, 2018. https://www.nytimes.com/2018/09/08/world/asia/china-uighur-muslim-detention-camp.html.

Burroughs, William. "The Limits of Control." *Semiotext(e)* III, no. 1 (1978): 38–42.

———. *Naked Lunch.* London: Flamingo, 1993 [1959].

Bush, Vannevar. "Report of the National Defense Research Committee for the First Year of Operation, June 27, 1940 to June 28, 1941." http://docs.fdrlibrary.marist.edu/psf/box2/a13f19.html.

———. "Science the Endless Frontier." Office of Scientific Research and Development, 1945.

Carney, Matthew. "Leave No Dark Corner." Australian Broadcasting Corporation. New York: Infobase, 2018.

Carr, Nicholas. *The Shallows: How the Internet Is Changing the Way We Think, Read and Remember.* London: Atlantic Books, 2010.

Carville, Olivia. "The Super Rich of Silicon Valley Have a Doomsday Escape Plan." *Bloomberg*, September 5, 2018. https://www.bloomberg.com/features/2018-rich-new-zealand-doomsday-preppers.

Catalist. "About Catalist." https://www.catalist.us/about.

CCB. "Exploring the Blue Ocean: 2017 Annual Report." China Construction Bank. http://en.ccb.com/en/newinvestor/upload/20180817_1534487897/20180817143224827527.pdf.

CDT. "White Paper Outlines Potential Uses of AI." *China Digital Times*, November 19, 2018. https://chinadigitaltimes.net/2018/11/white-paper-outlines-potential-uses-of-artificial-intelligence.

Cerf, Vint. "Sop Workshop 160: Global Trends to Watch: The Erosion of Privacy and Anonymity and the Need of Transparency of Government Access Requests." http://paranoia.dubfire.net/2011/11/two-honest-google-employees-our.html.

Chamayou, Grégoire. *A Theory of the Drone.* Translated by Janet Lloyd. New York: The New Press, 2015.

Chan, Tara Francis. "China's Social Credit System Has Blocked People from Taking 11 Million Flights and 4 Million Train Trips." *Business Insider,* May 21, 2018. https://www.businessinsider.com.au/china-social-credit-system-blocked-people-taking-flights-train-trips-2018-5.

Chang, Ha-Joon. *Bad Samaritans: The Guilty Secrets of Rich Nations and the Threat to Global Prosperity.* London: Random House Business Books, 2007.

Charlton, Graham. "Do 50% of Adults Really Not Recognise Ads in Search Results?" April 27, 2016. https://searchenginewatch.com/2016/04/27/do-50-of-adults-really-not-recognise-ads-in-search-results.

China State Council. "Opinions Concerning Accelerating the Construction of Credit Supervision, Warning and Punishment Mechanisms for Persons Subject to Enforcement for Trust-Breaking." China Copyright and Media, September 25, 2017. https://chinacopyrightandmedia.wordpress.com/2016/09/25/opinions-concerning-accelerating-the-construction-of-credit-supervision-warning-and-punishment-mechanisms-for-persons-subject-to-enforcement-for-trust-breaking.

———. "Planning Outline for the Construction for a Social Credit System (2014–2020)." China Copyright and Media, June 14, 2014. https://chinacopyrightandmedia.wordpress.com/2014/06/14/planning-outline-for-the-construction-of-a-social-credit-system-2014-2020.

———. "State Council General Office Some Opinions Concerning the Construction of a Social Credit System." China Copyright and Media, March 23, 2007. https://chinacopyrightandmedia.wordpress.com/2007/03/23/state-council-general-office-some-opinions-concerning-the-construction-of-a-social-credit-system.

Chomksy, Noam. "Destroying the Commons: How the Magna Carta Became a Minor Carta." TomDispatch.com, July, 22, 2012. http://www.tomdispatch.com/post/175571/tomgram%3A_noam_chomsky%2C_the_great_charter%2C_its_fate%2C_and_ours/#more.

———. *Profit over People: Neoliberalism and Global Order.* New York: Seven Stories Press, 1999.

Choudry, Aziz, ed. *Activists and the Surveillance State: Learning from Repression.* London: Pluto Press, 2019.

Chung, Heidi. "The Richest 1% Own 50% of Stocks Held by American Households." *Yahoo Finance,* January 17, 2019. https://au.finance.yahoo.com/news/the-richest-1-own-50-of-stocks-held-by-american-households-150758595.html.

Civis. "Our Mission." https://www.civisanalytics.com/mission.

Cohn, Carol. "Sex and Death in the Rational World of Defense Intellectuals." *Signs* 12, no. 4 (1987): 687–718.

Collinson, Patrick, and Rupert Jones. "Wonga Collapses into Administration." *The Guardian,* August 30, 2018. https://www.theguardian.com/business/2018/aug/30/wonga-collapses-into-administration.

Conway, Flo, and Jim Siegelman. *Dark Hero of the Information Age: In Search of Norbert Wiener the Father of Cybernetics.* New York: Basic Books, 2006.

Cook, William A., ed. *The Plight of the Palestinians: A Long History of Destruction.* New York: Palgrave Macmillan, 2010.

Cooper, Simon. *Technoculture and Critical Theory: In the Service of the Machine?* London: Routledge, 2002.

Couldry, Nick, and Andreas Hepp. *The Mediated Construction of Reality.* Cambridge: Polity, 2016.

Crampton, Jeremy W. "Platform Biometrics." *Surveillance & Society* 17, no. 1/2 (2019): 54–62.

Crosby, Alfred W., Jr., ed. *The Columbian Exchange: Biological and Cultural Consequences of 1492.* 30th Anniversary edition. Santa Barbara, CA: Praeger, 2003.

Cubitt, Sean. *Finite Media: Environmental Implications of Digital Technologies.* Durham, NC: Duke University Press, 2017.

Curl, John. *For All the People: Uncovering the Hidden History of Cooperation, Cooperative Movements, and Communalism in America.* Oakland, CA: PM Press, 2009.

Darby, Henry C. *Domesday England.* Cambridge: Cambridge University Press, 1977.

Davies, William. *The Happiness Industry: How the Government and Big Business Sold Us Well-Being.* London: Verso, 2015.

Davis, Angela Y., ed. *If They Come in the Morning: Voices of Resistance.* London: Verso, 2016.

Davis, Mike, and Daniel Bertrand Monk, eds. *Evil Paradises: Dreamworlds of Neoliberalism:* New York: The New Press, 2007.

Dayen, David. "The Android Administration." *The Intercept,* April 22, 2016. https://theintercept.com/2016/04/22/googles-remarkably-close-relationship-with-the-obama-white-house-in-two-charts.

Deleuze, Gilles. "Postscript on the Societies of Control." *October* 59 (Winter 1992): 3–7.

Denyer, Simon. "China's Watchful Eye." *Washington Post,* January 7, 2018. https://www.washingtonpost.com/news/world/wp/2018/01/07/feature/in-china-facial-recognition-is-sharp-end-of-a-drive-for-total-surveillance.

Desmond, Matthew. *Evicted: Poverty and Profit in the American City.* New York: Crown, 2016.

DeVos, Stephanie. "The Google-NSA Alliance: Developing Cybersecurity Policy at Internet Speed." *Fordham Intellectual Property, Media and Entertainment Law Journal* 21, no. 1 (2011).

Dick, Philip K. "The Minority Report." In *Minority Report.* London: Gollancz, 2002.

Donlon, J. P. "GE CEO Jeff Immelt on the Future of GE and of American Manufacturing." *Chief Executive,* March 10, 2014. https://chiefexecutive.net/ge-ceo-jeff-immelt-on-the-future-of-ge-and-of-american-manufacturing.

Donnersmarck, Florian Henckel von. *The Lives of Others*. Buena Vista International, 2006.

Donovan, Kevin P., and Emma Park. "Perpetual Debt in the Silicon Savannah." *Boston Review*. https://bostonreview.net/class-inequality-global-justice/kevin-p -donovan-emma-park-perpetual-debt-silicon-savannah.

Dorling, Philip. "Asio Eyes Green Groups." *Sydney Morning Herald*, April 12, 2012. https://www.smh.com.au/politics/federal/asio-eyes-green-groups-20120411 -1wsba.html.

Department of Social Services (DSS). "Cashless Debit Card." DSS, Australian Government. https://www.dss.gov.au/families-and-children/programmes-services/ welfare-conditionality/cashless-debit-card-overview.

Durand, Cédric. *Fictitious Capital: How Finance Is Appropriating Our Future*. Translated by David Broder. London: Verso, 2017.

Earnest, Lester Donald. "How the Biggest Military-Industrial-Congressional Fraud of the 20th Century Launched More Frauds and the Internet." Stanford.edu. https://web.stanford.edu/~learnest/nets.

Economist. "Creating a Digital Totalitarian State: China's Social-Credit System." *Economist* 421, no. 9020 (2016).

———. "Psychometrics: Tests of Character." *Economist*, September 29, 2016. https:// www.economist.com/finance-and-economics/2016/09/29/tests-of-character.

Edney, Matthew H. *Mapping an Empire: The Geographical Construction of British India 1765–1843*. Chicago: Chicago University Press, 1997.

Edwards, Paul N. *The Closed World: Computers and the Politics of Discourse in Cold War America*. Cambridge, MA: MIT Press, 1996.

Elahi, Amina. "Civis Analytics Lands $22 Million to Expand Data-Powered Problem Solving." *Chicago Tribune*, November 30, 2016. https://www.chicagotribune .com/business/blue-sky/ct-civis-analytics-funding-22-million-bsi-20161130 -story.html.

Ellsberg, Daniel. *The Doomsday Machine: Confessions of a Nuclear War Planner*. New York: Bloomsbury, 2017.

Engelhardt, Tom, and Nick Turse. *Terminator Planet: The First History of Drone Warfare, 2001–2050*. Lexington, KY: Dispatch Books, 2012.

Enloe, Cynthia. *Globlization and Militarism: Feminists Make the Link*. 2nd ed. Lanham, MD: Rowman & Littlefield, 2016.

Fan, Lixin. "Last Train Home." Canada: Zeitgeist Films, 2009.

Federal Election Commission (FEC). "Cambridge Analytica, 2015–2016." https://www.fec.gov/data/disbursements/?data_type=processed&committee_ id=C00580100&recipient_name=cambridge+analytica&two_year_transaction_ period=2016&min_date=01%2F01%2F2015&max_date=12%2F31%2F2016.

———. "Civis Analytics, 2015–2016." https://www.fec.gov/data/disbursements/ ?data_type=processed&recipient_name=civis+analytics&two_year_trans

action_period=2016&min_date=01%2F01%2F2015&max_date=12%2F31%2F2016.

Federal Reserve. "Consumer Credit." https://www.federalreserve.gov/releases/g19/HIST/cc_hist_mt_levels.html.

———. "Mortgage Debt Outstanding." https://www.federalreserve.gov/data/mortoutstand/current.htm.

Federici, Silvia. *Caliban and the Witch: Women, the Body and Primative Accumulation.* New York: Autonomedia, 2014.

———. *Re-Enchanting the World: Feminism and the Politics of the Commons.* Oakland, CA: PM Press, 2019.

Fitbit. "Fitbit for Corporate Wellness." https://www.fitbit.com/content/assets/group-health/FitbitWellness_InfoSheet.pdf.

Flemming, Andy, and Aureliein Mondon. *The Radical Right in Australia.* https://www.oxfordhandbooks.com/view/10.1093/oxfordhb/9780190274559.001.0001/oxfordhb-9780190274559-e-32.

Foucault, Michel. *Discipline and Punish: The Birth of the Prison.* New York: Vintage Books, 1995.

Frieden, Jeffry A. *Global Capitalism: Its Fall and Rise in the Twentieth Century.* New York: W. W. Norton, 2006.

Friedman, Milton. *Capitalism and Freedom.* 40th Anniversary ed. Chicago: University of Chicago Press, 2002.

Fromm, Erich. *The Fear of Freedom.* London: Routledge & Kegan Paul, 1960.

FSM. "About the World Social Forum." World Social Forum. https://fsm2016.org/en/sinformer/a-propos-du-forum-social-mondial.

Fuchs, Christian. *Digital Labour and Karl Marx.* New York: Routledge, 2014.

Funding, Anna. *Stasiland: Stories from Behind the Berlin Wall.* New York: HarperCollins, 2003.

Galeano, Eduardo. *Hunter of Stories.* Translated by Mark Fried. London: Constable, 2019.

———. *Open Veins of Latin America: Five Centuries of the Pillage of a Continent.* Translated by Cedric Belfrage. New York: Monthy Review Press, 1997.

Geertz, Clifford. "Form and Variation in Balinese Village Structure." *American Anthropologist* 61, no. 6 (1959): 991–1012.

———. *The Interpretation of Cultures: Selected Essays.* New York: Basic Books, 1973.

George, Susan. *A Fate Worse Than Debt: A Radical New Analysis of the Third World Debt Crisis.* London: Penguin Books, 1990.

Gerovitch, Slava. "The Cybernetics Scare and the Origins of the Internet." *Baltic Worlds,* February 11, 2010. http://balticworlds.com/the-cybernetics-scare-and-the-origins-of-the-internet.

Gilliom, John. *Overseers of the Poor: Surveillance, Resistance, and the Limits of Privacy.* Chicago: University of Chicago Press, 2001.

Gleick, James. *The Information: A History, a Theory, a Flood*. London: Fourth Estate, 2012.

Google. "How Search Works." https://www.google.com/insidesearch/howsearch works/thestory.

———. "Ten Things We Know to Be True." https://www.google.com/about/phi losophy.html.

Gould, Stephen Jay. *The Mismeasure of Man*. Revised and expanded edition. New York: W. W. Norton, 1996.

Graeber, David. *Debt: The First 5,000 Years*. New York: Melville House, 2012.

———. *The Utopia of Rules: On Technology, Stupidity, and the Secret Joys of Bureaucracy*. Brooklyn: Melville House, 2015.

Graff, Garrett M. "The Polls Are All Wrong. A Startup Called Vivis Is Our Best Hope to Fix Them." *Wired*, June 6, 2016. https://www.wired.com/2016/06/civis -election-polling-clinton-sanders-trump.

Gramsci, Antonio. *Selections from the Prison Notebooks of Antonio Gramsci*. New York: International Publishers, 1971.

Greenfield, Adam. *Radical Technologies: The Design of Everyday Life*. London: Verso, 2017.

Greenwald, Glen. *No Place to Hide: Edward Snowden, the NSA and the Surveillance State*. London: Hamish Hamilton, 2014.

Gregg, Aaron. "Amazon Launches New Cloud Storage Service for U.S. Spy Agencies." *Washington Post*, November 20, 2017. https://www.washingtonpost.com/ news/business/wp/2017/11/20/amazon-launches-new-cloud-storage-service-for -u-s-spy-agencies.

Griffiths, Philip Jones. *Agent Orange: "Collateral Damage" in Vietnam*. London: Trolley Books, 2004.

Guardian staff. "Bush Rejects Taliban Offer to Hand Bin Laden Over." *The Guardian*, October 14, 2001. https://www.theguardian.com/world/2001/oct/14/afghan istan.terrorism5.

Guerin, Daniel. *Fascism and Big Business*. New York: Pathfinder, 1973.

Hackernoon. "How Much Time Do People Spend on Their Mobile Phones in 2017?" Medium Corporation, May 9, 2017. https://hackernoon.com/how-much -time-do-people-spend-on-their-mobile-phones-in-2017-e5f90a0b10a6.

Hahnel, Robin. *Of the People, by the People: The Case for a Participatory Economy*. London: Soap Box, 2012.

Han, Byung-Chul. *Psychopolitics: Neoliberalism and New Technologies of Power*. London: Verso, 2017.

Hao, Cheng. "The Death and Revival of Usury in China: An Institutional Analysis." *Journal of Economic Issues* 52, no. 2 (2018): 527–33.

Hares, Sophie. "The Cost of Clean Water: $150 Billion a Year, Says World Bank." Reuters, August 28, 2017. https://www.reuters.com/article/us-global-water-health/ the-cost-of-clean-water-150-billion-a-year-says-world-bank-idUSKCN1B812E.

Harvey, David. *Abstract from the Concrete*. The Incidents. Cambridge, MA: Sternberg Press, 2017.

———. *A Brief History of Neoliberalism*. Oxford: Oxford University Press, 2005.

———. *The Condition of Postmodernity: An Enquiry into the Origins of Cultural Change*. Oxford: Basil Blackwell, 1989.

———. "Cosmopolitanism and the Banality of Geographical Evils." *Public Culture* 12, no. 2 (2000): 529–64.

———. *The New Imperialism*. Oxford: Oxford University Press, 2005.

———. *Seventeen Contradictions and the End of Capitalism*. London: Profile Books, 2014.

Haskins, Caroline. "Dozens of Cities Have Secretly Experimented with Predictive Policing Software." *Vice*, February 6, 2019. https://www.vice.com/en_us/article/d3m7jq/dozens-of-cities-have-secretly-experimented-with-predictive-policing-software.

Hatton, Celia. "China 'Social Credit': Beijing Sets up Huge System." *BBC News*, October 26, 2015. https://www.bbc.com/news/world-asia-china-34592186.

Hayek, F. A. *The Road to Surfdom*. London: Routledge, 2001.

Hinkel, Jason. "An Open Letter to Steven Pinker (and Bill Gates, for That Matter) about Global Poverty." *Climate & Capitalism*, February 4, 2019. https://climateandcapitalism.com/2019/02/04/letter-to-steven-pinker-about-global-poverty.

Hinkson, John. "Globalization and New World Order." In *Cold War to Hot Planet: Fifty Years of Arena*. Edited by John Hinkson, Paul James, Alison Caddick, Simon Cooper, Melinda Hinkson, and Dan Tout, 51–73. Melbourne: Arena Publications, 2016.

———. "New World or Worlds Unravelling?" *Arena Magazine*, June 19, 2018. https://arena.org.au/new-world-or-worlds-unravelling-by-john-hinkson, 2–3.

———. "Trump and the Fascist Prospect." *Arena Journal* 47/48 (2017): 33–56.

Hinkson, John, Paul James, Alison Caddick, Simon Cooper, Melinda Hinkson, and Dan Tout, eds. *Cold War to Hot Planet: Fifty Years of Arena*. Melbourne: Arena Publications, 2016.

Hinkson, Melinda. "In Humanity's Wake." *Arena Journal* 51/52 (2018): 1–9.

Hobsbawm, Eric. *The Age of Capital: 1848–1875*. London: Abacus, 2013. 1975.

———. *The Age of Empire: 1875–1914*. London: Abacus, 2013. 1987.

———. *The Age of Extremes: 1914–1991*. London: Abacus, 2013. 1994.

Hoffman, Samantha. "Programming China: The Communist Party's Autonomic Approach to Managing State Security." *Merics China Monitor* 44 (2017): 1–12.

Hoffower, Hillary. "We Did the Maths to Calculate How Much Money Jeff Bezos Makes in a Year, Month, Week, Day, Hour, Minute, and Second." *Business Insider Australia*, January 10, 2019. https://www.businessinsider.com.au/what-amazon-ceo-jeff-bezos-makes-every-day-hour-minute-2018-10.

Holloway, David. "Innovation in Science: The Case of Cybernetics in the Soviet Union." *Science Studies* 4, no. 4 (1974): 299–337.

HuffPostTech. "Google CEO on Privacy (Video): 'If You Have Something You Don't Want Anyone to Know, Maybe You Shouldn't Be Doing It.'" *Huffington Post*, December 7, 2009. http://www.huffingtonpost.com/2009/12/07/google-ceo-on -privacy-if_n_383105.html.

ICBC. "2017 Annual Report." Industrial and Commercial Bank of China. http:// v.icbc.com.cn/userfiles/Resources/ICBCLTD/download/2018/720180423.pdf.

Im, Heung-soon. *Factory Complex: The Exploitation of Female Laborers in the South Korean Workplace*. Video. 2015.

IMF. "Annual Report: Economic Surveillance." International Monetary Fund. https://www.imf.org/external/pubs/ft/ar/2017/eng/economic-surveillance.htm.

Introna, Lucas D., and David Wood. "Picturing Algorithmic Surveillance: The Politics of Facial Recognition Systems." *Surveillance & Society* 2, no. 2/3 (2004): 177–98.

iPass. "Two Thirds of Mobile Professionals Feel Anxious without Wi-Fi, Says Ipass Report." iPass, November 28, 2017. https://www.ipass.com/press-releases/two -thirds-mobile-professionals-feel-anxious-without-wi-fi-says-ipass-report.

iResearch. "China's Third-Party Mobile Payment Report." Beijing: iResearch, 2017.

Isserles, Robin G. "Microcredit: The Rhetoric of Empowerment, the Reality of 'Development as Usual.'" *Women's Studies Quarterly* 31, no. 3/4 (2003): 38–57.

Jamerson, Fredric. "Postmodernism and the Market." *The Socialist Register* (1990): 95–110.

James, Paul. *Globalism, Nationalism, Tribalism: Bringing Theory Back In*. London: Sage, 2006.

———. *Urban Sustainability in Theory and Practice: Circles of Sustainability*. London: Routledge, 2015.

Jay, Paul, and Lester Donald Earnest. "Cold War Radar System a Trillion Dollar Fraud—Lester Earnest on Rai." *The Real News*, December 24, 2018. https://the realnews.com/stories/cold-war-radar-system-a-trillion-dollar-fraud-lester-ernest -on-rai-1-4.

Jenkins, Holman. "Google and the Search for the Future." *Wall Street Journal*, August 14, 2010. http://online.wsj.com/news/articles/SB10001424052748704901104575423294099527212.

Jensen, Michael C., and William H. Meckling. "Theory of the Firm: Managerial Behavior, Agency Costs and Ownership Structure." *Journal of Financial Economics* 3, no. 4 (1976): 305–60.

Jiang, Min, and King-Wa Fu. "Chinese Social Media and Big Data: Big Data, Big Brother, Big Profit?" *Policy & Internet* 10, no. 4 (2018): 372–92.

Juergensmeyer, Mark, Manfred Steger, Saskia Sassen, and Victor Faessel, eds. *The Oxford Handbook of Global Studies*. Oxford: Oxford University Press, 2018.

Kain, Roger J. P., and Elizabeth Baigent. *The Cadastral Map in the Service of the State: A History of Property Mapping*. Chicago: University of Chicago Press, 1992.

Katz, Naomi, and David Kemnitzner. "Fast Forward: The Internationalization of the Silicon Valley." In *Women, Men, and the International Division of Labor*, edited by June C. Nash and Maria P. Fernandez-Kelly. Albany: SUNY Press, 1984.

Kim, Larry. "The War on 'Free' Clicks: Think Nobody Clicks on Google Ads? Think Again!" *WordStream*, August 19, 2019. http://www.wordstream.com/blog/ws/2012/07/17/google-advertising.

Kimery, Anthony L. "While Fending Off DOJ Subpoena, Google Continues Long-standing Relationship with US Intelligence." *Homeland Security Today*, January 25, 2006. https://archive.is/skEkN.

Kitchin, Rob, and Martin Dodge. *Code/Space: Software and Everyday Life*. Cambridge: MIT Press, 2011.

Klein, Naomi. *The Shock Doctrine: The Rise of Disaster Capitalism*. London: Penguin, 2007.

———. *This Changes Everything: Capitalism vs. the Climate*. London: Allen Lane, 2014.

Klinger, Bailey. "The Test of Entrepreneurship: Revolutionizing SME Finance." Organization of American States. https://www.oas.org/en/sedi/desd/IIDialogo/presentations/Bailey_Klinger.pdf.

Kornbluh, Peter. *The Pinochet File: A Declassified Dossier on Atrocity and Accountability*. New York: The New Press, 2003.

Kornish, Lorie. "Consumer Debt Is Set to Reach $4 Trillion by the End of 2018." CNBC, May 21, 2018. https://www.cnbc.com/2018/05/21/consumer-debt-is-set-to-reach-4-trillion-by-the-end-of-2018.html.

Kovel, Joel. *Against the State of Nuclear Terror*. Boston: South End Press, 1983.

Krishna, Sankaran. *Globalization and Postcolonialism: Hegemony and Resistance in the Twenty-First Century*. Edited by Terrel Carver and Manfred Steger. Lanham, MD: Rowman & Littlefield, 2009.

Kuzenkoff, Jeffrey H., and Scott Titsworth. "The Impact of Mobile Phone Usage on Student Learning." *Communication Education* 62, no. 3 (2013): 233–52.

Landes, David S. *Revolutions in Time: Clocks and the Making of the Modern World*. Cambridge, MA: Harvard University Press, 1983.

Lazzarato, Maurizio. *The Making of the Indebted Man*. Cambridge: Semiotext(e), 2012.

Lee, Amanda. "Alipay Rolls Out World's First 'Smile to Pay' Facial Recognition System at KFC Outlet in Hangzhou," *South China Morning Post*, September 1, 2017. https://www.scmp.com/tech/start-ups/article/2109321/alipay-rolls-out-worlds-first-smile-pay-facial-recognition-system-kfc.

LenddoEFL. "Unleashing Global Economic Potential with Alternative Data." https://include1billion.com.

Lenin, Vladimir Illich. "The Immediate Tasks of the Soviet Government." March–April 1918. https://www.marxists.org/archive/lenin/works/1918/mar/x03.htm.

———. "The Taylor System—Man's Enslavement by the Machine." March 13, 1914. https://www.marxists.org/archive/lenin/works/1914/mar/13.htm.

Leopold, Jason. "Exclusive: Emails Reveal Close Google Relationship with NSA." *Aljazeera America*, May 6, 2014. http://america.aljazeera.com/articles/2014/5/6/nsa-chief-google.html.

Levine, Yasha. "Google and Encryption: Why True User Privacy Is Google's Biggest Enemy." *Pando Daily*, January 27, 2014. https://archive.today/bDecl.

Levinson, Marc. *The Box: How the Shipping Container Made the World Smaller and the World Economy Bigger.* Princeton, NJ: Princeton University Press, 2006.

Levy, Steven. *In the Plex: How Google Thinks, Works, and Shapes Our Lives.* New York: Simon & Schuster, 2011.

Lewis, Avi, and Naomi Klein. *The Take.* Canada: First Run Features/Icarus Films, 2004.

Lewis, Paul. "'Our Minds Can Be Hijacked': The Tech Insiders Who Fear a Smartphone Dystopia." *The Guardian*, October 5, 2017. https://www.theguardian.com/technology/2017/oct/05/smartphone-addiction-silicon-valley-dystopia.

Lewis, Tim. "With Wonga, Your Prosperity Could Count on an Algorithm." *The Guardian*, October 16, 2011. https://www.theguardian.com/money/2011/oct/16/wonga-algorithm-lending-debt-data.

Livingstone, David N. *The Geographical Tradition: Episodes in the History of a Contested Enterprise.* Oxford: Blackwell, 1992.

Loach, Ken. *I, Daniel Blake.* eOne Films, 2016.

Lv, Aofei, and Ting Lou. "Authoritarian Practices in the Digital Age Asymmetrical Power between Internet Giants and Users in China." *International Journal of Communication* 12 (2018): 3877–95.

Lynch, Gabrielle, Justin Willis, and Nic Cheeseman. "Claims about Cambridge Analytica's Role in Africa Should Be Taken with a Pinch of Salt." *The Conversation*, March 23, 2018. https://theconversation.com/claims-about-cambridge-analyticas-role-in-africa-should-be-taken-with-a-pinch-of-salt-93864.

Lyon, David. *Surveillance after Snowden.* London: Polity, 2015.

———. "Surveillance Culture: Engagement, Exposure, and Ethics in Digital Modernity." *International Journal of Communication* 11 (2017): 824–42.

———. "Surveillance, Snowden, and Big Data: Capacities, Consequences, Critique." *Big Data & Society* (2014): 1–13.

———. *Surveillance Studies: An Overview.* Cambridge: Polity Press, 2007.

Makdisi, Saree. *Palestine Inside Out: An Everyday Occupation.* New York: W. W. Norton, 2008.

Malcolm, Lynne, and Muditha Dias. *The Myth of Multitasking.* Podcast: All in the Mind, September 2, 2015. https://www.abc.net.au/radionational/programs/allinthemind/the-myth-of-multitasking/6743356.

Marx, Karl. *Capital: A Critique of Political Economy.* Translated by Ben Fowkes. 3 vols. Vol. 1, Westminster, UK: Penguin Classics, 1976.

———. "Letter from Karl Marx to Nikolai Danielson in St. Petersburg, 10 April 1879." https://www.marxists.org/archive/marx/works/1879/letters/79_04_10.htm.

Marx, Karl, and Friedrich Engels. *The Communist Manifesto.* New York: Signet Classic, 2011.

Mattelart, Armand. *The Invention of Communication.* Translated by Susan Emanuel. Minneapolis: University of Minnesota Press, 1996.

———. *Networking the World: 1794–2000.* Translated by Liz Carey-Libbrecht and James A. Cohen. Minneapolis: University of Minnesota Press, 2000.

Mayer, Jane. "New Evidence Emerges of Steve Bannon and Cambridge Analytica's Role in Brexit." *New Yorker,* November 17, 2018. https://www.newyorker.com/news/news-desk/new-evidence-emerges-of-steve-bannon-and-cambridge-analyticas-role-in-brexit.

———. "The Reclusive Hedge-Fund Tycoon Behind the Trump Presidency." *New Yorker,* March 27, 2017. https://www.newyorker.com/magazine/2017/03/27/the-reclusive-hedge-fund-tycoon-behind-the-trump-presidency.

McChesney, Robert W. *Digital Disconnect: How Capitalism Is Turning the Internet against Democracy.* New York: The New Press, 2013.

McClelland, Mac. "I Was a Warehouse Wage Slave." *Mother Jones,* March/April 2002. https://www.motherjones.com/politics/2012/02/mac-mcclelland-free-online-shipping-warehouses-labor.

McCoy, Alfred W. *Policing America's Empire: The United States, the Philippines, and the Rise of the Surveillance State.* Madison: University of Wisconsin Press, 2009.

McKenzie-Murry, Martin. "How Reclaim Australia Hid a 'Terrorist.'" *The Saturday Paper,* August 13, 2016. https://www.thesaturdaypaper.com.au/news/law-crime/2016/08/13/how-reclaim-australia-hid-terrorist/14710104003610.

Medina, Eden. *Cybernetic Revolutionaries: Technology and Politics in Allende's Chile.* Cambridge, MA: MIT Press, 2011.

Melendez, Steven. "A Landmark Vermont Law Nudges over 120 Data Brokers out of the Shadows." *Fast Company,* March 2, 2019. https://www.fastcompany.com/90302036/over-120-data-brokers-inch-out-of-the-shadows-under-landmark-vermont-law.

Merchant, Carolyn. *Autonomous Nature: Problems of Prediction and Control from Ancient Times to the Scientific Revolution.* New York: Routledge, 2016.

Metzinger, Thomas. *The Ego Tunnel: The Science of the Mind and the Myth of the Self.* New York: Basic Books, 2009.

Michel, Arthur Holland. "How Rogue Techies Armed the Predator, Almost Stopped 9/11, and Accidentally Invented Remote War." *Wired,* December 17, 2015. https://www.wired.com/2015/12/how-rogue-techies-armed-the-predator-almost-stopped-911-and-accidentally-invented-remote-war.

Mills, C. Wright. *The Power Elite.* Oxford: Oxford University Press, 2000.

Mintz, Sidney. "Plantations and the Rise of a World Food Economy: Some Preliminary Ideas." *Review (Fernand Braudel Center)* 34, no. 1/2 (2011): 3–14.

Mitchell, Timothy. *Colonising Egypt*. Cambridge: Cambridge University Press, 1988.

Mitchell, William J. *City of Bits: Space, Place, and the Infobahn*. Cambridge, MA: MIT Press, 2000.

Monahan, Torin. *Surveillance in the Time of Insecurity*. New Brunswick, NJ: Rutgers University Press, 2010.

Monmonier, Mark. *How to Lie with Maps*. 2nd ed. Chicago: University of Chicago Press, 1996.

Montaño, John Patrick *The Roots of English Colonialism in Ireland*. Cambridge: Cambridge University Press, 2011.

Moore, Jason W. *Capitalism in the Web of Life: Ecology and the Accumulation of Capital*. London: Verso, 2015.

———. "The Capitalocene, Part I: On the Nature and Origins of Our Ecological Crisis." *Journal of Peasant Studies* 44, no. 3 (2017): 594–630.

Mosco, Vincent. *To the Cloud: Big Data in a Turbulent World*. Boulder, CO: Paradigm, 2014.

Mozur, Paul. "One Month, 500,000 Face Scans: How China Is Using A.I. to Profile a Minority." *New York Times*, April 14, 2019. https://www.nytimes.com/2019/04/14/technology/china-surveillance-artificial-intelligence-racial-profiling.html.

Mukerji, Chandra. *From Graven Images: Patterns of Modern Materialism*. New York: Columbia University Press, 1983.

Mumford, Lewis. *The Myth of the Machine: The Pentagon of Power*. New York: Harcourt Brace Jovanovich, 1970.

———. *Technics and Civilization*. New York: Harbinger Books, 1963 [1934].

Nasdaq. "Amazon.com, Inc. Ownership Summary." https://www.nasdaq.com/symbol/amzn/ownership-summary.

Newmyer, Tory. "Can a Silicon Valley Insider Save Ohio's Economy?" *Fortune*, June 3, 2012. http://fortune.com/2012/06/03/can-a-silicon-valley-insider-save-ohios-economy.

Noble, David F. *Forces of Production: A Social History of Industrial Automation*. New York: Alfred A. Knopf, 1984.

Nordman, Christophe Jalil, and Isabelle Guérin. "The Shock of Indian Demonetisation: A Failed Attempt to Formalise the Economy." *The Conversation*, April 3, 2018. https://theconversation.com/the-shock-of-indian-demonetisation-a-failed-attempt-to-formalise-the-economy-93328.

O'Neil, Cathy. *Weapons of Math Destruction: How Big Data Increases Inequality and Threatens Democracy*. New York: Crown, 2016.

OpenDomesDay.org. "Opendomesday.Org." https://opendomesday.org/place/TL4933/wicken-bonhunt.

Oppenheimer, Joshua. *The Act of Killing*. Det Danske Filminstitut, 2012.

———. *The Look of Silence*. Why Not Productions, 2014.

Osnos, Evan. "Doomsday Prep for the Super-Rich." *New Yorker*, January 30, 2017. https://www.newyorker.com/magazine/2017/01/30/doomsday-prep-for -the-super-rich.

Palumbo-Liu, David. "The Ongoing Persecution of China's Uyghurs." *Jacobin*, June 1, 2019. https://jacobinmag.com/2019/06/china-uyghur-persecution -concentration-camps.

Parenti, Christian. *Lockdown America: Police and Prisons in the Age of Crisis.* London: Verso, 2008.

———. *The Soft Cage: Surveillance in America from Slavery to the War on Terror.* New York: Basic Books, 2003.

———. *The Tropic of Chaos: Climate Change and New Geography of Violence.* New York: Nation Books, 2011.

Pasquinelli, Matteo. "Google's Pagerank Algorithm: A Diagram of Cognitive Capitalism and the Rentier of the Common Intellect." In *Deep Search*, edited by Konrad Becker and Felix Stalder. Piscataway, NJ: Transaction Publishers, 2009.

Pembroke, Michael. *Korea: Where the American Century Began.* Melbourne: Hardie Grant, 2018.

Phillips, Peter. *Giants: The Global Power Elite.* New York: Seven Stories Press, 2018.

Pieterse, Jan Nederveen. *Globalization and Culture: Global Mélange.* Edited by Manfred Steger and Terrell Carver. Lanham, MD: Rowman & Littlefield, 2009.

Piketty, Thomas. *Capital in the Twenty-First Century.* Translated by Arthur Goldhammer. Cambridge, MA: The Belknap Press, 2014.

Pinker, Steven. *Enlightenment Now: The Case for Reason, Science, Humanism, and Progress.* New York: Viking, 2018.

Poitras, Laura. *Citizenfour.* Radius-TWC (2014).

Polanyi, Karl. *The Great Transformation: The Political and Economic Origins of Our Time.* Boston: Beacon Press, 2001.

Popper, Karl. *The Open Society and Its Enemies.* London: Routledge, 2011.

Prahalad, C. K., and Stuart L. Hart. "The Fortune at the Bottom of the Pyramid." *Strategy + Business* 26 (2002).

Prashad, Vijay. *The Darker Nations: A People's History of the Third World.* Edited by Howard Zinn. New York: The New Press, 2007.

———, ed. *Letters to Palestine: Writers Respond to War and Occupation.* London: Verso, 2015.

———. *The Poorer Nations: A Possible History of the Global South.* London: Verso, 2014.

Privacy International. "Fintech's Dirty Little Secret? Lenddo, Facebook and the Challenge of Identity." October 23, 2018, https://privacyinternational.org/long -read/2323/fintechs-dirty-little-secret-lenddo-facebook-and-challenge-identity.

Raghubir, Priya, and Joydeep Srivastava. "Monopoly Money: The Effect of Payment Coupling and Form on Spending Behavior." *Journal of Experimental Psychology* 14, no. 3 (2008): 213–25.

Ramzy, Austin, and Chris Buckley. "The Xinjiang Papers: 'Absolutely No Mercy': Leaked Files Expose How China Organized Mass Detentions of Muslims." *New York Times*, November, 2019, https://www.nytimes.com/interactive/2019/11/16/world/asia/china-xinjiang-documents.html.

Rigi, Jakob, and Robert Prey. "Value, Rent, and the Political Economy of Social Media." *The Information Society* 31, no. 5 (2015): 392–406.

Robins, Kevin, and Frank Webster. "Cybernetic Capitalism: Information, Technology, Everyday Life." In *The Political Economy of Information*, edited by Vincent Masco and Janet Wasko, 44–75. Madison: University of Wisconsin Press, 1988.

Robinson, Geoffrey B. *The Killing Season: A History of the Indonesian Massacres, 1965–66*. Princeton, NJ: Princeton University Press, 2018.

Roderick, Leanne. "Discipline and Power in the Digital Age: The Case of the US Consumer Data Broker Industry." *Critical Sociology* 40, no. 5 (2014): 729–46.

Rogers, Peter. "Is China's Social Credit System Coming to Australia?" *The Conversation*, May 28, 2019. https://theconversation.com/is-chinas-social-credit-system-coming-to-australia-117095.

Rosenberg, Jonathan. "The Meaning of Open." Google Official Blog, December 21, 2009. http://googleblog.blogspot.com.au/2009/12/meaning-of-open.html.

Rossiter, Ned. *Software, Infrastructure, Labor: A Media Theory of Logistical Nightmares*. New York: Routledge, 2017.

Rotblat, Jozef. "The Hydrogen-Uranium Bomb." *Bulletin of the Atomic Scientists* XI, no. 5 (1955).

Rothwell, Nicolas. "Colonial Turbulence in the North." *Arena Magazine*, no. 148 (2017): 11–17.

Roy, Arundhati. *Capitalism: A Ghost Story*. London: Verso, 2015.

Ruff, Tilman. "Nuclear Promises." *Arena Magazine*, no. 162 (2019): 19–22.

Rushkoff, Douglas. "Survival of the Richest." *OneZero*, July 5, 2018. https://medium.com/s/futurehuman/survival-of-the-richest-9ef6cddd0cc1.

SABRE. "The Sabre Story." https://www.sabre.com/files/Sabre-History.pdf.

Said, Edward W. *Culture and Imperialism*. New York: Vintage Books, 1994.

———. *The Question of Palestine*. New York: Vintage Books, 1992.

Salame, Richard. "The New Taylorism." *Jacobin*, February 20, 2018. https://www.jacobinmag.com/2018/02/amazon-wristband-surveillance-scientific-management.

Scheer, Robert. *They Know Everything about You: How Data-Collecting Corporations and Snooping Government Agencies Are Destroying Democracy*. New York: Nation Books, 2015.

Scheppele, Kim Lane. "From a War on Terrorism to Global Security Law." 2013. https://www.ias.edu/ideas/2013/scheppele-terrorism.

Scherer, Michael. "Friended: How the Obama Campaign Connected with Young Voters." *Time*, November 20, 2012, http://swampland.time.com/2012/11/20/friended-how-the-obama-campaign-connected-with-young-voters.

———. "Inside the Secret World of the Data Crunchers Who Helped Obama Win." *Time*, November 7, 2012. http://swampland.time.com/2012/11/07/inside-the -secret-world-of-quants-and-data-crunchers-who-helped-obama-win.

Schmidt, Eric, and Jonathan Rosenberg. *How Google Works*. London: John Murry, 2014.

Schüll, Natasha Dow. *Addiction by Design: Machine Gambling in Las Vegas*. Princeton, NJ: Princeton University Press, 2014.

Schumpeter, Joseph. *Capitalism, Socialism and Democracy*. London: Routledge, 2006.

Scott, Brett. "In Praise of Cash." Aeon. https://aeon.co/essays/if-plastic-replaces -cash-much-that-is-good-will-be-lost.

Scott, James C. *Seeing Like a State: How Certain Schemes to Improve the Human Condition Have Failed*. New Haven, CT: Yale University Press, 1998.

Searchinger, Timothy D., Stefan Wirsenius, Tim Beringer, and Patrice Dumas. "Assessing the Efficiency of Changes in Land Use for Mitigating Climate Change." *Nature* 564 (2018): 249–53.

Sharp, Geoff. "Constitutive Abstraction and Social Practice." *Arena* 70 (1985): 48–82.

Shiotani, Naoyoshi. "Psycho-Pass." Fuji TV (Noitamina), 2012.

Shiva, Vandana. *Earth Democracy: Justice, Sustainability, and Peace*. 2nd ed. London: Zed Books, 2016.

———. *Monoculture of the Mind: Biodiversity, Biotechnology and the Third World*. Penang, Malaysia: Third World Network, 1993.

Siewert, Rachel. "Ten Years of Intervention." *Arena Magazine*, no. 148 (2017): 5–7.

Singh, Supriya. *Globalization and Money: A Global South Perspective*. Lanham, MD: Rowman & Littlefield, 2013.

Sly, Liz. "U.S. Soldiers Are Revealing Sensitive and Dangerous Information by Jogging." *Washington Post*, January 28, 2018. https://www.washingtonpost.com/ world/a-map-showing-the-users-of-fitness-devices-lets-the-world-see-where-us -soldiers-are-and-what-they-are-doing.

Smith, Adam. *An Inquiry into the Nature and Causes of the Wealth of Nations*. Chicago: University of Chicago Press, 1977.

Smythe, Dallas W. *Dependency Road: Communications, Capitalism, Consciousness, and Canada*. Edited by Melvin J. Voiget. Norwood, NJ: Ablex, 1981.

Sobel, Dava, and William J. H. Andrewes. *The Illustrated Longitude*. New York: Walker Publishing Company, 1998.

Soghoian, Christopher. "Two Honest Google Employees: Our Products Don't Protect Your Privacy." Slight Paranoia, November 2, 2011. http://paranoia.dubfire .net/2011/11/two-honest-google-employees-our.html.

Spielberg, Steven. *Minority Report*. DreamWorks Pictures, 2002.

Steger, Manfred. *The Global Studies Reader*. 2nd ed. Oxford: Oxford University Press, 2014.

Steger, Manfred B. *Globalisms: The Great Ideological Struggle of the Twenty-First Century.* Lanham, MD: Rowman & Littlefield, 2009.

———. *Globalization: A Very Short Introduction.* 3rd ed. Oxford: Oxford University Press, 2013.

———. *The Rise of the Global Imaginary: Political Ideologies from the French Revolution to the Global War on Terror.* Oxford: Oxford University Press, 2008.

Steger, Manfred B., James Goodman, and Erin K. Wilson. *Justice Globalism: Ideology, Crisis, Policy.* London: Sage, 2013.

Steger, Manfred B., and Paul James. *Globalization Matters: Engaging the Global in Unsettled Times.* Cambridge: Cambridge University Press, 2019.

Steger, Manfred, and Paul James, eds. *Globalization: The Career of a Concept.* London: Routledge, 2015.

Steger, Manfred B., and Ravi K. Roy. *Neoliberalism: A Very Short Introduction.* Oxford: Oxford University Press, 2010.

Ström, Timothy Erik. "Abstraction and Production in Google Maps: The Reorganisation of Subjectivity, Materiality and Labour." *Arena Journal* 47/48 (2017).

———. "Mapping Google Maps: Critiquing an Ideological Vision of the World." Thesis, Western Sydney University, 2018. https://researchdirect.westernsydney.edu.au/islandora/object/uws%3A47394.

———. "Twenty Years of Google: Abstract and Control." *Arena Magazine*, no. 156 (October-November 2018): 35–39.

———. "The Road Map to Brave New World: Cartography and Capitalism from Gulf Oil to Google." *Culture Unbound* 9, 2018.

Sullivan, Danny. "Google Still Doing at Least 1 Trillion Searches per Year." January 16, 2015. http://searchengineland.com/google-1-trillion-searches-per-year-212940.

———. "Google Still World's Most Popular Search Engine by Far." http://searchengineland.com/google-worlds-most-popular-search-engine-148089.

Sunkara, Bhaskar. *The Socialist Manifesto: The Case for Radical Politics in an Era of Extreme Inequality.* London: Verso, 2019.

Surin, Kenneth. "Hostage to an Unaccountable Planetary Executive: The Flawed 'Washington Consensus' and Two World Bank Reports." In *World Bank Literature*, edited by Amitava Kumar. Minneapolis: University of Minnesota Press, 2003.

Tagg, John. *The Burden of Representation: Essays on Photographies and Histories.* Basingstoke, UK: Macmillan Education, 1988.

Tao, Li. "You Will Soon Be Able to Pay Your Subway Fare with Your Face in China." *South China Morning Post*, March 13, 2019. https://www.scmp.com/tech/innovation/article/3001306/you-can-soon-pay-your-subway-ride-scanning-your-face-china.

Taylor, Astra. *Democracy May Not Exist, But We'll Miss It When It's Gone.* London: Verso, 2019.

Taylor, Fredrick Wilslow. *The Principles of Scientific Management*. Champaign, IL: Book Jungle, 2009.

Thompson, Derek. "Google's CEO: 'The Laws Are Written by Lobbyists.'" *Atlantic*, October 1, 2010. http://www.theatlantic.com/technology/archive/2010/10/googles-ceo-the-laws-are-written-by-lobbyists/63908.

Thompson, E. P. *Customs in Common*. London: Penguin Books, 1991.

Tiqqun. *The Cybernetic Hypothesis*. theanarchistlibrary.org, 2010.

Toscano, Alberto. "The Open Secret of Real Abstraction." *Rethinking Marxism* 20, no. 2 (2008): 273–78.

Trainer, Ted. "An Anarchism for Today: The Simpler Way." *Capitalism Nature Socialism* (2018): 1–17.

TRNN. "The Bizarre Billionaire That Backed Bannon and Made Trump President." *The Real News Network*, November 2, 2017. https://therealnews.com/stories/the-bizarre-billionaire-that-backed-bannon-and-made-trump-president.

Tsing, Anna. "Supply Chains and the Human Condition." *Rethinking Marxism* 21, no. 2 (2009): 148–76.

Turner, Fred. *From Counterculture to Cyberculture: Stewart Brand, the Whole Earth Network, and the Rise of Digital Utopianism*. Chicago: University of Chicago Press, 2006.

Turse, Nick. *The Complex: How the Military Invades Our Everyday Lives*. London: Faber and Faber, 2008.

———. "Donald Trump's First Year Sets Record for U.S. Special Ops: Elite Commandos Deployed to 149 Countries in 2017." *The Nation*, December 14, 2017. https://www.thenation.com/article/donald-trumps-first-year-set-a-record-for-use-of-special-operations-forces.

———. *Kill Anything That Moves: The Real American War in Vietnam*. New York: Metropolitan Books, 2013.

Vaidhyanathan, Siva. *The Googlization of Everything (And Why We Should Worry)*. Berkeley: University of California Press, 2011.

Vascellaro, Jessica E. "Google Agonizes on Privacy as Ad World Vaults Ahead." *Wall Street Journal*, August 10, 2010. http://online.wsj.com/articles/SB10001424052748703309704575413553851854026.

Vincent, Joshua. "Historical, Religious and Scholastic Prohibition of Usury: The Common Origins of Western and Islamic Financial Practices." Seton Hall University, May 1, 2014. https://scholarship.shu.edu/cgi/viewcontent.cgi?referer=https://www.google.com/&httpsredir=1&article=1600&context=student_scholarship.

Vinnies.org.au. "What's Wrong with the Cashless Debit Card?" St Vincent de Paul Society. https://www.vinnies.org.au/page/Publications/National/Factsheets_and_policy_briefings/What_s_wrong_with_the_cashless_welfare_card.

Vitali, Stefania, James B. Glattfelder, and Stefano Battiston. "The Network of Global Corporate Control." *PLoS ONE* 6, no. 10 (2011).

Wallerstein, Immanuel. *World-Systems Analysis: An Introduction*. Durham, NC: Duke University Press, 2004.

Wang, Jackie. *Carceral Capitalism*. South Pasadena, CA: Semiotext(e), 2018.

Ward, Adrian F., Kristen Duke, Ayelet Gneezy, and Maarten W. Bos. "Brain Drain: The Mere Presence of One's Own Smartphone Reduces Available Cognitive Capacity." *Journal of the Association for Consumer Research* 2, no. 2 (2017): 140–54.

Warren, Aiden. "Globalization, Security and Drones." In *Global Encyclopedia of Public Administration, Public Policy, and Governance*, edited by Ali Farazmand. Berlin: Springer, 2017. https://link.springer.com/referenceworkentry/10.1007%2F978-3-319-31816-5_3195-1.

Warren, Aiden, and Aleksei Hillas. "Lethal Autonomous Robotics: Rethinking the Dehumanization of Warfare." *UCLA Journal of International Law and Foreign Affairs* 22, no. 2 (2018): 1–28.

Warshaw, Jack. "If They Come in the Morning." *Misfits Migrants and Murders*, https://jackwarshaw.bandcamp.com/track/if-they-come-in-the-morning-2.

Waters, Colin N., James P. M. Syvitski, Agnieszka Gałuszka, Gary J. Hancock, Jan Zalasiewicz, Alejandro Cearreta, Jacques Grinevald et al. "Can Nuclear Weapons Fallout Mark the Beginning of the Anthropocene Epoch?" *Bulletin of the Atomic Scientists* 71, no. 3 (2015): 46–57.

Weber, Max. "Politics as Vocation." In *From Max Weber: Essays in Sociology*, edited and translated by H. H. Gerth and C. Wright Mills, 77–128. New York: Oxford University Press, 1946.

Weizman, Eyal. *Hollow Land: Israel's Architecture of Occupation*. London: Verso, 2017.

West, Emily. "Amazon: Surveillance as a Service." *Surveillance & Society* 17, no. 1/2 (2019): 27–33.

Westcott, James. "Written in Stone: In the Race for Geology's Highest Accolade—a 'Golden Spike'—Do Advocates of the Anthropocene Sell Their Ideas Short?" Aeon. https://aeon.co/essays/is-rushing-to-declare-the-anthropocene-also-human-error.

WHO. "Waterborne Disease Related to Unsafe Water and Sanitation." World Health Organization. https://www.who.int/sustainable-development/housing/health-risks/waterborne-disease/en.

Wiener, Norbert. *Cybernetics: Or Control and Communication in the Animal and the Machine*. New York: The Technology Press, 1948.

———. "A Scientist Rebels." *Atlantic* (January 1947).

WikiLeaks. "Amazon Atlas." https://wikileaks.org/amazon-atlas/releases.

Wilkinson, Richard, and Kate Pickett. *The Spirit Level: Why More Equal Societies Almost Always Do Better.* London: Allen Lane, 2009.

Williams, Raymond. *Communications*. Ringwood, Victoria: Penguin Books, 1966.

———. *Culture and Materialism: Selected Essays*. London: Verso, 2005.

———. *The Long Revolution*. Ringwood, Victoria: Pelican Books, 1971.

————. *Marxism and Literature.* Oxford: Oxford University Press, 1977.

Williamson, John. "What Washington Means by Policy Reform." Peterson Institute for International Economics, October 1, 2019. http://www.iie.com/publications/papers/paper.cfm?researchid=486.

Wilpert, Greg, and Alexander Zaitchik. "Amazon in Danger of Total Destruction under Brazil's Right-Wing President Bolsonaro." *The Real News Network,* July 12, 2019. https://therealnews.com/stories/amazon-in-danger-of-total-destruction-under-brazils-right-wing-president-bolsonaro.

Winner, Langdon. *The Whale and the Reactor: A Search for Limits in an Age of High Technology.* Chicago: University of Chicago Press, 1986.

Wolf, Eric R. *Europe and the People without History.* Los Angeles: University of California Press, 2010.

Wolff, Richard. *Capitalism's Crisis Deepens: Essays on the Global Economic Meltdown.* Chicago: Haymarket, 2016.

————. "Democracy at Work: A Cure for Capitalism." Chicago: Haymarket, 2012.

Wolfie, Christl. "Corporate Surveillance in Everyday Life." Vienna, Austria: Cracked Labs, 2017.

Wood, Denis. *The Power of Maps.* Edited by John Fels. New York: Guilford, 1992.

Wood, Ellen Meiksins. *Democracy against Capitalism: Renewing Historical Materialism.* Cambridge: Cambridge University Press, 1995.

World Bank. *The East Asian Miracle: Economic Growth and Public Policy.* Oxford: Oxford University Press, 1993.

Wright, Joe. "Nosedive." In *Black Mirror.* Endemol Shine, UK, 2016.

Wu, Xiaolin, and Xi Zhang. "Automated Inference on Criminality Using Face Image + Responses to Critiques on Machine Learning of Criminality Perceptions." arXiv.org, May 26, 2017. https://arxiv.org/pdf/1611.04135.pdf.

Xuanzun, Liu. "Social Credit System Must Bankrupt Discredited People." *Global Times,* May 20, 2018. http://www.globaltimes.cn/content/1103262.shtml.

Zand, Bernhard. "A Surveillance State Unlike Any the World Has Ever Seen." *Der Spiegel,* July 26, 2018. https://www.spiegel.de/international/world/china-s-xinjiang-province-a-surveillance-state-unlike-any-the-world-has-ever-seen-a-1220174.html.

Završnik, Aleš, ed. *Big Data, Crime and Social Control.* Abingdon, UK: Routledge, 2018.

Zhangke, Jia. "24 City." China: MK2 Diffusion, 2008.

Zhou, Yingnan Joseph, and Shuai Jin. "Inequality and Political Trust in China: The Social Volcano Thesis Re-Examined." *China Quarterly* 236 (2018): 1033–62.

Zuboff, Shoshana. *The Age of Surveillance Capitalism: The Fight for a Human Future at the New Frontier of Power.* London: Profile Books, 2019.

INDEX

About the Author

Timothy Erik Ström is a writer based in Melbourne, Australia, whose research focuses on the overlapping realms of technology, ecology, and capitalism. He works as a casual lecturer at the University of Melbourne, coordinating the masters' courses digital politics and global media policy and governance. He is also precariously employed as a researcher for Western Sydney University's Institute for Culture and Society and as a teacher of global political economy at RMIT University. He lives with his partner, UB, and daughter, Mirolima; is an editor and regular contributor to *Arena*: and writes science fiction. More of Tim's writings can be found on his website, *The Sorcerer's Apparatus*: www.sorapp.net.

GLOBALIZATION
Series Editors
Manfred B. Steger
University of Hawai'i–Mānoa and Western Sydney University
and
Terrell Carver
University of Bristol

"Globalization" has become *the* buzzword of our time. But what does it mean? Rather than forcing a complicated social phenomenon into a single analytical framework, this series seeks to present globalization as a multidimensional process constituted by complex, often contradictory interactions of global, regional, and local aspects of social life. Since conventional disciplinary borders and lines of demarcation are losing their old rationales in a globalizing world, authors in this series apply an interdisciplinary framework to the study of globalization. In short, the main purpose and objective of this series is to support subject-specific inquiries into the dynamics and effects of contemporary globalization and its varying impacts across, between, and within societies.